COLORS OF AMBER
A Memoir

Amber B. Skylar

Roots Publications
Sterling, Virginia

Editing by Stephanie Gunning:
www.stephaniegunning.com

Cover and interior design by Gus Yoo:
www.coroflot.com/azraeltrigger

Cover illustration by Rassouli, A Visionary Artist:
www.rassouli.com/artist.htm

Roots Publications
877-248-7109
www.rootspublications.com

978-0-9899068-0-7 (paperback)
978-0-9899068-1-4 (ebook)

1. Memoir 2. Family relationships 3. Women's studies
4. Inspiration 5. Spirituality

To my beautiful son, Ringer, and our long lost dog, Neo.

CONTENTS

I saw the full moon this Christmas.
It sheltered me with light.
I felt the coldness of winter . . .
She is forcing me within.
What a mystical place to be in:
The opening of my eyes . . .
To the discovery of Amber.

(December 1996)

INTRODUCTION

 One night, I dreamed of flying. It had been a long time since I'd had such an exhilarating dream. This time, however, I was in the middle of a war zone. I was trying to tell my sisters that it was possible to fly. "See. Watch me lift right up." No one in my dream could see that I was actually flying. My sisters went back to their task of building white-shelled bombs to provide the men in the dream with the ammunition needed to destroy their enemy.

The softest breeze held me in the air. As I zoomed back and forth over the battleground, I dipped low and blew out smiles like bubbles, trying to get the people in my dream to see.

Rockets were built and launched. I struggled for air. Smoke smothered the sky. I could sense a delicate presence around me.

People were screaming in tones of misery and mourning. Death lingered quietly. An unusual calmness surrounded me. I understood things. Strangely, joy and bliss filled me like a balloon. I swooped and hovered over the battlefield, directing my gaze into the souls of the suffering.

A glow of compassion spread across the battlefield. Death was present to take people home. Tenderness enraptured me. It illuminated me and gave me strength to complete my task: to uphold the flame of love to safely guide people on. In that awareness, I was free.

The dream faded. I slid toward the edge of my bed and when I opened my eyes I found my furry black cat looking at me.

When I was a teenage girl, I noted in a little blue diary I kept that I'd one day write a book about my life. I had no idea at the time that I had so much more life to live before I would begin that task. But I knew that I would write it one day. *Colors of Amber* fulfills that promise. Writing has allowed the unspoken to be spoken. It has helped me frame and see reality. Somewhere on a piece of paper a record now exists.

Mine is a story laced with pain, suffering, tender beauty, confusion, razor-sharp anger, and delicate buds of joy and rebirth. Woven within these pages are real life examples of the potential of the human body's ability *to persevere and adapt in order to survive, to learn, to live.*

For a good portion of my life, people scared the hell out of me and so I spent time alone. Yet, I was driven, pressed forward into maddening personal growth, which required me to interact with others. Seeds of curiosity about life coaxed me into the next moment. Curiosity's presence was like a good dog to me: loyal, serving, reliable, and generous. It never left my side and uplifted me from the bitter bite of anxiety and depression. As I harvested the budding nectar of change throughout my life, it fed my barren soul and developing mind. Curiosity brought me face to face with my own innate goodness and it invited me into the next moment of possibility—against the odds.

Human kindness, love, and compassion would drop me to my knees into a puddle of humility. They softened me. Transformation waited on the other side of my suffering. Compassion's delicate salve allowed me to let go of the warrior's edge and to just let things be—for a while. I never walked this path alone. There was always someone close by to extend a hand.

You may want to judge and blame the people you read about in this story. You may get angry with them. There may also be moments, while you are reading, in which you feel hopeful for me, only to be subsequently plunged back into the emotionality of my experiences, my choices. I invite you to allow these experiences, and your interpretations of them, to flow, to pass, and to transform. I have. I have transcended the archetypal role of being either a victim or a rescuer.

Today, I am responsible for my life. As a twenty-first-century woman, I have more opportunities to walk away and begin anew. It is not easy, but neither is staying in a bad, destructive situation.

I have made many choices throughout my life. As an adult, I am now responsible for their effects, regardless of how those events were shaped or by whom. I am aware that in the past I have been a victim of circumstance and that in many of those moments I was unschooled in healthy decision making. Different choices were not possible. Many of the decisions I made were laced in intense fear. As a woman, I was terrified, for instance, when I became pregnant. Fear, anxiety, and depression loomed over every decision I made as I embarked on the possibility of bringing a child into the world and *protecting* it. Domestic abuse composed intense symphonies of fear and anxiety in my adult life. I was a product of all I had learned at home and in the world: messages about women, fear, marriage, sex, social status, and social expectation. I made choices from that collection of information within my experiences. That's what people do.

Why does a battered woman stay in a relationship? Is it possible that historically, women have been trained, invited, and supported to remain in a bad situation as a means of survival? Perhaps while reading my story, you may begin to understand how a mind is developed, how behavior is shaped, and how people who are able to help, look the other way when reality asks of them to do otherwise.

I am a strong and resilient person. I invite you to seek out every moment in my story when another has stepped in to guide, protect, uplift, and support me. That's the message in this memoir.

Writing this book has pushed me over the edge and into the depths of my darkest self-judgments and fears. I have hated myself. On different occasions I've burned the manuscript, buried it, or tossed it gleefully in a dumpster with ideas about "getting over it," "putting it all behind me," and other concepts that I allowed to deter me from completing the task of putting forth my story. Writing this book was painful and a difficult undertaking. But when I put forth the effort and faced the deep waterways of emotion, sweetness would seep into my being. Each sentence was like a runner's last step toward the finish line. In pain and agony, and still pressing on, completion of this achievement became possible. Every word provided a nourishing breath as I looked at my life, let go of what I could not control, and accepted responsibility for the change that needed to be done.

I still have dark moments. Knowledge has been food for my mind. Studying the evolution of human achievements and deriving inspiration and respect for the human body to persevere has profoundly pressed me to fulfill this one dream of a young girl.

As a yoga student and teacher, I can feel my body today without shame. I can feel the outer layer of my inner existence and I can participate in life with other people in community where religion does not divide us. It's hard sometimes, but coming back to the breath and listening to its sound, coming into my flesh and experience its communication help ground me and keep me safe. My personal evolution is embedded and encoded with a collective collaboration of connections and experiences with other people.

I share with you one other dream.

In the dream, I awakened and found myself seated on the ground and encircled by four women: one in front of me, one behind me, one to my right, and one to my left. On a foggy grayish day, on top of a medium-sized hill, I then gazed out further and saw an endless number of circles within circles of other women seated around ours—women of all ages and all colors, facing me. One by one, a woman or girl would stand and say, "You said you would!"

"You said you would," an old, old woman challenged.

"You said you would," from a softly spoken voice of a young girl.

"You said you would," from a Native American woman holding hands with her daughter.

"You said you would," came from the strong, resounding voice of a black woman.

A soft humming noise surrounded me as each ghostly woman spoke her challenge to me.

I have had this dream on several occasions.

In my worst moments, therapists, strangers, friends, and one of my sisters fed me, gave me money, supported me, and cared for me. People fed my mind and nurtured the possibility of what I have become today. *I did not want or desire to get up.* I had become accustomed to pain and fear. I was familiar with it and found myself to be comforted by it. Depression was the nap I needed to lay down and give up. My story is one that people make excuses for such suffering. I have had very good reasons for giving up. Instead,

I have learned that my greatest talent, my deepest empathy, and most courageous passion arise when I face the pain.

It seems so poetic.

I write to express, to record, and to show people the power of creative expression. This book offers the possibility of healing through the written and spoken word, through the creative process of self-examination, self-expression through art, sharing, through connection and community engagement and interaction. No matter how hard-wired the mind is programmed, guided, or directed to "forget the past," it does not. The past is forever stored in our internal network of neurons and chemistry. We need to talk about it in order to change it. Negative, aggressive, and violent behavior is the obvious outcome of such attempts to hide or wash away human history. Media expresses this quite well.

A healthy, non-destructive expression of anger can provide enough momentum to insight great change and healing.

I have discovered that when asked, "How are you?" I reply honestly. Sometimes my answer is, "I'm good." Other times it's, "I am not happy today." Whether I am teaching yoga, talking to a cashier, or getting gas, I have found that most of the time people will stop when they hear me express my truth, and then they'll say things like, "Me, too. I have just never heard anyone say that before." Conversations ensue when all of us are reminded of our place in a community, when all of us are reminded of our mutual vulnerability as human beings.

Positive thinking is helpful, if we believe what we are trying to tell ourselves. Modern-day folks in healing circles are all trying to say the right things to be enlightened. I offer to you that enlightenment is not a trip off the planet to some far-off place, but the ability to be human, the ability to bear our humanity, and having the courage to admit that we are not anything more than one human being among many.

Quite often, I find myself still surprised by the ebb and flow of life. I have a few days of feeling good and then experience great challenges. My question to myself when I realize the tide is turning is, "Can you handle it, Amber?" Some days I allow myself to say, "Not today." On those days, maybe I curl up with my cat, a blanket, or a friend and cry.

I love science, I really do. But it has not yet been able to put its hand or mathematical mind on the body's expression through "emotions." I do not feel sadness in my ankle. It hurts in my chest and heart area. We cannot "touch" emotions, measure them, or see them. Cleverly, we tell ourselves that we are weak when we cry or better yet, we quickly follow the guidance of scientists and doctors and attempt to medicate it away. We mock psychotherapy and then apply layers of social shame to people who get it. We socially brand them and as a result deter people from reaching out for help. It becomes a sign of weakness to talk about what is going on inside of us.

I think we refer to our emotional challenges as "baggage." We are a people who lack courage to feel, to express, and when those who do, we call them "artists" and give them a pass for such experiences—or better yet we call them "women." Powerful leaders know this human vulnerability and we are available to be manipulated, commanded and managed. We have been emotionally branded to look away from our inner experience. Men have been castrated of their natural ability to feel. Transformation calls for the softer more feminine values like love, compassion and—nonviolence.

In this book, you will see how a life can be shaped by layers of ignorance and suppression. You will see how a person can do things without truly and consciously making a choice to do so. You will see how a few people's actions guided me to the possibility of change. You may begin to understand how and why people become victims.

What I hope you will learn is that although you cannot fix anyone, offering one small supportive gesture for someone else may have an impact so great that it inspires change, inspires possibility, for someone like me to rise up and transcend.

I am not happy every day, but for the first time in my life I know what it feels like to be happy. I have developed the skill to be able to look at reality and to manifest enough strength to speak out in my own voice about my life's truth, be heard by all, and still live my life as best I can. The human spirit can be broken, just like a branch on a tree or a wing on a bird. It can. The mind and the body however, are still available to repair, restore and renew what remains. In that awareness, I have discovered that the human being, can still feel the warmth of the sun, the green edgy grass in the spring, the delicious sensation of a hug, the silliness of pets, and the ultimate realization that the highest calling is to be a human. Nothing can destroy that until the body itself lets go.

I invite you to be an observer as you read my story. See what comes up for you. Watch when you want to blame me or someone else for these events that have already passed. Look into yourself and see what is possible for you to accept about yourself, what is possible or what interests you to change, get help, connect, or make a difference in your life before it's gone. Time is abundantly waiting for you to make a contribution to humanity, starting with yourself.

Starvation of the mind, body, and soul brings out the crumbs of depression, which attract the mice of misery to slowly nibble away at the human spirit. Support is out there. Can you allow yourself to reach out for it? Can you allow yourself to accept it? Can you reach out and make connections?

PART ONE

THE ILLUSION

It is recognized that a house, job, dog, fish tank, marriage, cars, children, and holidays are the essence of life or reality, inasmuch as they are socially safe methods of measuring the intrinsic value that is placed on the worth of a human being.

The age of innocence is behind us when we embark reflectively on the reality of our choices. Whether the will of any person was swayed, seduced, or even violated during her life, inevitably the choice remains to look and see what truths she has created, lived by, and hidden behind in order to cleverly avoid what stands right before her.

In *The Vampire Lestat,* Anne Rice writes an intriguing observation of mortals through Lestat, her leading character, a vampire. "Well, I was very quickly to learn an important lesson about mortals and their willingness to be convinced that the world is a safe place . . . and this lesson about mortal peace of mind I never forgot. Even if a ghost is ripping a house to pieces, throwing tin pans all over, pouring water on pillows, making clocks chime at all hours, mortals will accept almost any 'natural explanation' offered, no matter how absurd, rather than the obvious supernatural one, for what is going on." Living in the land of the obvious, the illusion has become the exact behavioral representation of Rice's mortals. People make sense of the most unnatural observations in life and none as mysterious as the supernatural.

Allow me to illustrate such things.

CHAPTER 1
WHITE — INNOCENCE

 A bride four times, I met my first husband when I was twenty-three. Sam, a Jewish man with rich black hair, had a red sports car and a black leather jacket. My Christian mother once ran her fingers through his chest hair just to tease me about how attractive that was on a man.

I was barely surviving as a night cashier at a convenience store, and spent most daylight hours in darkness beneath my blankets. Roaches scampered over the floor and nibbled at the little food I had stolen to eat. I would awaken around 2:00 P.M. in overwhelming panic, not understanding why. I hated the hour and the sun that went with it. Because of this, I would usually try to bury myself until darkness fell again. I was such a fearful human being that even breathing was painful.

It was summer.

Occasionally, I would bask outdoors until golden amber covered my body. Tanned, I felt clothed while nude. Nudity was shameful. It lured people to want to touch me in ways that I had become accustomed to, but was afraid of.

Sam was my fairytale prince who glistened in the sun and had come to take me away and keep me safe. He looked the part with his nice car, good job, stylish clothing, and college education. Best of all, he seemed to like me.

During the first month of our three-month courtship, Sam took me to Myrtle Beach, South Carolina, for a weekend of fun. I had never seen the ocean before and at first I was frightened by the waves' powerful sound as they rolled onto the shore.

I was overwhelmed.

I noticed the bare skin of the almost-nude people scattered about eating, tanning, flirting, and swimming. Incredibly shy on this, my first, time in a bikini, I felt exposed. People feasted their eyes upon me as I walked past them.

We settled on the sand, which burned my feet. I was irritable and extremely uncomfortable with everything. Sam asked me if I wanted to go into the water. Nervously, I agreed. I accepted his hand and held it tightly as we walked further and further out into this strange collection of blue. It mirrored my mood.

My scorched and tender feet were now immersed in gritty sand, and seaweed slithered around my legs. What mysterious creatures lived beneath the moving waters? I held Sam tighter.

He kept walking. It did not matter to him that I was afraid. He had no intention of turning back. I was chilled with fear. I shivered. The water was shoulder high, and I desperately clung to him. He stopped and turned to face me with a strange smile, and then began to remove my bikini. He lifted my legs, wrapped them around his waist, and lustfully thrust himself inside of me.

People watched.

The protective shelter of the ocean covered me. The experience was one of fear and naiveté. I was unschooled in the ways of living and loving. The door to my heart was guarded, but my inner beauty was still there and desperately believed in love.

My mind was blank at this stage in my life. I listened to those around me for advice, as I was literally unable to make decisions on my own. I simply did not know how.

Sam was my first consensual sexual relationship and he was in charge of everything that happened. That weekend I performed sexually for meals. He decided to feed me only once a day, but he did allow me to call my mother.

When I told her I was eating little, she said, "You should be grateful for the trip, Amber. He probably doesn't have enough money to spend on food and the trip."

Most of my time that weekend was spent in bed. I believed that if I gave Sam my body I would be loved, protected, and fed. My own unedited version of love was ingrained in my mind from all I had been taught at home. I believed I was doing as I should. What else was there to do?

I gave my body often after I moved in with Sam. He allowed me to eat only yogurt. He felt I needed to lose weight because my muscular frame was not attractive to him outside of the bedroom. I had a bed, a marriage proposal, and yogurt to fill my stomach.

During the days, I played house as I had when I was a little girl, waiting for Sam to come home. I prepared dinner when he provided the ingredients, and many nights I bided my time waiting for him to come home by candlelight, smoking a joint in the sexy lingerie he bought me. Alcohol and marijuana provided bandages for the open wounds I carried in my heart and mind. Many nights he would be up to three hours late with no call. When he did return, we had sex, and then he dropped off to sleep.

One day Sam brought a woman to our queen-sized waterbed as I lay sleeping. They entered the apartment laughing and reeking of alcohol. He wanted me to have a ménage à trois. Sam said I should do it because I made no other contribution to our home. I felt small and afraid as I scrambled to get out of the bed. In shock, I ran out of the room as they rolled around on top of each other, kissing and laughing. I grabbed a coat and left the house to wander the streets.

The moon was half full and I could see the stars. The fall air was crisp. For warmth, I walked the streets until a teary-eyed fatigue swept over me. It was after midnight when I curled up against a wall in an alleyway for comfort. Garbage, broken glass, and rough-edged pebbles were scattered about as I brushed clear a space to sit. A cat meowed hesitantly as it moved out of my way. I reached out for it and it purred its way into my arms. I could hear what sounded like rats scampering in the alley. The moon cast an indirect, bluish light into the darkened space, allowing me to see. The purring cat was now skittish and squirmed its way from my arms into the night. I leaned my head on the wall, pulled my legs toward me, wrapped my coat around me, and cried.

I was awakened by the shuffling sounds of heavy feet and an odorous smell of alcohol. A strange man approached and tried to force himself on me. I felt his grimy, callused hands awkwardly grasping at my coat and hair. He slurred and mumbled words of his intention. I screamed and kicked him, managing to cause enough pain for him to release me. I ran home with my heart racing faster than my feet. I heard it thumping as I crept upstairs to our apartment. I did not have keys, but was able to open the door and slip inside.

Sam must have been too drunk to lock the door. He and his lady friend occupied our bed. I made my way across the living room and slept in the darkness of the closet.

Sam and I were not yet married.

Gleefully, I thought I was going to miss my own wedding. When the bride is not nearly as important as the fully stocked bar, things are forgotten. I'd asked my maid of honor, members of the wedding party, and my family for a ride to the wedding. No one was available. Everyone assumed someone else was giving me a ride.

My younger brother, Adam, forgot his sport coat. When he went to his apartment to retrieve it, he heard noises in our apartment above it. He came up to see who was there and was surprised to find me. Dressed in a forty-dollar white gown, I stood with my eyes glazed over, hair tinted a Cyndi Lauper red, and baby-blue eye shadow smeared on my eyelids. Beauty was not my forte. I felt like a Barbie doll waiting for someone to play with me.

I had already drunk a good amount of whiskey that morning. I did not want to marry Sam, but I did not know what else to do or where to go with my life. My brother looked at my tears and said, "Oh, Sis, you've got cold feet and that's normal."

I tried to convince him to take me far away. I felt very anxious inside because I knew the man I was about to marry did not love me.

I did not know I was supposed to love him.

Already an hour late and the church another hour away, my brother picked me up and literally carried me to his car. On the way to the church, Adam stopped at a roadside stand to buy me flowers. He said, "What the hell, everyone's waited this long, they can wait a little longer."

My head spinning, I smiled and said, "Thank you. I will never forget this." I was miserable. Then I pleaded once more, "Please take me away from here. I do not like this guy."

He told me, "I love you, sis. Don't be afraid. Everything will be okay."

I'd hoped he would have said something else. But he didn't. What else was there to say? He simply did not know that something better might be out there for either of us. We had survived all of our lives in scenes of chaos. Seven children, one working mother, poverty, and the ever-changing seasons moved the stream of my fatherless childhood. Daddy disappeared. He came back once, never to return. It would be some years more before I would decide to contact him.

Before meeting Sam, I spent most of my time hiding in bed, believing my dream of love would someday come true—a love my mother spoke of often in reference to my absent father. In her illusion of him, she romanticized their love. I therefore grew up with the same illusion of a man who would wisp in, love my body, leave, and then I would spend my life hoping he'd come back for me. This twisted fantasy fed the acidity of my emotional digestion. It played out over and over in my life as a woman, depleting me of the necessary nutrients of a healthy relationship. Instead, my sight grew darker; my interior being became the essence of depression. Through the emotional window of that depression the world was bleak and miserable. Getting married seemed to be the only way out. In fact, it was a road leading me back through the past.

I do not really remember the wedding ceremony—only bits and pieces of it, like vomiting in the toilet. How could people have known what I was going through? After scolding me, my mother smiled at me. Her smile led me all the way down the aisle for the sacred ceremony between a woman and a man. If Mom thought this was a good idea, then I felt better about it. She only wanted the best for me. So I staggered down the aisle with a sick feeling in my stomach, partly from the alcohol, but also from fear because I felt exposed to the eyes of the onlookers.

My mom might have had another opinion of Sam if she had accompanied us on our honeymoon. We went to a snow-covered and isolated small town in Tennessee. Sam had reserved a room for us and had pizza delivered. I went into the bathroom to put on my nightgown. I peeked out the window, as if trying to prepare an escape. My mind filled with the deafening silence of the snow and I felt the emptiness of this remote valley.

When I entered the bedroom, Sam was lying stark naked on top of the covers. He patted the bed for me to join him. Shyly, I lay next to him as he picked up the television remote while explaining that he had rented some movies. I was relieved. I smiled and sat up in bed, trying not to look at his nudity. I grabbed a slice of pizza and settled in for what became my first exposure to pornography.

I watched a beautiful young lady being raped by two men. Sam liked her innocence and the way they violated her. I was horrified when Sam grabbed his penis and tried to force my head down to perform oral sex on him as he watched the girl. I pulled away and ran out the door barefoot into the white night. I found a bush and curled up beneath the hollow of its branches. I cried and shivered.

I hated people. They made me sick.

I don't know how long I waited, but Sam had called the police. A cop soon appeared, peeking under the bush, asking, "Are you all right in there?" I did not move. He introduced himself, removed his jacket, and handed it to me. For a while we sat in silence. Then he asked me if I was in danger. I was so frightened I could not speak, but his presence soothed me.

I could hear Sam and the hotel manager talking with another officer. I was not planning to move, but was shivering so badly my teeth were chattering. The policeman promised he would keep me safe. I climbed out from beneath the bush. My feet were freezing and I stumbled as he put out a hand to catch me. I climbed into the police cruiser as the officer spoke harshly to Sam. Then Sam spoke softly to the other policeman and I heard them loudly chuckle.

I was no longer safe.

The policeman who had helped me came back to the car looking frustrated. He opened the door and knelt down to ask if I was feeling better. It was clear he wanted to help, but I did not believe that he or anyone else could help me. I simply nodded my head to indicate that I was fine. Truly, I was silently screaming for him to take me with him, away from Sam. I walked back into that hotel room. I chose to do so because I didn't have a voice to speak and ask for help. I went in silence, and carried with me the gentleness of that policeman. It comforted me to know that such kindness existed.

I had become a wife.

About three months later another surprise awaited me. Sam decided to join the Army. He wanted to become a warrant officer to fly military aircraft. He said he was wasting money on our marriage and blamed it and me for his frustrations.

One evening, an Army recruiter named Juan Ventura came to visit. I remember his accent, his cologne, and his polished black boots. He was all military until it came to talking to prospective military spouses and what their lives might be like. He had a cocky smile and something in his eyes made me uneasy. I kept my distance from him.

There was a knock at the door. It was a young woman named Cassy, who introduced herself as a military wife. She had come to talk to me. I invited her in and noticed an intimate exchange between her and the recruiter. She positioned herself between Sam and the recruiter. Uneasiness was building in me. Something was off. I tried to calm myself. I went to the kitchen to prepare drinks for everyone. I glanced into the living room to see the recruiter caressing Cassy's leg and showing this to my husband. Cassy whispered something into Sam's ear as I reentered the room. I felt angry because I was the only one who had a problem with what was happening.

Storming in from the kitchen, I shouted, "Get out!"

Everyone was shocked.

"Take that bitch with you and get out!"

The recruiter looked at Sam as he got to his feet.

"I don't know what your problem is, but get lost!" Sam hollered back at me. "Get outta here now!"

I did not trust Juan or Cassy and I wanted them gone, but they were not leaving. That was obvious. So I left. I was too angry to stay. With nowhere to go, I wandered the streets until dark and then made my way back to the apartment. The lights were out and there was no one inside. Angrily, I assumed that the three of them had gone elsewhere to be together. After smoking a joint, I fell asleep on the couch.

When a person becomes enmeshed in this type of life, there seems to be no way out. I felt trapped and did not understand that any other possibility existed. Everyone I knew or met seemed to be "messed up" or "weird" in one way or another. So I slipped further into darkness.

Months later, after Sam had gone into the Army, I received a tearful telephone call from Cassy. She asked if we could meet. I walked to where she lived and she told me the entire truth. Juan Ventura had recruited her husband into the Army also. He had been instrumental in sending her husband to Korea immediately after Basic Training and Advanced Individual Training. At that time, Korea was considered a "hardship tour," where spouses were not allowed to travel. Then, Juan had begun calling Cassy in order "to do his job and provide her comfort."

Emotionally distraught one day, she called Ventura and tearfully told him how lonely she was without her husband. This U.S. Army recruiter took it upon himself to take care of this poor Army wife. That is how they became lovers. He visited her almost every day until she became pregnant. Then, he was no longer anywhere to be found. He relocated almost immediately after she told him she was pregnant. Cassy told me that afternoon that she had also slept twice with my husband.

What occurred to me then was the old saying, "If you can't beat 'em, join 'em." And that is exactly what I did. I took the tests for all the military branches and swore I would accept the first available assignment. The U.S. Army was first to call, and so within two weeks I was at Basic Training in South Carolina.

I really did not know what was in store for me. Technically, I was still married to Sam, and the Army attempts to assign couples together. But I was not looking forward to that because, as far as I was concerned, we were no longer a couple. I received my first assignment even before I completed Basic Training. I was told that I would be sent directly to Korea after finishing Advanced Individual Training. I was happy about it, believing that my new "top secret" security clearance meant that I was special, and also because I wanted to be as far away as possible from Sam, who was stationed in El Paso, Texas.

My mother learned that I would be close to the Korean Demilitarized Zone. She felt this was too dangerous and that I needed to be with Sam. She wrote letters to the President of the United States and to four senators complaining.

In the military, when you "make waves," you are in a dangerous position. When my mother wrote to her politicians, she triggered a Congressional Inquiry. I was a private first class and one of the few women soldiers in my platoon who would not give in to the pressure to sleep with the drill sergeants. Mom's letters made big "waves." Male drill instructors, who already hated me for refusing to submit to them sexually, could not wait to swarm over me with ridicule, threats, and as much filthy talk as they felt would break me down. I vowed that the disdain I felt for these men would fuel my body so I could outdo them. Each time they made a sexual move or a bold, arrogant comment about my body, it added fuel to my fury.

I got up early, slept less, polished my boots in the middle of the night, and awakened the other members of my all-female platoon as early as 4:30 A.M., thirty minutes prior to formation. I did this to prevent male drill instructors from entering our rooms and showers as we readied ourselves for the day. They had a habit of sneaking in early to feast their eyes on partially clad females while they yelled obscenities at us. This battle could not be won by telling higher-ups. And no one did tell. It became a war and I was determined to win it in any way I could. This did not make me popular with my platoon, but as acting platoon leader I was in charge. I cared about my body and the fact that it was being viewed without my permission.

The drill sergeants' goal was to disempower me in my role as platoon leader. When we had road marches, my platoon would be told to run instead of walk. The women who had traded sex for cigarettes and other privileges were spared from having to run in full gear.

The drill instructors had no idea that I had so much anger toward them, or that I focused on it purposefully to push myself beyond expected limitations. I can remember the heavy helmet; the rucksack filled with an entrenching tool, MREs, and other supplies; the 7.65- pound M-16; the ammo pouches; the water canteen; the poncho; the stinging sweat in the 103-degree humidity; and most of all, the numb legs of those road marches. If we had a five-mile run, I just kept running. I didn't care if I died in the process. It seemed better than not finishing. Instead of earning respect, however, I was isolated from my peers and was challenged even more by my drill instructors. As pressure mounted, they began referring to me as Tough Guy.

When it rains in South Carolina, red fire ants make hills as much as ten inches high. During drills involving a low crawl with weapons, I was forced to crawl through small anthills, which though not as noticeable as the tall ones, are just as deadly. I would be eaten alive by these ants and spend nights fantasizing about collecting bags full of them and using them to torment my drill instructors. I especially hated to have to lie in prone position, stomach down with elbows propped up holding an M-16 rifle, legs spread out behind me. Drill instructors would make the women hold the position while talking about our asses.

One afternoon, as I got up from the prone position, I was ordered to lie back down. I refused. For my disobedience, I was ordered to do pushups in the 100-degree weather, one foot away from an anthill. Being in excellent physical condition, I could do pushups until the stars came out. But I was sweating profusely and the ants raced to bite me. I don't know how many pushups I did, as two drill sergeants watched, but as the ants bit me, I pushed faster and harder. I was determined that they were not going to beat me, and they did not. When they finally allowed me to stop, I picked up my weapon and gear and marched off. I was miserable, but I kept silent. I walked with pride and an arrogant attitude.

Boot camp recruits are assigned a buddy. Everywhere one goes, the other goes as well. My "buddy," Mina Cho, hated me. Late that same night, awakened by the same drill instructors, I ended up in a wooded area with Mina because the sergeants wanted to put more pressure on me. It was pouring rain. We had been instructed to get our entrenching tools and rain gear, and then we were loaded in the back of an open military vehicle and driven to this sandy, wooded area. The drill sergeants told us we would spend our night digging foxholes for two people, as deep as the tallest person's armpits. They left us there, in the middle of nowhere, with rain pouring down.

Mina began to curse me in Korean. Understanding why she was mad, I took off my poncho and built a lean-to for her. I told her to use it to get some sleep.

With the drill sergeants gone, I began digging, which served as a release for some of my anger. I dug ferociously. Soon I had sand in my underwear, ears, hair, and fingernails. I did not care. I saw someone smoking in the distance and heard a female voice giggling. I decided to sing as loudly as I could, just to irritate whoever was out there. I bellowed out "O Christmas Tree" and a bunch of other Christmas carols I could remember.

Eventually one drill sergeant returned to find out what was going on. I looked him square in the eye as he surveyed the situation. He looked at the sleeping Mina Cho and back at me. He had no choice other than to admire my indomitable spirit.

After I finished digging one foxhole, he came back for us. The other drill sergeant had left with the mysterious smoking woman. We rode to the barracks in the back of a pickup truck while the cool rains cleansed me. I had survived. I was victorious.

I was exhausted.

I carried Mina Cho up the barracks stairs. She was tiny and very weak, and the exposure had been too much for her. I put her in the shower fully clothed to rinse her off and then got her undressed and into bed. I then cleaned every inch of my body and went back to my own room, knowing another day awaited me. We had to get up in one hour.

From my bed, I looked out the window and wondered if I would ever have to stop fighting to protect my body. There was no one to tell and I had no peers who would side with me. They would rather give themselves to the drill instructors than to go through what I did. I began to doubt my own convictions, wondering what was ahead. Was this all the world had to offer women?

After my mother's desperate plea to the government officials to spare her daughter from Korea, I was stripped of my three stripes, my rank, and demoted to the lowest possible level in the military: a private (no stripes). I was then reassigned to Fort Bliss, Texas, to be with Sam. Whining to one's congressman is considered an act of weakness. In the military, you simply do not tell. I had spoken a few times with Sam. He said the Army had "straightened him up some" and he "needed me badly." He said he was sorry for his past behavior. But it was obvious all he wanted was sex. I almost became physically ill when I arrived at the apartment he had selected for us to share. He had hung all of my lingerie on hangers after having them shipped from our stored household belongings. Not one other article of clothing was unpacked or folded.

It did not take long for Sam to find other women to bed. It became known that he was sleeping with Emily Springer, who was one of only four other women in my battalion. Sam decided he would work a night shift while I was on day duty. He spent his off-time playing tennis and other games with Emily.

The dark mood within me grew until, once again, I felt worthless. It is against the U.S. Military Code of Justice to sleep with someone other than one's own spouse. However, anyone reporting such activity usually got in some kind of trouble. Military people of all grades and ranks slept with others outside of their marriages. My first sergeant once informed the men, especially the married men, that if they intended to use their "peter beaters" they had better use a "damned good condom."

I generally didn't like the men and women in that battalion. Of the five women, I was the only one not sleeping around. The male-dominated culture of the military seemed to have its own rules regarding sexual conduct and women. I found it very much a man's world.

One day, I came home to an empty apartment. Nothing except my clothing and military gear was left. Furious, I drove to Sam's helicopter unit. As I walked into the hangar, everyone stopped what they were doing. The highest-ranking official on the floor told me to "get the hell out." They knew who I was and apparently believed they were protecting one of their own. All of our household belongings had been removed from our apartment only hours earlier. I was nervous and angry. I found my voice and demanded that they return my belongings. "Where is Sergeant Sam Berg?" I asked.

Sam and some of his buddies laughed.

I turned to face them. "Where is our furniture?" I demanded.

I was on the verge of tears when a captain from upstairs overheard my shouting. He said, "What's going on down there?"

The chief warrant officer told him that everything was under control.

"Who are you, soldier, and what are you doing in my hanger?" the captain asked me.

I stood my ground stubbornly trying to maintain my composure. "I am Specialist Berg, Sergeant Berg's wife," I answered, "and I believe some of these men helped him to take my furniture from our apartment this morning."

The captain invited me upstairs to explain further. As I told him about Emily and Sam and me fighting, he seemed angered, but maintained his composure. He apologized to me and said that although he could not correct my husband's immoral behavior, he could get my furniture back. As we descended the stairs, I wondered what was to happen. The captain looked me squarely in the eye, as if to say, "Straighten up, soldier." His eyes were kind, and so I lifted my head high and followed him.

The captain ordered the men in the hangar to get as many trucks as needed and deliver all of the furniture to my apartment immediately. He ordered his chief warrant officer to personally oversee the task and ensure my safety. He also ordered my husband to keep only his clothing, military gear, and anything that clearly belonged to him. The captain advised Sam to cooperate fully. Everyone moved to his command, and as I waited, the captain said, "I hope I have honored you as you should be."

That's how Sam and I became officially and unexpectedly separated.

Not long afterward, Sam appeared at my door. He had a young, blond woman in his car. Even so, he had the nerve to beg to get back with me, saying he was miserable without me. I asked about the woman in the car. He replied, "She doesn't mean anything to me. I love you and I want you back." I swiftly moved him to the door and told him it was finished between us.

Looking back on it now, I think he just wanted the extra perks you get for being married.

Shortly after that last incident, he filed for divorce.

I was living on my own when I met Richard Bellamy. He was handsome and charming. His gentleness and attentiveness seemed genuine.

I was pretty reclusive at that point in my life. I felt like a misfit who didn't do what others do. I spent much of my time talking to myself or on the phone with my mother. Her opinion of the ending of my marriage to Sam was, "It's all in the past. Leave dead dogs alone." In the meantime, work, alcohol, and my new boyfriend, Richard, could not drown out the weight of the depression I carried. What was it? Did everyone feel this way? It seemed not.

Richard was as smooth as silk. I truly thought I loved him. He would go out of his way to impress me. Still lacking in social skills, I was grateful to be noticed at all. I was still feeling shame about the breakup with Sam and the fact that Emily was in my battalion where she was continually flaunting her ability to lure him away from me.

Richard and I met at a disco. He was dancing alone in the middle of the floor, like John Travolta in *Saturday Night Fever,* with women surrounding him. That turned me off. He noticed that I was not taken as the others were with his performance. Thus, it became his mission to convince me that he was lovable. I had doubts about him.

Richard's alcoholic father had been killed while driving drunk and his mother had abandoned him to an aunt. He had joined the Army as soon as he turned eighteen. Little did I know how desperately he needed love. All I knew was that he would bring flowers to my apartment. I would wait for him on hot summer evenings in El Paso to come and love me. I was severely depressed and desperately needed his love. I trusted it.

I felt safe.

Richard's touch was tender and he constantly professed his love. He went to great lengths to do special things for me. What I did not realize at first was that Richard was stealing my money to do them.

One day I awakened from sleep after a long night of passion and took a shower. Emerging from the bathroom, I noticed that the money I had left on my dresser was missing. Richard seemed to be sleeping, but I decided to confront him about it because I had noticed money missing before. His anger over my distrusting him startled me, so I was convinced that I must have been mistaken. How could someone who loved me so much steal and lie to me? It just wasn't possible. There had to be decent people out there.

Soon I began receiving roses on my bed at night when Richard wasn't there. I would awaken in the morning to find them at my feet. I would call Richard to thank him and ask how he got into the house. He would always laugh and say it was a "secret." Finally, I asked him not to do this anymore and he agreed. However, his promise was empty.

A few days later, I came home from work to find five after-dinner mints in tin foil stacked like dominoes on my kitchen counter. Previously, on two separate occasions I had returned home from work to find that someone had prepared my favorite snack of a ham and Swiss cheese sandwich on wheat bread and tomato juice, and left it partially consumed in my kitchen. Apparently, Richard thought this kind of behavior impressed me. He continued to claim that the flowers on my bed at night were from him, as well as the partially eaten food and the chocolates. He said he wanted me to know how much he loved me.

I noticed some of my lingerie was missing. When I asked him about it, Richard claimed to have taken these items because he "wanted to have something to hold on to while he was not with me." I lived in an apartment with ground-level entryways in front and in back. The back entrance had French doors and a little patio. The windows were large, taking up almost half of the back wall above the French doors. My bedroom was a loft, open on top and also open enough to see in from the outside. Admittedly, I was exploring my sexuality with Richard, as I had never done before. My body was ripe and deprived, and I needed to be touched. Sex was the only means of nurturing that I knew. I wanted to believe that Richard was the mystery man surprising me with gifts. However, I was uneasy about him entering my home without my permission. Furthermore, money turned up missing whenever we were together.

Ultimately, I discovered that Richard was not the one sneaking into my house to leave food and flowers. He had stolen my money, but not my lingerie. I found out that Richard was lying to me when I went to his barracks to find him one day. He was not there, but I met his roommates and they set me straight. They said Richard had been telling tales about our relationship, and that he would say or do anything to keep me. They told me Richard was very jealous of whoever was really giving me the flowers and that he had been caught stealing from his buddies to impress me with clothing and other gifts.

Richard's stealing and lying was bad enough, but I had another problem: If Richard was not the one entering my home at night, who was?

I lived next door to a police detective. After demonstrating how easy it was for someone to break into my apartment, he gave me some suggestions as to how to secure my home better.

I broke off my relationship with Richard. Shortly afterward, I found a single white rose at the foot of my bed. I was terrified and called the military barracks. The First Sergeant told me to file a report with the Military Police and suggested I move to the barracks if things did not change. That was the last thing I wanted to do. I loved my privacy more than I hated the terror that was emerging within me.

For safety, I invited a couple of my male platoon friends to stay with me for a while. These were good guys. Though I did not know them well, we had partied together in Ciudad Juarez, Mexico, which is directly across the Rio Grande from El Paso where we were based. We all had looked out for each other then, so I trusted them with my home and safety. They liked the idea of moving in because they hated living in the barracks. Their presence was useful. We slept to-gether platonically on my living room floor for at least two weeks and nothing else strange happened. They were serious about protecting me and it felt like I had a family of brothers.

When Richard telephoned, the guys would say I was busy. Be-cause he kept calling, I started to believe that maybe the nocturnal intruder was Richard after all.

One evening my platoon friends and I went out dancing. The guys were having a good time with some of the women at the club. I felt they needed some fun, so I told them I was going home by myself and they were welcome to bring their friends by later. I drove home and entered the apartment feeling apprehensive as I made my way through the rooms.

To quiet my nerves, I checked under my sink and under the stairway. I searched behind my shower curtain, behind my clothing in the closet, and under the couch. My cat jumped and frightened me. I opened the back door to the patio and searched the storage room. Everything seemed fine. I'd spoken with my mother about what was going on and she'd suggested that if it made me feel better to look under the sink, then I should do it, no matter how ridiculous it seemed. Having done so, I was beginning to feel safe. I reentered my apartment from the back patio and locked the door behind me.

I started to undress downstairs as I was not certain I wanted to sleep upstairs. I had had several glasses of Scotch and was beginning to feel relaxed and sleepy. I went upstairs, brushed my teeth, combed my hair, put on my nightgown, and checked that my .357 Magnum pistol was in the drawer next to my bed. I had purchased the weapon for self-defense and gone to the shooting range at least twenty times with it and now was an expert shot. My bed was adorned with cream-colored fabric draped around the four bedposts to create a canopy effect. When I lay down and began to fix the covers around me, I saw something beyond the canopy out of the corner of my eye. Fear began to creep over me again.

My nightstand light was still on. My telephone and gun were right next to me on my left. I decided to face the icy fear I was feeling and look directly to my right. When I did, I saw my stalker not twenty feet from me, standing on the ledge outside my window. Not Richard.

I remembered having discussed using the gun with my neighbor. He had informed me that if I were to shoot someone outside my home, I would have to drag him inside. The law very clearly allowed you to shoot someone in self-defense inside your own home, but not outside. The thought of dragging in the stalker terrorized me. Fear raced rapidly through me, rendering me powerless to think.

I screamed.

The stalker had a lot of black hair and dark eyes. I could see the whites of his eyes standing out from his dark features. He had a totally clear view of me. His hands and body were pressed against the window. He remained as he was. I picked up the telephone, pressed zero, and had the operator call the police. I could not remember my phone number or address. I just kept screaming and the man kept watching me with a strange smile on his face. I dropped the phone as soon as I heard a voice tell me that my call had been traced and the police were on the way. They had advised me not to do anything and told me that the police would arrive without sirens. I was so frightened of what might happen meanwhile that I took the gun out of the nightstand drawer, stood up, and pointed it directly at the intruder. He never budged. He just kept smiling at me. I could not stop the gun from shaking. My body must have gone into shock. I could not have fired that weapon even if I'd wanted to.

Moments later the police arrived with their lights flashing. The stalker jumped from the window ledge and vanished. The cops gave chase, but could not find him. Afterwards, they questioned me about him and I told them the whole story, but I had no helpful answers. Later, once they were gone, I called the barracks. My buddies had not yet returned. My unit sent over two other male friends to stay with me overnight. The police would never catch the stalker.

After this incident, I felt I could not handle life anymore. Three days later I began to plan for suicide. I was in soul shock. I saw people as being full of darkness and I felt I was being enveloped by it. By my mid-twenties, I had seen enough to know just how dark life could be from growing up and the way Sam had treated me. Even so, I had no idea of the greater darkness that was ahead of me.

I knew I would not be able to shoot myself, so I went to the nearest grocery store at 3:00 A.M. to buy as many over-the-counter drugs as I could. I was crying uncontrollably as the store piped in the voice of John Denver singing "Sunshine on My Shoulders."

That night I lit my bedroom with candles and put on my prettiest nightgown. I then swallowed every aspirin and diet pill I had purchased and lay in bed crying while feeling sick to my stomach. In the drama of my anticipated departure from life, I had no idea that these pills would not kill me. They just made me incredibly sick.

At this critical juncture in my existence, Staff Sergeant John Kinder entered the picture. He was my immediate supervisor, and I did not know that he was fond of me or that he hated the military. He was a cyclist and an artist. Though he had always maintained a professional demeanor he had been nicer to me than he was to most soldiers under his command. For some reason, he felt a strong need that very evening to come and talk to me, although he'd never entered my home before.

I do not know how John got into the apartment, but he did. There he found me, in my bed, sick and crying. He used my phone to call someone. Then he picked me up in his arms and took me to a non-military hospital where I had my stomach pumped. Honestly, that felt worse than the misery I was experiencing trying to leave this earth.

After I was released from the hospital, John took me to his home to stay for a few days. He also arranged for me to be reassigned due to personal hardship. When he offered me the option of going to Germany, Japan, or Hawaii, I chose Hawaii, thinking the sunshine would help me. I was afraid of the darkness of Germany and longed to see the ocean once more. Thanks to John Kinder, two weeks later I was on my way, leaving my stalker behind me.

CHAPTER 2
RED —
WARRIOR
OF THE HEART

 In Hawaii, I slid into the worst depression of my life. The descent into overwhelming darkness within me was a nightmare day in and day out. I hated the sunshine and the shiny, happy people. They were too bright for me to bear.

While I was in uniform, I performed so well I became known as "strat", meaning I was hardcore: "sharp," "tough," "the best." However, I had no place to hide and nurse my emotions because I was required to live in military quarters due to my low rank and the high cost of living. As a Specialist Fourth Class at this point, having worked hard to earn my stripes back and more, I had a room to myself in the barracks, but no real privacy. We were in coed barracks, but females were not allowed to have males in the rooms except during daylight hours. At twenty-five, after all that I had experienced, I now found that I had a curfew and I was miserable. I was an adult and desperately needed privacy. Furthermore, in addition to the other indignities, residents of the barracks had to perform janitorial duties and were responsible for noise control. I also had nosy neighbors who were always trying to create something out of nothing.

I had been teaching aerobics at my previous post. When I arrived at Fort Shafter, I was asked by my commanding officer to teach morning physical training. This came as a surprise to a particular Sergeant First Class from my new barracks. Up until my arrival Sergeant Berringer had been instructing physical fitness training. She did not like me at all because I replaced her. She outranked me by four stripes. The military was her life and she felt that I was a threat to her. Her face screamed jealousy.

It was August 6, the eve of my twenty-sixth birthday, and I was scheduled to leave at 5:00 A.M. the next morning for Advanced Leadership Training on another part of the island. I was so pumped up I couldn't sleep, so several friends and I went out dancing. At 2:30 A.M. I was walking down the street with them. From across the street, someone called out to me. I looked over and saw a tall, cute guy. He crossed the street and came up to me. I liked him. He invited me to hang out with him and his friends. I did. I did not know at the time that Jeremy Bradshaw knew anything about the military or that his father was an Army officer at Fort Shafter.

I told Jeremy that the next day was my birthday and that I would be leaving within a few hours for Advanced Military Training. We were getting along so well that he said he wanted to see me on my birthday. I let him know that if I passed an inspection in the morning I would be allowed visitors at the training location. He said he would be there that very night to wish me a happy birthday. I thought he was romantic and funny, but I never expected to see him again.

The next day, because my gear was "tight," I passed inspection and earned the evening out. In the afternoon, someone from the staff came and told me I had a visitor waiting in the visitors area. I was also advised to inform this unexpected guest, whoever it was, about the speed limits on the base and tell him that if he ever wished to see me again he had better obey them. Evidently he had zoomed in there on a crotch rocket motorcycle. I did not know who was waiting for me and was pleasantly surprised when I got to the visitor area to discover that it was Jeremy.

Jeremy was nicely dressed, tall, and handsome. He brought me candy. He was carrying legal books and told me he was a law student. Though he was only nineteen, I thought he was exciting. He had a motorcycle, and rode it arrogantly, like a god. He followed me on his bike as I drove in my little two-door sedan to the military post's swimming pool. Seeing me in my swimsuit, he complimented me on my figure in a gentlemanly manner. He did not gawk or stare, but simply stated his admiration of my beauty. Later, we rode his motorcycle together and I had to hold on to him. I was quiet and felt frustrated by my shyness, but otherwise it was a great date.

Jeremy subsequently became an inspiration to me while I was training. I excelled in my instruction. He came to visit me whenever I was allowed company. He was even there when I was turned down for visitation.

Not long after my training period ended, we were together in my barracks room. We had a disagreement, and argued up until curfew. He left with one minute to spare, and I went to sleep, not realizing that my nemesis, Sergeant Berringer, was guarding the only unlocked entrance to the barracks attempting to catch me and my boyfriend in an infraction. Jeremy knew she hated me. To avoid getting me in trouble, without telling me he decided to sleep in the small hallway just outside my room. He thought he was doing a decent thing for me, but the military being as strict on rules as it is, in fact it was a dumb thing to do. He might have gotten out if he'd rushed, but he did not want to take the chance.

Berringer was suspicious, as she had not seen my male guest leave. She was out to discredit me in any way she could. By morning, she had contacted the Base Commander with her suspicions. I awoke to the sound of an alarm, and shouts of "fire drill." I heard pounding on my door. It was Jeremy. I was surprised he was still in the building. He explained that he had tried to get out of the barracks but thought that Berringer had seen him. I was in a panic so I hid him in my footlocker. I went outside with everyone else and heard rumors that someone had been seen in the barracks. I was nervous. I'd never been in trouble in the military before and took great pride in my work.

Jeremy was discovered in my footlocker. It was locked, but the MPs shook it until he made a sound. That gave them authority to break the lock.

Berringer was determined to prove to my captain that I was not as strat as everyone thought I was. Retrospectively, I can see that her jealousy infected all of us. Her insecurities, such as they were, spilled over on anyone and everyone in her path. She lacked the ability to contain her emotions, or to understand herself enough to respect other people instead of fearing them. Her behavior was typical of people in power. Due to her hostility, her actions redirected my life's course in a way that I now believe happened exactly as it should to help me become who I am today.

My captain could not believe this incident had happened considering my excellent performance until then. Around the base, the scandal of me violating the rules made my life a bowl of popcorn as people crunched down on the popping gossip. Everyone made jokes about my predicament and chided me about this incident.

Jeremy's father was a high-ranking officer. I learned this shortly after meeting Jeremy. He now threatened to have me reduced in rank, as if I was responsible for his son's behavior. He made it clear that Jeremy and I were not to see each other again.

"One failure after another" is the way I felt about myself. Depression and the humiliation of people's projections on me weighed heavily on my mind. I sought out an Army psychiatrist under the guise that I was distraught over my divorce and the stalker. My captain approved the care and I began to see Richard Pollard, M.D. On my first visit I agreed to return voluntarily at least twice a week.

Later on I agreed to allow the doctor to film me. I remember feeling shy and self-conscious sitting on the couch when Dr. Pollard made this request. Looking back, I can tell that he suspected I had some serious issues. And I did. He knew I'd been abused—though not to what extent—but to me at that point in my life, it was just my normal life. Dr. Pollard said he would use the films for evaluation purposes and to train other Army counselors. I had no problem with that. They could have tossed me out of the Army at any time. Because I cooperated, they did not. I was desperate for help. I saw him for six to eight hours a week for the next eight months.

Meanwhile, I still wanted my privacy and Jeremy wanted to be free from the emotional drama of his family. If we married we would receive an allowance from the Army to move off post. So within a month of knowing each other, we got married. We talked about him getting a job and staying in school.

The ceremony was romantic. As my groom looked into my eyes, he professed to love me until death we would part. My heart melted. We were young. We were infatuated.

In reality, we were running.

Considering my life history, Dr. Pollard asked if I was in love with love. Jeremy was tall, handsome, charismatic, funny, playful, romantic, wild, and mysterious. How I felt about him seemed like love to me. Dr. Pollard was concerned by my quick decision to marry. After the wedding, he increased my therapy sessions. He also questioned me about my intense desire for privacy. I told him I thought I was crazy and did not want people to know it.

Shortly after getting married, I became pregnant. I had been on birth control pills for seven years to control a hormonal imbalance. Two of my three sisters had been unable to conceive and I was thought to have the same health issues as them. Thus, I could not believe I was pregnant.

I found out during a routine weekly Army weigh-in. I was a lean and muscular physical training instructor. The private who weighed me joked about muscles weighing more than fat because I had gained ten pounds. I could not understand my weight gain since my uniforms still fit me perfectly. Furthermore, I did not feel any differently.

Periodically, we were screened for drugs and it was our unit's turn to be tested. My urinalysis showed where the excess weight had been hiding. A major holding the test results asked me the biggest question of my life when he said, "Did you know that you are pregnant?" I slapped him in the face, and then almost fell down. As stunned as we both were, he quickly assisted me to a chair and calmly asked, "Are you all right?" I had just struck an Army officer, but all I could think of was his question, whirling around in my mind. "Did you know that you are pregnant?"

Dr. Pollard encouraged me not to keep the child because he felt that I was still a child myself emotionally and needed a lot of help. He showed enormous concern and compassion for me as he listened to my life unfold in our sessions. I felt like a freak sometimes when he filmed me, but Dr. Pollard knew he had to continually justify providing me services to the military. I don't know how he did it exactly, but he was successful and I was grateful. When my tour of duty in Hawaii ended, I knew I would not see Dr. Pollard again. I was scared.

The final time I saw Dr. Pollard, he suddenly reached out his hand and touched mine. I tore his office apart trying to get away from him. He just sat quietly watching me while a tear slipped down his face. I was crouched in the corner with his papers scattered and a bookshelf knocked over. He simply sat there and said, "You will know you have grown when someone can reach out to touch you and you do not run away." He then invited me to sit back in the chair.

Hesitantly, I sat down. I maintained my distance while he shared something else with me. I was afraid. He said, "Amber, under other circumstances I would have had to put you in the psychiatric ward and had you released from the Army. But I fought to protect you because you are the only patient I have met in twenty years who was so willing to grow. You have courage and I will miss you."

I left that final session feeling weighed down by the sorrow in my heart. I had felt a connection to Dr. Pollard, but realized that I had never fully opened up to him due to fears I myself could not understand at that time.

Naturally, bring pregnant, my life changed drastically. Among other things, I could no longer use alcohol to run away from my troubles. Images of a dead or deformed baby haunted me. I was so nauseous that I did not want to eat. If I did not eat, I believe I would have fainted. I did not like that I had to "eat for two," I worried about my figure.

Even though my weight gain was not yet noticeable, I began to feel sluggish and attributed this to food and weight gain. I felt burdened that I would have to endure this aspect of my femininity. I was totally unaware of the hormonal symphony rehearsing inside of me in preparation for the birth of my son. I was clueless, and tenderly curious.

As a little girl, I had a doll I loved whose name was Marguerite. One day, something bad happened to her—and to me—that made me decide I would never have children. I was a child, and there had been no protection for me against bad things happening, so I believed that I would not be able to protect a child of my own from the danger that exists in this world.

While pregnant, I would lie in bed and wonder what was happening to my body. After blood work came back to confirm my pregnancy, it still was not determined when I had conceived. I was scheduled for a sonogram, prior to which I was to drink a gallon of water. Each time they tried to look through the thickness of my stomach muscles, I was sent back to drink more water.

Two young lieutenants, doctors in training, were there to assist and learn. My breasts and lower body were covered so I felt safe. These men seemed too innocent to harm me. A nurse, the two lieutenants, and a lieutenant-colonel, who was the senior physician, searched for my baby using the sonogram. It took almost two hours for them to find my son. When they did, he was only two millimeters long. I did not understand why my body was gaining weight with such a small thing inside of me. When they gave me a picture of the fetus, I began to cry. What was growing inside of me?

Pregnancy was customary in the obstetrician's office, but not in my experience, so I was terrified. After my appointment, I found the first place I could hide, curled up, and cried. Later, when I went home and told Jeremy the news, he was worried, shocked, confused, and afraid. The first words from his parents when he told them were, "She and that baby are not welcome in our home, now or ever." I presume they believed I was pregnant before we were married.

Mean-spirited people joked about the paternity of my baby behind my back, but none cared enough to ask me who the father might be if it weren't my husband.

Jeremy was unemployed, disconnected from his parents, and despite initially telling me he was studying law, uneducated at nineteen. He was used to living a reckless, happy-go-lucky lifestyle with his motorcycle. He relied upon a small inheritance from his grandmother to fund his partying, food, and the things he did when I was not with him. But we were pregnant now, and I needed him to be more responsible. I was becoming a mother and had to take care of my body. This nineteen-year-old son of a general, who cruised around in his parents' red BMW convertible, was not happy that I was no longer his drinking buddy.

My pregnancy was a nightmare for us. We got married for the housing money, fun, and a romantic idea of the love we had. Both of us were running from things we were too young to understand. Each day we grew apart from each other, regressing into our survival patterns and blaming each other for our situation. We were afraid. Jeremy took a job at a pizza parlor. I was still in the Army, but had been scheduled for early release as a result of my pregnancy.

I continued reporting to duty, but was given a lighter workload. One day, I started to leave for work, thinking Jeremy long gone. As far as I knew he was supposed to be working the early shift preparing for the lunch crowd. I decided to take the stairs down fifteen flights because riding the elevator made me nauseous. Who did I find, but my husband, Jeremy, sleeping in the stairwell. Anxiety, panic, and abandonment flooded my thoughts like a dam being released due to pressure.

When I saw him, I remembered what my mother had once said to me when I told her I was pregnant. I could hear her voice in my head, saying, and "He's a compulsive liar who will leave you alone with this baby." She was referring to the numerous times my father had impregnated her and left for booze and other women, eventually never to return.

My life had become very much like that of the environment I was brought up in: I had become irresponsibly pregnant without a partner to help, without education, and naively depending on the culture at large to help me solve my problems.

Jeremy sleepily stood up and said, "I wasn't supposed to go in this morning and I didn't want to wake you up. So I slept in the hall." I didn't know if he was being truthful. I was so used to the suffocating feeling of anxiousness. In that moment, I was so filled with panic that I chose to believe him because it washed away the terrible feelings I was experiencing. I called it love, and offered it to him graciously because I was so desperate for it to be true.

Denial would become a behavior pattern I would often use as a coping mechanism. It was my mind's conjured up, patchwork perception of reality. It was too difficult to manage my over-stimulated reactions to events in my life. I did not have the ability to deal with the truth. It was more bearable to cope and survive than to feel the pain of another person's harmful and thoughtless ways. Later, therapists would challenge me and call my behavioral style co-dependency.

A few days after avoiding the reality of the stairwell incident, I hid in the hallway, watching to see if my husband was being truthful. To my despair, I witnessed him sneaking back into our apartment thinking I had left. I wanted to die. I felt as if I couldn't breathe. My entire body registered shame like I was burning inside. I could not comprehend it. I had believed that my beauty, my lovemaking, my homemaking, and the vulnerability I felt while carrying the baby would snap him into reality, into responsibility. They didn't. Was I really that bad now that I was pregnant and getting bigger?

I blamed myself for Jeremy's behavior. Another pattern. Victimization had become a role for me to play in many situations, a reason to blame someone else for what I perceived to be real. Perspective allows me now to understand the overwhelming feelings he must have had at barely nineteen. We were both scared. Neither of us had the life skills or maturity to deal with the responsibility of the truth of our situation.

That day, I stayed in the hall for at least half an hour, afraid he'd get angry with me if I confronted him immediately. Finally, I called my commander to say I would be late for duty "because I'm not feeling well." And then I walked in the door.

Jeremy was sleeping inside. But he heard me and woke up to realize he had been caught in a lie. He began yelling at me, "You bitch, just like my mother, always in my business!" Jeremy's fury peaked when I cried.

There it was again, something he'd learned from his home life. I actually understood what he was saying. I was now going to be a "mother" and he did not like his own very well. I could understand all of that, and yet remained clueless to understand how to redirect and understand my own life and future.

He smelled of alcohol and I remembered he had been out late the previous evening. I was terrified. As beautiful and fragrant as it is in Hawaii, its beauty sickened me and always would remind me of the terrible fights we'd been having. The warmth of the morning and the sounds of Honolulu stirred below at street level. I wondered if the neighbors could hear Jeremy's raised voice. I could not fight him. He kept screaming at me as he dressed, and then stormed out of the apartment.

I ran after him and cried, "Jeremy, please don't leave me this way," but he slammed the door and left anyway. Ten minutes later I heard him yelling again, fifteen floors below, and beeping my horn. He had taken my car, my only means of transportation to work. I thought he had changed his mind, so I raced out to our balcony with an uplifted heart. I can still see him, tall and handsome, car door open on my little white car, yelling up at me, "You fucking bitch, you need to mind your own business!"

Our neighbors looked down and yelled at him to go away, but he screamed back that he was "living with a bitch in Apartment 1513." I was so devastated that I wanted to die because I felt unworthy to be carrying a child. Already I was doing to my child what had been done to me: depriving him of a father and a stable home. I made my way to the bathtub, the smallest, safest place in the apartment, where I slept for the rest of the day, paralyzed with fear and despair.

Sometime in the middle of the night, Jeremy came home. He had been drinking. When he found me in the tub, he cried. He picked me up, carried me to the bed, and wrapped me in blankets. He said he was sorry, over and over, and begged for forgiveness. Since I knew of nothing else to do, I forgave him. It was the only thing to do at the time, because quite frankly he was all that I had.

Later, I wondered how much of my motivation truly was forgiveness and how much was his codependency on me. How do we endure trials and tribulations, holding out for love, hoping it may lift a heart and change its course? There was codependency in our relationship, but also definitely compassion, because I still feel it in my heart for him. We created our son, which provided huge growth opportunities for me, as my love for my son challenged me to move away from the edge of destruction and over the years led me to reconstruction, helping me become the stronger, more mature, and capable woman I am today.

Jeremy was struggling with problems he did not know how to handle, and a family who did not support him in the way he needed. We were two wounded human beings struggling side by side with life's strange and unpredictable experiences.

Our fighting continued.

I tried not to butt into Jeremy's business, but my own rage was mounting. I grew to resent my womanly body. No mother should have to give birth without being able to provide her child adequate food, clothing, shelter, healthy love, and safety. I had believed I was a failure even before I became pregnant so I was certain I did not qualify to bring life into this world. I loved and needed Jeremy now because I was vulnerable and scared to death. If nothing else, I needed him as a friend to talk to me, hold me, and help me, because this baby was coming and I knew nothing about being pregnant.

This is a great moment in my story to want to blame him, but let's be really honest with ourselves. He was nineteen. He did step up and do what he thought he could. His efforts just fell short of optimal, as anyone who knew him back then could have predicted.

To his credit, Jeremy joined the Army and went off to Basic Training. He felt proud of doing the "right thing" and set out to be a responsible father. After I got my "early out" from the Army, because I was his wife I was shipped to Jeremy's first assignment at Fort Polk, Louisiana.

Jeremy's father, who wanted to use his rank to influence his son's training, overshadowed Jeremy's attempts at achieving success in the military. Letters I received from Jeremy when he first entered the Army showed that he was really nervous. But that he was determined to do it on his own and take responsibility for the baby and me. Sadly, his burgeoning self-esteem dwindled as his father weaved his way into his training. He was striving towards self-improvement, but his father's interference put unbearable pressure on him—so much, in fact, that he barely made it through Basic. When he returned from Basic, we managed to obtain an off-base house out in the country. It was an older home, but one with personality. Jeremy's mother sent all the baby items one might imagine, including an entire set of bedroom furniture. Evidently, she had always liked me, but had not been allowed to show her feelings until then, acceding to the wishes of the head of her household, Jeremy's domineering father. She was excited about the baby and I was grateful for her kindness.

Loneliness had become my new companion. Its presence felt violent, its intensity constantly stabbing away at my sanity. Any sign of affection was welcomed. The volume on preexisting depression gets dialed way up during pregnancy, as hormones saturate the body. Jeremy had become extremely distant due to conflicting feelings of his own self-worth and the comparison to his father. Even when he made supportive statements to his son, his dad was gross-ly condescending. The message was that Jeremy never would be good enough and that his father never would help him financially be-cause he had married me. Jeremy was constantly being negatively reinforced by his narcissistic father's message that he was a failure.

As tensions mounted for Jeremy during duty hours, he came home later each night without calling. He drank heavily, yelled at me, and physically pushed me around. He would shut down verbally or leave suddenly, giving no information as to where he was going or for how long. He would just walk out. There is an old saying that the "best way to a man's heart is through his stomach." My mother had told me that. I adopted the belief that if I made good meals and had the house clean when he came home he would be happier: the old, 1950's feminine model for marriage engrained in women's psyches. Thus, I spent a lot of time creating meals I thought would please him. I actually loved taking care of the hearth and home.

My neighbors often complimented me on my housekeeping skills. I shared this knack for domesticity with my mother and she had taught me well. Our home was always clean, with fresh sheets drying on the line out in the sunshine. Not only did I provide Jeremy with clean clothing and delicious meals, but with all the sex he want-ed. Throughout my pregnancy, I physically enjoyed him even more than before.

Late one summer evening, I made lasagna and a salad. I had picked wildflowers as a centerpiece for the dinner table and was waiting for Jeremy to arrive. Since I was no longer the slender, sexy young woman he had met I had taken great care of my appearance. After all, I was eight months pregnant and lovemaking was still very good. I had gone to great lengths to look and smell pretty so he would be amorous. When he arrived, I was happy he was home. Loneliness had spent the day massaging me. As he changed out of his uniform, I took the food from the oven and placed it on the table.

When we finished dinner, Jeremy informed me that he was leaving to spend the evening with friends. I was angry, hurt, and lonely. I challenged him, and we began to argue. We were standing up screaming at each other when Jeremy punched me in the face. I fell to the floor with a dual pain of the body and of the soul. *How could he hit me?* I was pregnant for God's sake.

I held back my tears as Jeremy stormed out of the room. His fury was heightened by his realization of what he had done. I whimpered as silently as possible until he left, and then lay on the floor for hours. As sad as I was, tears would not come. I selfishly began to hate the baby and myself because I could not commit suicide without killing my child.

I used the same pattern of thinking I had used most of my life, blaming my femininity and myself for Jeremy's abusive actions. The combination of loneliness, lack of knowledge, fear, and hormones flooded my mind and interfered with my ability to cope effectively. I truly was in great need of help. Jeremy was barely old enough to understand that he needed help as well.

The gifts of womanhood made me feel shameful: love of the hearth, carrying and birthing large babies through our tiny bodies, and tolerating intense pain to bring forth life. These were some of the gifts of being female. I was in deep shame about having a vagina, breasts, and an enlarged belly. These were constant reminders to me that I was unwanted as a whole being, part of a less desirable gender, other than for what was necessary, things like sex and mothering.

I slipped into deeper depression as the darkness of that summer evening faded and eventually called the Army chaplain for support.

He came to my home immediately and offered me shelter on the base, where I would be protected from Jeremy's violence. I stayed for one night and realized that these people could only do so much for me. They were not going to take me in and help me raise my baby. I felt I had to believe Jeremy would get help and that things would get better. Believing I had nowhere else to go and making excuses for what was really going on were my codependency at work, just as I'd learned from my mother. Many women throughout history have done the same.

My naiveté and limited life experience led me to hold unrealistic hope that Jeremy would "simply" change and love the baby and me. It seemed so logical in my brain.

He said he loved me, but he'd learned from his father that love meant to cause others pain. He learned from his mother that if she really loved her man, she would tolerate a man's behavior and stay. A "real man" was in control and could basically do as he pleased. Being in a military culture, women were to do as they were asked by their husbands—and as soldiers they were forced to tolerate unregulated male behavior. I was stuck smack in the middle of my own intelligent rage and the cage of social conformity.

After that night, I spent most of my days waiting for the birth resting, cleaning house, washing laundry, hanging it on the line, and folding it cocooned in a web of loneliness. I did find beauty in nature. There were a handful of precious moments that fed my naked soul and my vulnerable belly, swollen breasts, and slaughtered, ignorant heart.

A few days after my early September due date a flying cockroach whizzed into the kitchen. My stomach was so big I could not see my feet and tripped over the cat trying to avoid the insect. I twisted my ankle and could not move. I crawled to the telephone to call Jeremy's unit. He had to come home and take me to the hospital. On the way to the hospital, he called me a "stupid bitch, just like my mother." Although I felt like crying, I knew that if I cried, it would irritate him and he would completely shut down, so I held back my tears.

Once at the hospital, Jeremy turned on the charm and became the best father-to-be. Just like his father, he was a charismatic social butterfly. He hovered over the doctors and nurses who tended to my injured foot. The whole time I felt like a child watching a movie, going with the flow of every moment, totally unprepared for what would come next. I felt safe in the hospital. Everyone, including Jeremy, fussed over me, being so pregnant and having a twisted ankle. I never wanted to leave.

On the way home, Jeremy dropped the charade and resumed the verbal abuse. He said disgustedly that he had to take the rest of the day off to care for me. When we arrived, he got out and went into the house, leaving me to get myself from the car to the house forty-five feet away. Over his shoulder, he told me to get my own ice for my foot, again called me a "bitch like my stupid mother," and then promptly went to bed.

A neighbor ran over and assisted me to the door. I refused her offer to help me into the house because I did not want to risk disturbing Jeremy. Thirty-seven weeks pregnant, hobbling on my injured leg, I dragged myself to the kitchen for ice. Jeremy was annoyed by the sounds of my struggles so he stormed into the kitchen. He was so agitated that he swung open the freezer door, grabbed the ice trays and dumped them on the floor. I slipped and fell on the ice.

His eyes were dark with anger and disgust as I lay on the floor dodging tumbling ice cubes. But he also had a smile on his face, as if this brought him satisfaction. As he walked out of the kitchen, he told me I was pitiful. I lay on that floor in the fetal position, crying as quietly as possible. My head was on the floor and I noticed ice cubes melting all around me. I was thinking this had to be the worst moment of my life, just as I had begun to have hope with life growing within my body that something beautiful existed on this earth.

I understood Jeremy's anger and suffering as if it was my own, and it was—as long as I stayed around to make it so. I wanted to believe that love would help both of us heal. I felt a deep, shy love for the baby within me, and a deeper longing for Jeremy, a need for his protection and support. For these reasons, I constantly forgave him. He was all I believed was available for the baby and me. Part of my need came from an illusion of safety related to my storybook image that the simplicity of cooking and cleaning would solve all of the problems between us. While my love illusion felt as if it were the path to healing, it also prevented me from accepting the responsibility of the truth. I had no talent or skill yet for coping with reality.

I had no one to turn to and no other place to go, so I gathered the ice cubes, put them in a dishtowel and tied the towel to my purse, which I dragged into the bedroom. All of my six-foot-two husband was sprawled out on our queen-sized bed. I pulled myself up onto the bed, took as little space as possible, placed the ice on my ankle, and fell into a deep sleep.

On September 10, Ringer was born. I was twenty-seven years old. Jeremy was barely twenty.

Jeremy's mother came to visit for two weeks. It was to be the best time I ever spent in that small Louisiana house. While she was there, Jeremy was good to me. He made sure his mother had plenty to drink and he joined her. She would stay home at night with me while Jeremy went out to "de-stress." His mother told me that this was a privilege that men enjoyed that women were not entitled to.

She babysat for us one evening so we could go together to the only nightclub in the area.

The club was where I first met Jeremy's girlfriend. She had long, brown hair, was very slender, and had a beautiful face. I knew he was cheating on me the moment they "bumped into" each other. She worked at the Army Post Exchange as a cashier. I was angry and jealous. I had too much to drink, became obnoxious, and was asked to leave. By that point, I could not find my husband and he had my car keys—thankfully. He had already left and I had no way home. As I stumbled through the parking lot, some soldiers from Jeremy's unit offered me a ride. It was a good thing, or else I might not have made it home alive.

As we were getting ready to depart, Jeremy and his girlfriend pulled up. He got out of the car and asked what my problem was. His buddies were trying to calm me down when Jeremy slapped me across the face and said, "Put the bitch in the car." His friends asked about his girlfriend. He told them he was giving her a ride home. I felt humiliated. I wanted to kill her right there, as she snuggled against my husband while I rode in the back seat. Fortunately, I was too drunk and too weak after delivering the baby just two weeks earlier. I passed out.

When we arrived home, Jeremy woke me and disgustedly told me to "get in the house." I stumbled in and watched them pull away.

Jeremy's mother was sleeping on the living room couch. I could tell she had also been drinking. Thankfully, the baby was asleep.

Ringer slept in his bassinet with me right next to him. Even in my drunken state, I could hear each time he made a sound. I had to feed him twice that night from the breast milk I'd pumped earlier in the day. I did not want the alcohol to hurt him. I loved to love my baby. He smelled so clean and beautiful. What a gift I had in front of me. My jealousy and anger seemed to fade and I finally slept sometime around 5:00 A.M. I am certain the alcohol numbed my pain.

Early the next morning, Jeremy returned. His mother asked no questions and he went directly to bed. I tried to talk to his mother, but she reminded me of the rules for men and the rules for women. I felt trapped and hated life again.

It was only in quiet moments with my son that I knew love, joy, and mystery in those days. I felt like a scientist and a doctor rolled into one, caring for this living entity. Each hour seemed to provide a new experience for which I lacked the necessary skills to cope. I existed in my life as I created it in my mind. I had begun to feel new things in my heart with the birth of Ringer, but I also felt deep shame about feeling love.

During the first winter of Ringer's life, one snowy evening he awoke for his routine love, feeding, and diaper change. Jeremy slept through most of these moments, since he worked long hours and he was always out. My feet were cold on the hardwood floors as I rocked back and forth while breastfeeding. This night I played Tchaikovsky's "O Come Emmanuel" and in the candlelight I gently swayed back and forth holding my son close to my shoulder. I could hear the wind outside and a branch tapping on the window.

Newborns do not have full control over their heads, and Ringer suddenly jerked so his little face touched mine. I felt the warmth and abruptly put him on the couch. I felt shame at this type of innocent, loving touch. Ringer wiggled uncomfortably wanting the warmth of me, so again I picked the little guy up. I looked guiltily around the room to see if anyone could see me, as if anyone would be watching at 3:30 A.M. I let Ringer snuggle close to me so I could smell his hair and skin, and allowed him to nestle on my shoulder and touch my face. Ringer's little legs touched my sorrow-filled heart. I began to cry as I held him closely and wondered if he understood. I felt the purity of his presence and his love for me.

Finally I let go of my fears and danced to the music with Ringer long after he was sleeping. I did not want to let him go while I experienced the miracle of love through pure human touch. I placed him in his bassinet and cried until dawn. I had discovered something new—healthy human touch—and I felt guilty about it. I was troubled because I did not know how to continue to love and receive love from this baby, but I became determined to protect him—though I had no idea how.

In the quiet moments during Jeremy's daily absences, I began to grow mentally and spiritually from the seed of love that had been planted by my intimate connection with Ringer. I was careful not to express love to Ringer too much in front of my husband, fearing he might become angry with me. I was desperate to keep the depth of this love a secret.

Jeremy struggled daily with his emotions. He was torn between his love for me and Ringer and the hatred he felt for himself. His projection of my neediness, like his mother's, disturbed and distanced him from me. He would not allow our connection to penetrate his own dark fears. I never stopped believing that our love would help him to overcome his self-hatred. Eventually he started sleeping in the garage, but sometimes he would come into the house to hold and love Ringer. Still, distance remained even though it was clear that he loved the baby.

Jeremy made many attempts to better himself, but he always regressed into old addictions and habits. His self-worth had been built on the façade his father and mother had created for his life. His father had a military career to protect, and his family followed orders as if they were his troops. His favorite saying was, "Don't air your dirty laundry in public."

What power some people seem to wield over others.

The fear and rage in Jeremy regarding his father and mother would consume him at times. He had opportunities to rise above these emotions, but could not. His anger was fueled by his mother's self-victimization and codependency, and his father's abusive and reckless contributions to their cycle of violence. These things outweighed Jeremy's desire for love and fueled his hatred for his parents. Jeremy's alcoholic mother was fed liquor as if it was normal. This gave wind to a flaming darkness in her that no one wanted to discuss, but more and more it affected their daily lives. The image of "correctness" in society seemed to be all that mattered, even at the price of one's body, mind, and soul.

During Operation Desert Storm, the Army's Inactive Ready Reserve (IRR) troops were called up to support the mission. Being an IRR, I was called to serve in Washington, D.C., for ninety days, which turned into eighteen months. Fourteen-month-old Ringer stayed with one of my sisters for the first three months of this duty. I was in contact with Jeremy . . . when I could reach him. It turned out he had pawned our stereo, television, and other items for a trip to Texas and to purchase a motorcycle. He was not paying our bills and was living recklessly. He also was on the verge of being discharged from the Army.

Meanwhile, I was caught up in the military life once again, including having to cope with individual soldiers' lack of ethics. We were well paid to serve on temporary duty, given luxurious living quarters, good meals, hardship funds, uniforms, and enough free time to become entangled in the lives of others. In many ways, the Gulf War brought freedom for my compatriots to party hard and sleep with others, married or not. Many people I worked with in Washington who received these perks barely performed their duties, while the men and women stationed in Saudi Arabia and at other home posts got only regular pay for serving their country.

Many things I experienced then were unfair, and my loneliness for Ringer was only deepened by the negative atmosphere of my peers and leaders. After my first assignment of ninety days was extended, I flew out to Oregon and brought Ringer to Washington with me. I could not bear missing him any longer. Not one other person on the planet cared either way.

I worked in the division of Mortuary Affairs and was dedicated to my duties, but I was disgusted with the sexual advances made toward me by the men there, including by my commanding officer (a reservist). I was judged a prude and often left out of social events because I would not play along. Jeremy had been communicating with my main commander, the Adjutant-General of the Army. She was the one who informed me that Jeremy had been discharged from the military and that I needed to ship my household goods somewhere because we were no longer entitled to military housing. She also let me know that Jeremy had been complaining about me and trying to cause problems. Fortunately, I had put forth extra effort to serve my country well. It paid off. The Army provided me with protection and allowed me to ship my belongings anywhere I wanted.

When my assignment in Washington ended, I decided to stay in the D.C. area. I had no other place to go. Shortly thereafter, Jeremy and I were divorced.

I was nervous about finding a job, but had put away money and invested in some nice business suits. I was hired by a small engineering firm. As an administrative assistant, I worked on contracts for the Department of Energy. I hated my job. More often than not, most of the staff had absolutely nothing to do. I was motivated and energetic, so the absence of responsibility left me frustrated and bored.

The engineering firm had an unspoken rule that women would wear skirts, preferably at least two inches above the kneecap. For spite, I wore pantsuits the majority of the time. Thus, I became known as the "one who doesn't follow orders." At a company meeting, I questioned the owner about this unspoken, unwritten policy. I was tired of my managers harassing me to comply. I could not understand why female employees even put up with this rule. We were not selling legs or sex. We were supposed to be selling services that support systems engineering.

I stood up in front of the entire company and said, "Mr. Barnes, I have been told that I have to wear skirts to work, and my job has been threatened if I do not comply. Nobody seems to know the answer, and most people only whisper about this. Is it true that we are required to wear skirts to work?"

There was a hushed silence and people slouched in their chairs. Some covered their faces and someone laughed out loud. "That is ridiculous," replied Mr. Barnes, "I cannot dictate what women wear to work unless it is inappropriate or unsuitable for the work environment." He swiftly moved on to the next topic. It is amazing what people will endure to keep their jobs. I watched his senior executives look at me as if I were dead meat. I am certain they thought I was stupid, but I felt good about speaking the truth, even if it could cost me my job.

Immediately afterward, the harassment and threats doubled. I was called into the company president's office due to complaints about me for all sorts of little things. I was nervous and frustrated with the blatant cycle of ignorance. I worked almost fifty hours a week. Every time Ringer got sick I was told that if I took leave I would be fired. The managers did not care that I was a single parent. I needed a job, but somehow I got the idea to quit the company and start my own business. And so I did.

It began with my friend, Jake Barlow. We had shared an office and I started to tell him about my life. He would stare at me as if he were glued to a television drama because he could not believe the stories I told. My life unfolded for the first time to someone who not only accepted it, but also offered enormous compassionate attention to me. We spent endless hours talking about my crazy life. Jake began to give me positive feedback, using statements such as, "So much courage," "So much strength," and "You should write a book."

During this frenzied time of my life, Jeremy was harassing me about having to pay child support. He tried to get out of it by accusing me of sleeping with other men. I desperately needed the money, because I was not making enough to support Ringer and myself. When I reached out to Jeremy's family, they said, "If you cannot take care of Ringer by yourself then we are going to take him away from you." I was angry and afraid of their threats, but did not have enough money for an attorney. I wrote to the top three attorneys in Washington, D.C. Two replied that I made too much money for them to be of any assistance.

The third, Robert Madden, laughed and said, "You have balls of steel to walk into my office asking for free service. That is why I am going to help you, young lady." Pride does not have a place when you need help, and pride did not prevent me from seeking it.

I felt shame and unworthiness, but I knew that Mr. Madden did not know that—and it was irrelevant, because my son needed care. At the time, Jeremy was in California. With Mr. Madden's representation, we won $500 per month in child support and I was awarded full custody of Ringer. There was no contest for custody. I felt that was unfortunate, because it showed that my son's father did not want to be a part of his life. Mr. Madden also inspired me to go into business. He told me that he had two master's degrees, one in law and one in psychology. He said I was too bright to "go to college just to learn to work for someone else." I quit the engineering company with a grand exit. Another woman in the firm decided to move on as well, so we shared a farewell luncheon.

Ringer became my life's motivation, inspiring me in the presence of enormous fear and doubt. My love for him fueled my flaming heart to move out into the world of possibility. I was on my way, with no idea of where I was going or how I was going to get there.

CHAPTER 3

BLUE — DROWNING

 When I left the engineering firm with my last paycheck of $762 in hand, I had an eviction notice and a child to feed. I ran a small ad in *The Washington Post* offering to manage businesses. My first client was my psychotherapist. I had begun seeing her while still on active duty, using my military insurance to offset the expense. She pre-billed the insurance company for extra visits to come so that she could be paid when my insurance ran out. When the payments ran out, she invited me to manage her affairs in exchange for therapy sessions.

This woman was different from other therapists I'd had. She seemed to really believe in me and encouraged me to believe in myself. She was a bit unusual, however. Her hair was a rat's nest and her clothing was always wrinkled and smelled dirty. She even wore snagged, torn pantyhose. Though her appearance was off-putting to me, she had a soft voice and cried occasionally, and I felt she really understood me. What I did not know was that the lives of her patients were like therapy for her. I thought that a therapist had all the answers and understood what I could not. A clear lack of maturity had led me to that delusion. I felt that she truly believed in me. She may not have been the best alternative, but for me there was no one else to trust. When she asked me to work for her I really believed she thought I had talent.

I worked for both my therapist and her husband. I organized her home and her patient files. Problems began when she asked me to "doctor up" her client records so that she could obtain more insurance money. I had a problem with recreating session notes. It did not feel right. It made me wonder how she handled my records, and what they said.

One thing we talked about was a new relationship I'd formed with a coworker from the systems engineering firm. It just didn't feel right. I had a bad feeling about him, and I wasn't convinced that he really was a good guy. But I did not have faith in my own feelings of doubt.

It's demoralizing when you are an adult living in society and do not know how to make up your own mind about things. That was me. I did not trust myself, believing both of these powerful people in my life, my boyfriend (and soon-to-be fiancé) and my therapist knew more than me. They were educated, successful, and came from good families. So I listened to both of them, as they were the two most influential people in my life. Nonetheless something was causing me enormous feelings of anxiety and I was convinced that it was me, my fear of being in relationship.

My boyfriend, Mitch, told me one day, "Amber, I come from a family where my mother and father have been married for over forty years. We have never had any family troubles like what you've been through growing up and in your previous marriages. You are just scared because of your background. I am a good guy. Ask all of my friends."

One evening my therapist took me out to dinner, unknown to me, another ethical violation. During our meal, I asked her two questions.

"Do you think that what I am doing with your client files is legal?" I asked.

"Of course! I just get behind. You have no idea what these insurance agencies require in paperwork. Just don't let anyone know you have read my clients files. That's why I've hired you as a professional. You have to keep this confidential."

"Okay, I guess you would know. I am just not so comfortable with this." Trying not to make her mad, I changed the subject, "Anyway, do you really think I should marry this guy?"

"He is a nice guy, Amber. You can trust me."

"Will you be my maid of honor? I don't have anyone to be in the wedding."

She smiled, "Of course I will. And maybe my husband can be an usher or something."

Trust is a funny word with an even funnier definition. I have hated myself most of my life for my inability to trust effectively. Are people really *that* manipulative? Do I *always* have to be on my guard with them? How would I ever learn to trust myself? There are many things that happen in humanity that are not addressed, are hidden and ignored, and those that choose to speak up can be the target of unjust punishment. I had learned this as a little girl. My doubt's fearful dominance over me allowed me to ignore my own intuition and instead to buy in to someone else's version of reality—that person's illusion—over and over again. It did seem safer, for a while, to trust in a fantasy of hope and safety, even if it was inauthentic, instead of my primal instinct of doubt and discernment. I had been taught to subordinate my will to the will of others as a female. Now I did it again.

Mitch Gilroy of Fredericksburg, Virginia, became my fiancé. When we had worked together he had flirted with me while I was sharing an office with Jake Barkley. Jake and I discussed my goals for the future prior to my leaving the company. My quest centered on finding a husband to love and protect my son and me. I was looking for a clean-cut, tall, strong, employed, church-going Caucasian. Three men were introduced to me within a week. One was a gardener, one an accountant, and the third was Mitch.

Deciding he was worth pursuing, I asked Mitch to go to the bookstore with me on our lunch break, as I needed a book on etiquette for a workshop I was going to be teaching. When it was time to leave the bookstore, Mitch said, "If you can guess what is in that glass bottle, I'll take you to lunch." He was very flirtatious. I smiled, told him what was in the bottle, and we went to lunch. There was a strong sexual chemistry between us from the beginning. My body was on fire for him. He made comments about my beautiful legs and assisted me in getting into his car. He had gorgeous eyes and I was blinded by his presence.

During lunch Mitch revealed that he was engaged to be married. My heart sank. What were we doing flirting over lunch? He felt that marrying this woman was what everyone expected of him and he wanted to please his parents. His fiancée had never been married and was very sweet. They lived separately, but he would go to her house for occasional meals and to pick up the laundry she had done for him. He told me he did not love her.

I don't know what I was thinking, but my heart was nauseated by Mitch's shared confidences. Why were we flirting and touching when he was engaged? Mitch said I was the prettiest girl he had ever met who was interested in him. He asked, "Why are you interested in me? I am just a country boy." He was tall and handsome, and very nice. In some ways, he reminded me of Ringer's father.

That night I was depressed—again. I could not understand why a man engaged to another woman was being so flirtatious with me. I struggled with my feelings, because when I had picked up my little boy from preschool, I already had told him I had met the best man in the world to be a father to him and that he wasn't available. That was way too much to share with a two-year-old child. He did not understand my tears, but I could see it hurt him to see me cry. The feelings of abandonment I'd experienced as a child without a father intensified my desire to provide a father for my son. He also wanted a father desperately.

Knowing what I do now, if I could go back and make a different choice I would listen to the depression. I believe that my body, my nervous system, was trying to protect me. The depression was a direct message to do something differently than I had done in the past.

Unable to sleep that night, I slipped into anxiety and an overwhelming sense of fear. I was completely untrusting of the possibility that the fear and anxiety were healthy clues for me. In therapy, I had learned that I feared intimacy. In my home I had been taught that I needed to have a man protect me. Therefore I believed that because he was a Christian, Mitch was good and desirable, and that it was me who was damaged and lacked sense. I felt a lack of self-worth, fear of not having protection for my son, fear of losing a nice guy, and fear of my overwhelming loneliness. In panic that my emotions would swallow me, the only escape was to pursue Mitch. I told myself he could not be happy about his impending marriage, or *why else would he have flirted with me so much?* I had to find out. My therapist agreed with me.

Mitch and I began to spend one romantic evening after the other with one another. I did everything I knew to captivate him. We were cheating on his fiancée. He talked about how he was torn between his feelings for me and his obligation to her, a dilemma that was intensified by the fact that his family loved her. I used all of my sexual knowledge to please this passionate lover. I believed he loved me. I believed he was afraid to stand up to his parents. Why else would a guy risk losing his relationship? Fear stricken, I convinced myself that I was doing the right thing and pushed him to be honest with his fiancée, friends, and family.

Although I pushed Mitch to be honest, I forgot to do the same for myself. I was in a triangulation with him and his fiancée, making myself the victim again, desperately and fearfully rescuing him and persecuting her. In reality, I had no conscious idea of what I was doing except that I "needed" to be with him and "needed" him to be a father for Ringer. I was afraid on my own. I did not feel safe, especially at night. I was terrified that someone would kidnap my son. I was afraid of the rapist the news said was on the loose in my neighborhood.

Everything is perfect in the beginning of relationships, isn't it? I pressed him to announce that his wedding was off. Mitch spent time pondering this, but made no move. His hesitation became an emotional nightmare for me because I was engrossed in him and tormented by the thought of losing him. I felt miserable, but didn't have the courage or strength to walk away. I didn't have the emotional intelligence to understand what was happening.

Mitch had Bible passages ingrained in his mind about my being a divorced woman. His parents were deeply imbedded in their own religious reality and had impressed it upon their children. He was struggling with his attraction for me, teachings of the Bible as interpreted by his parents, and the potential shock to his fiancée and family. After he finally announced our relationship to everyone, his fiancée called me.

"Hello, is this Amber Bradshaw?"

"Yes, who's calling?"

"I am . . . I was . . . Mitch's fiancée until you took him away."

I felt shame run through my veins like fire. My heart beat rapidly. I felt territorial and defensive, but also empathetic. Mitch had met her two years earlier, after her previous boyfriend had been killed. He'd told me that at first he felt sorry for her. Then he felt marrying her was the right thing to do. It seems warped to me now, but at that time he sounded like he was being a nice guy to me.

"I hate you, you bitch. Do you know what I am going through? I can't eat, or drink, or go to work. I can't even sleep. Why did you do this to me?" she angrily asked me. "How long has this been going on? I knew something was going on, but how long?"

I started to say something, but she yelled, "Shut up! I don't want to listen to you." She was devastated.

In a strange way I felt glad for her that she did not have to be with this man, and was glad it was me instead of her. This, too, had become one of my patterns of behavior—telling myself that I was taking on the pain of others, thinking I was doing something for them, heroically. It is very clever how we can create stories to justify our behavior. I had no idea at the time that I was doing this. I actually believed at some level that I was doing everybody some good in this situation. Where did I learn how to do that?

When I did get the chance to speak, I did not lie about my relationship with Mitch. I felt the woman's pain as she lashed out at me. This was devastating for her and I felt terrible about my involvement with Mitch. I allowed her to scream at me.

"I hate you! I hate both of you!" she screamed. Then she said, "You deserve each other. He is not as nice a person as he seems. You will find out, and I hope you get what you deserve."

I thought it was the pain talking, but little did I know that her words would come back to haunt me. Looking back, I am glad that she did not have to endure what I did. I was a fool. I was about to bring pain not only into my life, but into my son's as well. Very quickly, the illusion of my "perfect" relationship would be shattered.

This period was painful for Mitch because his mother was relentless in heaping biblical guilt on him. After Mitch told his parents of the breakup with his fiancée, his mother sent him Bible quotes such as: a "spoiled and divorced woman" is not fit for a husband. According to her, I was fit only to remain unmarried for the rest of my life, because I had been married before and had carried a "seed" from that marriage. Her judgments only pushed Mitch to try to rescue me from my treacherous past. I saw him as a hero, someone who cared enough to rescue me. I thought I needed a father for my son so I could fit in with society. However, the harsh judgments from Mitch's family stayed with me and deepened my own ruthless judgments of who I was. This strange, complicated web of events brought many truths to light for all of us.

Mitch wanted to elope, but I thought it would be more respectful to allow his family to see their son get married. Disillusioned as I was, I actually believed that getting married and involving the family would soothe things over. I selected a conservative wedding gown to please his strict Christian family. Because I felt like gutter trash I was trying to dress up my own perception of myself—another self-harming misjudgment. Despite my attempts to please them, his family regarded me with open hostility and criticism and barely spoke to me on my wedding day. They were not happy.

I decided to be patient, believing that in time they would get to know me and see how wonderful I could be. I thought I knew what I was doing and had my heart wide open to be accepted and loved by his family. I was still a young lady in hopes of having a loving family. Even after everything I'd been through already with Sam and Jeremy, I was still very naïve. Armed with their strict Christian morality, I simply did not have a chance against Mitch's family. I was trash to them, plain and simple.

Ultimately, I became a threat to them as my truest nature burst from the soil during our marriage together. Family truths were exposed and I began to see more clearly that I was not all that bad.

Mitch's strange, awkward ways began to manifest themselves on our honeymoon. These somehow went back to vacation trips he had taken with his family. Something about traveling seemed to bring out the demon in him. Everything had to be absolutely perfect. We were in the Bahamas, in a lovely little cottage overlooking the bay. It was very expensive there. Right away, a problem. Anything to do with spending money or wastefulness bothered Mitch.

I cannot remember what happened to make him throw me across the room and onto the bed. But he did. My head hit the headboard. He then walked over and sat on me, using his arms to force me to lie there. I was beginning to freak out. He would not let me go, he said, until I calmed down. He wanted me to be quiet. It was as if he knew that what he was doing was not right, but felt he could make things better by forcing me to cooperate and calm the situation. I was not supposed to be alarmed or frightened. His eyes told me that he was both.

The beautiful illusion of my world collapsed around me. I heard the sounds of the ocean outside and my thoughts tossed and swirled with the whipping water being thrown upon the shore. I crashed deep into the depths of my mind. Where would I find an answer to bring me back to the surface? I died inside. I had no will to face this type of violence again and I felt a part of my mind shatter into a million tiny pieces. I lay in silence like a dead fish floating in the water. I wanted the water to rise up high and pull me under. I could not breathe.

This was my fault, I believed, because I had stolen him away from his fiancée.

How had my mind become this way: ignorant, blind, and self-deprecating?

I did not shed a tear. Mitch did not like tears. I'd observed this while dating him, when Ringer cried. Ringer was three and even so Mitch told him tears were "for sissies." Tears fueled Mitch's fury. Now, lying on the bed, I saw a monster in my new husband and so-called protector of my son. I lay there in surrender as he kissed me "to make things better." Visions of my son flashed in my mind. I had been raised in a fatherless home for a good portion of my youth. Bad things had happened in my youth. I had to care for my son better than I had been cared for. I had to live for him if not for myself. I wanted to make this marriage work for Ringer.

I could not grasp that those types of demons were living everywhere behind the smiling faces of so many people. I didn't know how I could have missed seeing this violent characteristic in this man. What would I tell my clients, my friends, his family, and my son? Nobody would believe me. I remembered his ex-fiancée's wish for me to get what I "deserved," and hoped she somehow felt fulfilled. Throughout that miserable honeymoon, I became an actress to fool Mitch into thinking I was happy. It soon became evident that if he thought I wasn't happy his tension would rise and he would press me for answers about how much I was enjoying myself.

I discovered that he lacked in social graces and the ability to fit in with society outside his scope of control. He had problems ordering from the menu and often got very uptight if service was not perfect. So many things made him upset. I had never seen this before then. Maybe the pre-wedding bliss had blinded me to his nature or perhaps I was too naïve to have seen it before. He had a deep sense of unworthiness that drove him to insist on perfection in all things. If everything seemed all right then it was, and he felt safe. He had to feel *in control.*

My most interesting memory of our honeymoon occurred after the first attack. Once he was certain that I would remain calm on the bed, he took the hotel Bible into the bathroom and frantically read the scriptures. I did not understand what had happened to him, but it terrified me. It all seemed related to the very God to whom I had prayed to bring this man to me in love. I had sought guidance outside of myself to some source known as God, when all along my own nervous system flooded me with anxiety, clearly trying to communicate with me that the relationship was not safe. I know this now.

After the honeymoon and back on the job, Mitch was recognized for his "invaluable and dutiful service" that year to his company. It was important to him that he "do the right thing" publicly because then he fit in and felt a part of something dignified. He desperately wanted acceptance. On this occasion, he was accepted publicly, but it placed him in conflict with his deep yearning to be free from his biblical chains and the strict rules his parents had ingrained in him. He was not the man he portrayed himself to be, and I was the only one privy to this dichotomy. Out of the public eye and in the privacy of home, all of his frustrations in life surfaced in ugly ways. He hated himself and desperately wanted to be liked.

Mitch insisted on visiting his family at least twice a month. I hated these visits because there was some unspoken evil in their household, hidden under the guise of good Christian behavior. It was ugly to me and I feared it. I wanted to love away all the pain these people had neatly placed deep within their beings. They sought God and Christ outside of themselves, and I wanted to show them that God was already living within them.

Mitch's father powerfully controlled the behavior of others. Everyone around him was on bended knee in fear. One weekend at his parents' house, I was putting three-year-old Ringer to bed when Mitch came into the bedroom. He was concerned that I was not participating in the ritualistic evening card game that was always followed by prayer and Bible reading. If you were in that house you were expected to attend. I became anxious as Mitch insisted, "Leave that child alone." In a hushed, harsh whisper, he then told Ringer, "Shut up, you brat. Go to sleep now or I will whip your ass."

Mitch and his family were evil in the darkest way. They were in hiding behind the Christian story, and Jesus was their costume. I began to hate them all. Looking back, I can see it was healthy for me to feel that way.

Usually at bedtime Ringer wanted me to read to him and I wanted to read to him. It was the safest time to snuggle and be close without Mitch's jealousy surfacing. Ringer and I clung to each other as we moved through our new life with Mitch, but usually only when Mitch could not see us. But this time, I told Mitch I wanted to stay with Ringer for a while longer and that I would join his family shortly. He left, but within minutes he stormed back into the bedroom, jerked me away from my son, and said, "You are an asshole. We are all waiting for you."

I was provoked, whispering, "Why can't you play without me? I am tired."

Angrily, Mitch said, "This is the way we do things around here. When Dad wants to play cards, that's what we do."

Ringer was scared. Mitch had a strong hold on my wrist, so I calmed myself for Ringer's sake, "I'll be alright honey. Get some sleep for Mommy." I smiled and kissed him. "I'll be back shortly to check on you. I love you, baby," I said as I walked away.

I was furious when I reached the kitchen and sensed the nervousness of both Mitch and his mother. They smiled at me and casually asked about Ringer. Mitch's father mumbled something in his Southern mumbling accent that I couldn't understand.

I said, "I didn't hear what you said. Can you say that again?"

Mitch and his mother almost fell out of their chairs. Why were they so afraid? I did not understand the man and had simply asked for clarification. Mitch's father smiled at me. I sensed he had some respect for me because I was the only one ever to stand up to him and speak directly to him other than to chitchat.

He said, "Are you ready to play cards now that the baby is asleep?"

This was my opportunity; "Well Ringer is not asleep yet, as I understood you were waiting for me to play cards. I will probably go in and check on him soon."

"Well, all right then, let's play. Want something to drink?"

"No, thank you."

Ringer fell asleep while we played cards. I won. It was a small victory for me.

The card playing ended when Mitch's father decided it was time to read the scriptures. This ritual seemed stupid to me because no one even listened to what was being read. I did. They always read the same passages over and over as if these were the only ones they agreed with. That night, not caring about consequences, I asked, "Can anyone explain the Bible passage we just heard?"

They were all stunned. I was highly irritated at being forced to sit and listen to Mitch's father read words that were so muffled no one could understand what he said. What was the purpose of reading scripture when we couldn't hear it?

Whatever and wherever God and Christ were, they seemed to be screaming from within me, as if these acts were outrageous. Mitch kicked me hard under the table and his father mumbled through a half smile. His mother jumped up and busied herself serving refreshments to escape this uncomfortable moment. I asked her to stay in the room. I wanted to know what they believed the scriptures meant. I was angry about the misuse of the Bible. I felt they read merely from habit and without heart, simply to justify themselves as dutiful Christians.

Mitch's father reread the scripture. He said it was about love.

Provoked, I asked all of them, "If I didn't play cards with you and chose to put my child to sleep instead, would you think I did not love you?"

When the spirit speaks through you, there is no reply, but I touched the heart of Mitch's father with this and I could see the suffering he had experienced in his life. Mitch's mother dropped her eyes in shame, I suppose. Maybe it was fear of what her husband would say. My husband was too damned angry with me to say a word. He knew he could get to me later. I hugged Mitch's father goodnight and was flooded with a mixture of emotions.

People are strange. Why do we live in our world in such ways?

His father was not upset, so Mitch did not know whether to scold me or love me. And so he slept. I lay awake in the full realization that I was living in the absence of safety and of genuine, unconditional love. I felt that maybe I did not deserve such things.

Love has no boundaries, no judgment, no controlling mechanisms, and no repression. It nourishes cracked hearts and buried souls. This family was dying of spiritual thirst, and I was hardening to human love.

As I began to understand my husband better, I recalled things I had learned about love and how it often seemed to bring out the ugly side of people instead of their beauty. I closed the petals of my heart so completely after that that I even challenged God to try to reopen them. I gradually slipped away from showing open displays of love for my child. These would intensify Mitch's need for approval. He wanted all the affection for himself. He saw me as the sexual, sensual, and free-spirited mother he had never known.

During the first three months of our marriage, I would run miles on the treadmill at the gym, thinking about the hatred that blinded me and trying to pump every ounce of love out of me. My love, insecurity, and stupidity had created this situation. There seemed to be no way out. One of Mitch's new rules was that when he arrived at home he wanted me at the door to greet him with dinner on the table. This was what his mother did all of her married life.

I ran my own business and earned more than he did, in addition to tending to the needs of my child. One day, when Mitch got home from work, Ringer was in the kitchen with me, playing on the floor. For some unknown reason Mitch used his cowboy-booted foot to kick Ringer across the room. Stunned, he began crying. Before I had time to react, Mitch picked Ringer up by his head, a parenting skill he had learned from his older brother, and yelled at him to stop crying.

I was in a rage, near tears, and I could have murdered Mitch on the spot. Instead, I took a deep breath and told Mitch to put Ringer down. I could feel a storm brewing.

To this day I do not know what triggered Mitch's behavior. But he released Ringer. Terrified at the realization of what he had done, Mitch looked to me for help.

I turned away, knowing that if I showed any attention to Ringer, Mitch's fury would explode. I told Ringer to go to his room and that I would be there in a few minutes.

At this point in my life I wanted to express nothing but rage. I had fantasies about the hundreds of men I would kill. I would leave a few men alive while women ruled and trained them to behave properly. Men were sick, and I had become like the women who allowed them to be so cruel. I was a coward.

As usual after a violent episode, after kicking Ringer Mitch went to get his Bible to seek forgiveness and try to erase what had happened. Somehow he'd learned that forgiveness was granted to those who read their Bible, tithe at church, and praise Jesus. He was repenting while I was becoming murderous in the other room.

While he sat at the desk in my home office asking Christ for the forgiveness he would receive due to his Christian status, I came over and whispered into his ear, "If you ever hurt my son again, I will get you while you sleep." There she was at last, the mother bear!

After that, I went into Ringer's room and told him that Mitch would never hurt him again. I tried to ease his fears because I knew of nothing else to do. I thought of all that had transpired since our wedding, and the image I had concocted about being a family. My mind was shattered and my heart splintered. I had nothing to give this child. I was afraid that if I opened up, all the sorrow I was carrying would spill from me into Ringer. This was not appropriate for a child to bear, so I kept the misery to myself.

Was it strength that kept me alive or was it weakness? Why didn't I believe in myself enough to leave this relationship? What had happened to the fighter in me? Why couldn't I at least do this for my own flesh and blood, Ringer?

Within those same first three months of marriage, another incident occurred. Mitch had been having problems with the tenants renting his condominium. He'd had a discussion with them, but feared the responsibility of being the landlord. He never wanted to make waves with people so he talked nicely and agreed to things he did not like. Then he would take his frustrations out on us at home. Somehow it was always our fault. We did something to set him off.

Ringer and I were in the living room when I felt Mitch's mood shift. It was like a strange and invasive dark energy had crept into our home. It encircled me. I could see nothing, but my heart beat loudly and my blood chilled.

Intuitively, I took Ringer to our bedroom and told him to hide in the closet behind my long dresses. I told him to stay there and not to make a sound. I went back to the living room. Suddenly, Mitch realized that Ringer was not around.

"Where is Ringer?"

"He's playing in his room," I responded.

"Why did you take Ringer to his room? Is something wrong?" His voice was elevated and I could feel intense fear rising within me.

As I recall that scene, I am still overcome by it. As I write, my hands tremble, my heart races, and words pour out as if I am releasing the stale blood from my heart through my fingers. I am miserable reliving this.

Mitch called out, "Ringer, where are you?"

I stated, "Let's leave Ringer to play and tell me what was bothering you. You seem upset."

"I am not angry," he shouted.

"I didn't say you were angry," I replied in fear.

I hoped Ringer was hiding. I could not bear to fight in front of him. It ripped the fiber of my soul to see his little tormented face. I felt shredded and unable to protect him from the storms. Ringer could make no sense of such rage. Neither could I.

Mitch called out again, demanding that Ringer come out. I knew Ringer would not move. I had shut the door to his room to make it look as though he was inside. By the volume of Mitch's voice there was no way Ringer could avoid hearing; therefore, he was disobeying Mitch. My husband ran past me and into Ringer's room. This man, who had once held me and told me he loved my son and me, now was in a blind rage. Who was this man?

He grabbed me and shook me, yelling, "What did you do with Ringer?" Mitch felt as if I had hidden Ringer because he was about to do something wrong. He was right.

Because I had hidden Ringer, it was now my fault that Mitch was so angry. I followed Mitch as he stormed into our bedroom, searched the bathroom, and peeked into the closet. He could not find the boy. He turned to me and pushed me to the floor, banging my head harder and harder against the floor, totally beyond his ability to realize what he was doing.

I said nothing. My head was pounding from the beating and my mind was too shaken to think. In fear for his mommy, Ringer began to whimper.

Mitch stopped. He heard Ringer. He walked over to the closet. I sat up and cried while I hyperventilated. Mitch tore through the hanging clothes and spotted tiny, whimpering Ringer. Mitch dragged him out into the bedroom. I never will forget the fright on that child's face. Ringer pleaded with me to do something, but despite being an adult, mother, birth-giver, and protector of my son, I felt powerless to act, even on behalf of my child.

What was wrong with me? Why didn't I fight back?

Mitch told Ringer not to move. His face was beet-red from screaming. He stood still. We were about three feet from each other. I looked directly into my son's eyes to calm him as best I could. Mitch went to the door and locked the three of us in the bedroom. He began to yell so loudly that I thought the building would shake. I felt like a child myself. I was petrified. Ringer and I felt our hearts and souls reaching out to each other. The pull felt like a magnet. Suddenly my three-year-old son ran to my arms and I fought to hold back my tears. I had no idea what Mitch would do. I grabbed a strong hold on Ringer and wrapped him around me. I turned my back to Mitch and ran for the door.

"Mommy, hurry," screamed Ringer.

I ripped the door open with an unknown strength and ran into Ringer's room. I locked the door as quickly as I could against the push from the other side. The only things I could actually feel were fear and the tears running down my face. Through the door, I said, "Mitch, leave us alone before the neighbors call the cops." I had no idea if they could hear us.

"I am going to yell out the window if you don't stop!" I screamed. Why didn't I do it anyway?

I puked. Sweat covered my body. Ringer was in shock. Then things seemed quiet. I grabbed a desk chair and lodged it under the door.

I heard Mitch crying outside the door.

"I am so sorry. God, please forgive me."

He ran into our bedroom. I heard the bathroom door slam.

I knew it was over for then. Still standing, Ringer showed a sign of relief. He collapsed into my arms and clung to me. I will not allow myself ever to forget that moment. I was responsible for protecting my son. Police could do very little to protect women from abusive husbands who were so highly respected in their respective social circles. There had to be evidence of physical abuse, bruises, and marks on the body. A restraining order was the best that could be done and it would only be temporary.

I carried Ringer to his bed and tried to normalize things. I held him close. I never wanted to let go. He fell asleep.

I heard Mitch at the door. He was now crying and begging for forgiveness. He started reciting Bible scriptures. I remained silent and pressed against the door.

I heard him go into the kitchen and call someone. I crept out into the living room to listen. It was his mother. He spoke as normally as someone who had just called to check in with his parents. Thankfully, Ringer had fallen asleep.

When Mitch got off the phone, he saw me. He acted like a repentant child. He coaxed me to the bedroom, this time onto the bed. He kissed me, fondled me, and forced me to stay with him. It was as if I was having sex with a child and it felt incestuous. For Ringer's sake, I did, even though I felt filthy. I wanted Ringer to rest through this ordeal. He'd had enough trauma for one day.

You can't make sense out of violence like this. It just doesn't compute to a newlywed bride. It doesn't compute on any level for any reason for anyone. By this point, I'd had several years of on-and-off therapy. You would think I would have known how to make healthier decisions in life. I didn't.

We attended my church in Washington, D.C., which Mitch had joined. He insisted on attending church regularly, while I went only periodically. I often found myself frustrated with the sermons and meaningless conversations I had with church-going people. I was mentally shut down and did not want to hear comments like, "It's in God's hands, so let it go" and "Turn the other cheek, he just needs your love" from the old ladies whose cultural upbringing taught them that tolerance of abuse was love.

The only thing I loved in the world was Ringer. Otherwise, I would have killed myself.

I was a woman. And, as far as I knew, because of the way I was raised, society had very little respect for women outside of our sexual parts, our housecleaning abilities, and our pretty faces. My wish for death was twofold: first, it hurt so bad to feel that powerless; and second, and more importantly, I did not feel men deserved the beauty of women.

Mitch became a deacon as a gesture of service to the church. This holy act provided a Christian cloak for the darker side of him outside the church. Often I would get angry with Mitch for falling asleep during the sermon. He would chastise me about my own beliefs and urge me to respect his conscious contributions and remain loyal to his religious upbringing by merely attending services. He said even his father slept in church, so it was not a big deal. Mitch was considered such a pillar that he was asked to play the role of Jesus Christ for the Last Supper service. That is the wonderfully perfect image he portrayed in public.

People seemed to distort reality in order to avoid facing it. To "turn the other cheek" was noble, honorable, and cleverly used to seduce people like me into suppression.

One spring Sunday, we were on our way home from church. I was driving and Ringer was falling asleep in the back seat. Mitch reached back to tickle Ringer and said, "Look at the little boy, so cute, curled up trying to sleep."

Mitch was very peculiar after church, overly excited. It seemed as though he felt he'd done his duty and was now free to let go, as if his sins had been cleared. He acted weird and childlike.

"Stop it, Dad," Ringer said, annoyed. He was very sleepy.

Mitch persisted and Ringer said more firmly, "Stop it. Leave me alone."

When a three-year-old child sits through two hours of a Catholic mass it's understandable that he is tired, especially when they've loaded up the children with sweet punch and cookies. The sugar alone can knock most of us out. Mitch would not accept this as a viable option. He only saw rejection and he was not going to tolerate it.

Mitch reached to the back of the car and pushed Ringer up from his lying position.

"You don't treat me that way!" he yelled at the top of his lungs. "Get up. You are not going to sleep. You will stay awake until we get home."

Ringer was screaming in the back seat, terrified of Mitch. I began going eighty-five miles per hour in a fifty-five-mile-per-hour zone, hoping a police officer would pull me over. I pleaded with Mitch to stop yelling or I would stop the car. He told me that if I stopped the car he would get out and leave us.

"How can you defend him? He is obviously being disobedient," Mitch yelled.

Mitch reached into the back seat, grabbed Ringer and began to violently shake him, trying to get him to stop crying. I slammed on the breaks and stopped the car.

"Get out of the car!" I screamed.

Mitch jumped out of the car. I pulled away and left him there. I should have never, ever gone back.

Ringer and I went home and waited. Mitch came back later that evening, quiet and apologetic. I slept in Ringer's room that night with no trouble from Mitch. I realized that I was terrified to be alone. I didn't think I could raise Ringer on my own. I felt I needed this relationship to work. I felt I had no other place to go.

Where did I learn this weakness, this notion of dependency—and why?

The first time we went fishing in Mitch's motorboat, he wanted to please us and he tried. But his uncontrollable anger would spill out unexpectedly. He would go into a sudden rage and call me a bitch and Ringer a whiny little boy. On this day, he stopped the boat for us to swim. We were on the Potomac River and I had concerns about polluted water. As any child would be, Ringer was apprehensive. Mitch decided the best way for the boy to overcome his fears was to be thrown into the water without a life jacket. He laughed while watching Ringer struggle as he surfaced. "That's how we do it in the country," he said.

I immediately dove into the water, whereupon my husband accused me of being overprotective. I did not have on a life jacket, and Ringer clung to me so hard I thought we both were going to drown. Mitch jerked us out of the water and into the boat. We were shivering as he whipped the boat around to head back to the dock. Ringer was fuming in silence as we clung to each other.

Emotional trauma is worse than being hit, a nightmare from which there seems to be no way out. Other than my mother, most people I recounted this story to said, "Maybe he had a bad day," or "Did you do something to cause him to have such a reaction?" That is society's first option: Blame the victim. Convince the victim that they need to change, especially when the predator is so handsome, so respected at his work and at his church. It couldn't possibly be him.

I hated myself and began to put on an extra fifteen pounds, as I cared less and less. Mitch criticized my cooking and compared it to his mother's wonderful country cooking. Under all of this stress, Ringer and I frequently became ill. That meant going to the doctor and getting medicine. One afternoon Mitch called home to check on us and I said we were no better. I told him we needed to go to the doctor's office the next day, and he replied that Ringer and I were "nothing but money-sucking pigs." I prayed to swallow myself and disappear. I was nothing but a disappointment to my husband and myself. I never could communicate with him. I never questioned his behavior. I was afraid. Confusion nibbled at my intuition, my instincts. Anxiety took my breath away, while Ringer's presence and my responsibility to care for his needs kept pointing me into the unknown territory of reality.

Exhaustion became the leash that kept me from leaving Mitch.

I was sick for two weeks. I slept day and night. I went to the doctor, who told me I had chronic fatigue syndrome. On the next visit, she questioned me, "Are you depressed?"

"No, I don't feel depressed. I don't feel much of anything these days."

She tried to prescribe medicine for me, but stubbornly, I would not take it. I didn't feel that I needed medicine. I needed to work this out.

So I slept. Fatigue swallowed me. I dreamed of sinking to the dark depths of the ocean. The water got colder as I made my slow, murky descent to the bottom. In a garbled voice, I cried out for help. I felt an enormous pressure in my lungs. I felt as if they might burst. Groggily, I awoke between sleep intervals, only to feel the sluggish weight of my existence. I slipped in and out of this coma-like sleep.

One day I felt my foot touch the cold, icy, prickly clay bottom of the ocean floor, then the other foot, and my legs slid to the bottom. My body landed next and I lay wrinkled and soggy, being absorbed by the mucky surface of the ocean floor. I desperately wanted to sink further.

I felt my body being tossed back and forth. I could hear a voice calling out to me, "Mom!" Shake, shake. "Mom, wake up!"

I could not move. I could not open my eyes. I did not want to. Who was calling me? I cried in my sleep and the voice disappeared.

Some hours later I awoke, still on the ocean floor. I had done it. Was this death? I moved about in the watery atmosphere, which made movement seem difficult. I found my footing and began walking around in the dark. Each step I took was draining. I could barely move because the mush was so thick. Where was I going? Was I dreaming or was I alive? I questioned myself from the darkness of my mind. I wearily dredged my way across the ocean floor, and then I heard the voice again. "Wake up, Amber, wake up!"

Where was this voice coming from? I looked up in the dark waters and saw a tiny light above me. "Wake up, wake up, Amber," I heard myself saying.

I cried hard in my sleep and remembered Ringer. Where was he? I had to find him. I had no more strength left. My lungs were exploding and I realized I was drowning. I felt close to death and knew Ringer was not there with me.

I began to swim to the surface. It was a long, long struggle. I was drained of energy, but my desire to see my son again gave me the strength I needed to keep going.

I could see the water turning blue and the sunlight shining through.

"I can't make it. I'm too drowsy. Help me, please! I want to live." I burst forth from my intoxication and gasped for air. I looked around my room and felt my sweat on the bed. My mind was clouded and I cried. I realized that I had almost given up on myself, and more importantly, my son.

I vomited and crawled to the shower to cleanse myself. I was alive. It was all a dream.

Each evening when Mitch came home, Ringer and I would make ourselves look busy. This made Mitch happy. *Work* and *chores* were words Mitch used daily. It was important to him that Ringer spent his Saturday's working until Mitch told him to stop. My husband would not set boundaries or time limits on chores, simply to antagonize Ringer. The boy began to argue with Mitch, and became bolder in his challenges as his school grades dropped. Ringer spent most of his days disconnected from his surroundings, trying to go unnoticed in school. His spirit was broken.

One night Ringer had a dream. The next morning he told me he had seen an angel.

"You did? What did it look like?" I was curious to know.

"Well, I was sleeping and I heard it call out to me. I opened my eyes and all I could see was light coming from a face."

"Were you afraid?"

"No," he said calmly without giving more information.

"Was it a boy or a girl?"

"I couldn't tell. All I could see was that it stood by my fish tank and light came from its face."

"Did it say anything?" I asked.

"It said I was a very good boy."

He was so calm. His face glowed. I knew it was true. I looked at the space around the fish tank to see if there was anything left for me. How selfish for a grown woman to want this. I felt guilty.

Ringer defiantly told Mitch about his dream. "Dad, guess what."

"Yeah, son. What do you want to tell your dad?" Mitch asked.

"I saw an angel last night in my room. It told me I was a very good boy." Both Ringer and I were sort of proud of this. It let us know, and most importantly let Ringer know, that the hell he lived in was not his fault.

Super-Christian Mitch denounced such a wonder. "Well, son, we all think we see things when we don't. Someday when you're old enough you can be saved and ask Jesus to forgive you for your sins. Then maybe you'll get to see an angel."

Puke! Vomit! Let me shove him out the window, the pompous, arrogant, self-righteous Christian fool that he is. Talk about sinning! This man was way beyond his sin and forgiveness quota, but was egotistical enough to bestow such advice on a tolerant and loving child.

How dare he say stupid things like that to Ringer?

Ringer was a good boy and why wouldn't an angel tell him so? The dream became our secret. Ringer had other dreams, especially one about a tiger chasing him as he slept.

The fighting with Mitch was too much for him, so Ringer began therapy with a child psychologist. The therapist told me of Ringer's fears of going to bed at night, and of life in general. She was very concerned for the amount of fear Ringer had when he went to bed at night. "It's more than is usual for a child his age." She asked me many questions that I could not answer, but I knew Ringer was changing and he was calling out for help.

I was also living in fear of Mitch, but as I had deadened a part of myself in order to cope I could not relate to Ringer's pain. Ringer became dependent on the manipulative niceties bestowed on him by his stepfather. Ringer felt sorry for Mitch and wanted to fix things so that we could be a family. He was starving for a happy, perfect family.

During one of Mitch's episodes, I called the only friend I had and begged her to come and get Ringer. She did not want to get involved and said she was angry with me for putting her and her family in jeopardy.

I called my mother. She told me to call the police and press charges. I did not listen because I believed the situation was my fault. In addition, I did not think my mother was a good source of advice because I had spent my childhood watching her make similar poor decisions.

I called the police many times and they told me they could do nothing unless I was willing to press charges. They did come to the house on one occasion, but I felt I could not tell them the truth or press charges. They told me they had a safe house where I could go, but I declined. I had visions of my worst nightmare lingering in my mind. If I tried to press charges I would lose my home and be thrust into poverty. I did not *believe* I could make it on my own talent.

My health was deteriorating and I did not have a place to go. I told Mitch's mother and called members of his family about the violence, but they did not believe Mitch would behave the way I described because he was considered the good child in the family. They judged me because of my past, and like them I judged myself unworthy, referring to myself as "damaged goods." All his life, Mitch had seen his father treat his mother and siblings in this same way and he didn't try to do better. Mitch had learned this from his family. For their part, his family did not want to acknowledge it. They had found Jesus. They had been forgiven. I was the villain who brought out the dirty laundry. I brought up the past. Why didn't I just leave it alone?

People make me sick sometimes. Everywhere people know that bad things are happening, like alcoholism, incest, violence, and rage—and the list continues. It seems easier to turn away and badger those that try to talk about it, than to do something!

Blame is too often placed on the ones that try to get help.

"It's over," "Just put it behind you," "Why do you always have to look at the past?" I am so sick of these types of useless comments. They're the coward's way of avoiding responsibility for coping with the truth. There is no other path to healing than to go back and look at the truth we try to hide. Healing hurts, as the truth can be extremely painful. But masked memories can come out in strange and destructive ways, harming not only ourselves, but also the ones we love.

While all of this drama and chaos was going on in my personal life, I had become somewhat successful outside my home. My business was prospering and even I began to see the talent I had. As a child, I organized and cleaned everything I could. It was the only control I had over my environment. I couldn't change the people in my life, but I could move the furniture. I created visual harmony in hopes of changing the energy in our home. My business became a matter of going into people's homes to bring order out of chaos and balance to disharmony in exchange for money. I became a successful businesswoman.

During this time, an Associated Press reporter interviewed me for an article about blaming. She was looking for human interest stories. My therapist had been interviewed by her and asked me if it would be alright to give the reporter my information so she could hear about my difficult childhood and how it affected me in my adult life. I agreed. Mitch was indifferent.

Once the reporter's article was out, a producer for the *Oprah Winfrey* television show picked up the story and contacted me. She wanted my mother and me to appear together on the show to discuss why I did not blame my mother and father for the unpleasant parts of my life. At first I thought this would help me professionally. I actually felt like I was growing. That was the ending to the story that I wanted to be true. Socially, I was beautiful, I smiled often, and I had a good business. People wanted me to be happy. I was ashamed of telling the truth of my current marriage, because quite frankly most people really want to see only the best, the pretty lady with a handsome son and husband.

In the end, I declined the interview. I felt my life was a lie. I was out of integrity. How could I go on television and act like I was doing so well? I could not have women look up to me. I would have portrayed a strong, young woman who'd overcome challenges. Behind the façade was the truth of my shame and the fact that I did not have the strength or the skill to change it.

One day, Mitch's brother came to visit us. He drank heavily and smoked plenty of marijuana. As he got high, he asked me how I overcame some of the things I had encountered in my life. It was a good question, because I was barely coping at that point. He pressed on and on, sharing childhood stories of the way he was continuously beaten brutally by his father as a child, while his mother did nothing. In his drunkenness, he shared other family secrets about his uncles and his sisters. His mother had spent her life with her motherly and wifely Christian responsibilities. She turned her head from the things she saw and her children paid the price for it. It was easy to listen. I found restless comfort in knowing that I had not been the only person in this new family of mine who had suffered at the hands of ignorance. It helped me understand the illusion of Mitch I'd created and to see just how much we were all alike, behind our Christian behavioral robes.

I loved my mother-in-law empathetically, but hated her for what her son was doing to me. As his brother talked, Mitch got up and went to bed. I don't know if he just wanted to tune it out, but he did not try to stop me from talking with his brother. This was unusual, because he was normally very protective of his family and tried to prevent me from talking to them about such things. I could see his brother's anger and how vulnerable he was as I gained more insight into Mitch and his family. My heart opened with compassion, knowing the risk involved with someone so tormented.

As I suspected might happen, the very next day Mitch's brother lashed out at me and would forever remain distant after that, never to have another discussion with me. I became a target of his ridicule from then on to divert attention from him. He would tell his children that I was weird and strange. The only good thing to come of this was that it confirmed my suspicions about Mitch's family. Theirs was not a *Leave It to Beaver* home life as he had tried to make me believe. Mitch knew about my childhood, but his brother and family did not.

One Sunday before church, Mitch's mother was mechanically cooking, sewing, washing, gardening, cleaning, and trying to hold her family together in the face of her own vulnerability.

"Patty, if you are not feeling well, why don't you take it easy?" I asked her.

She replied, "It's my duty because it says so in the Bible. Amber, why do you press on so?"

My heart responded and I blurted out, "Because, I love you."

I believe that God uses all of us in different ways. For me, words seem to be God's choice of direct communication with people. God's words can come through us. I feel as if my words are not always mine because I am not always pre-thinking what I will say. Words just spill over from my heart. I was as surprised as she was to hear myself say this.

The softness I had within me remained and I welcomed her into my arms that morning as she cried. Tearfully, she said, "I don't know why my husband is the way he is, but he has had a hard life. You are a sweet and loving person, Amber." I believe the twenty or so tears she shed as we were speaking were the first she'd shed in a very long time.

The moment she realized her vulnerability, she quickly began to compose herself.

I never said so, but I felt as if God loved her right through my own being, even if it was just for a few moments. That was all the time I had to love her, for time was passing and children were waiting to get to church on schedule. I lingered a minute or two, knowing that Mitch's mother had distanced herself again, and that she would likely never allow herself to be so vulnerable with me again. It was a sad and beautiful moment.

Mitch's family members feared me because I spoke open-ly, asked questions, and stirred things up. I wanted to be close to them, and to love all the hurt away from that family. It was easy for them to target me and blame me for Mitch and my marital problems because I had the "sordid" past and was different. I really loved one of Mitch's sisters and I reached out to her repeatedly, but she had barriers I could never get through. I learned from her and she influenced me. She had a natural beauty, grace, and lifestyle, and occasionally I felt jealous of her. I wanted to be more like her, but she kept her distance from me.

The first Christmas after our marriage, I bought the most beauti-ful gifts I could find and wrapped them with great care. Mitch's family felt that I had overdone it and the shame blew through the air like the heat from the furnace. It was unspoken, but I noticed and suffocat-ed in it. I was trying to love them and gift giving had always had a special meaning for me. I poured out as much love as I could, spent too much money, and was embarrassed by the looks on the faces of the family. Loving is such a delicate thing.

Over the three-year period of our marriage, I would endure hu-miliation, oppression, and verbal and physical abuse, as well as seeing Ringer's heart hardening. When I had the chance to love

Mitch, I would break into that "cut in the fabric of time" and try to love him with all the gentleness of God pouring through me. Mitch would feel it and cry. He managed to reach out for help by turning himself in to a spousal abuse program through the county, and through a men's experiential psychology weekend. We tried marital therapy, but once again were blocked, this time by the Almighty Himself in the form of our pastoral counselor.

This so-called man of God told me such things as, "It is your job to give your husband sexual pleasure no matter what is going on. It is in the Bible" and "A woman does not have the right to withhold her body from her husband."

He also blamed me for Mitch's anger. The pastor said I provoked it, as if it would not exist without my presence. At last, I could see what was happening. My mind was being twisted, turned, manipulated, and scorched. I remember suddenly laughing with both Mitch and the pastor looking at me. I rose from the sofa and boldly told them, "Gentlemen, fuck off." I walked out the door with a smile on my face as the pastor called, "Amber, this is no way to behave."

I walked out into the sun that day, knowing they both believed that I was evil. I suspected otherwise, and decided to take my chances on my own. Shortly thereafter I moved out of our home. Finally courage had reached out its arms and embraced me.

CHAPTER 4
AMBER — HIDDEN

With the burst of new freedoms, I found that I had a few battles to contend with. One was the hunger for independence and sexual self-discovery. Another was motivation to live.

Underestimating my ability to secure housing for both my son and myself, I rented a one-bedroom apartment. He was little and did not need much space. That was the story I told myself over and over as I hid all of his toys and stored his clothing. Out of sight, out of my mind. I could not bear to look at him. I became enraged by his presence, as if he were a mirror image reflecting a part of me I did not want to see. I was a bad mother, or so I told myself. I felt selfish and wanted nothing more than to regress back to my old ways of coping with pain.

Nightclubs! The lights, the music, the alcohol, and men all created the platform on which I was convinced that I was a star. I was admired and sought out. In that arena I found comfort, as I escaped as much reality as possible. I was always in search of a man to tell me I was beautiful or worthy. However, this was a world that could also be cold and ruthless, a world where women danced as if they were in bed and allowed men to fondle them publicly. The more flesh a woman exposed, the more popular she was.

None of us were actually women; we were young ladies in search of attention or love. We used our beauty to seek out what we thought we wanted—more love—and we were willing to deal with abuse to get it.

When women use beauty or sex to attract a man, we get, "Oh baby, you are so beautiful," as they reach up and suckle our breasts like hungry little boys. Or they lift up our skirts and say, "I'm not going to do anything, baby," as we hide in our projected innocence, totally aroused, but living by the message that if we sleep with a guy too soon he won't respect us. And when he says the magic words, "Baby, I think I love you," we spread our legs as he prematurely, and selfishly, ejaculates before he enters our body. Then he falls asleep and we cuddle, for it feels so good just to be held.

In the morning, a man says, "I'll call you later," and we wait by the phone all day and night until he doesn't call and we see ourselves as ugly in the mirror. The message we give ourselves is, "If I'm beautiful, then why didn't he call?"

Madonna said, "Rejection is the greatest aphrodisiac." And she was right. The more I was rejected, the more I wanted to be with the idiot who'd just used my body and abandoned me. Why didn't he want me? Why did I want him?

In September 1996, I attended a women's weekend. For several years a good friend had been telling me about an international organization called Woman Within, which utilized Jungian experiential psychotherapeutic techniques to help women access their shadow sides: the parts that we try to hide, both our pain and our joy. This weekend of theirs was described as a place women go to heal and to discover the "love within us."

Yuck! Who would want to spend an entire weekend with women? The gossiping, jealous, cat-like behavior, and worst of all, the whining about their pathetic lives! This was not something I was interested in. I hated women more than I hated men. They had taught me to loathe myself and to use my sexuality as my greatest asset.

One day I finally agreed to talk to a woman about the program. I was miserable inside and I trusted my friend who referred me. I figured it couldn't hurt. In speaking with the woman, I found her to be grounded and not as I knew women to be. She explained that she'd been working for a mysterious undercover government organization for most of her life. She, too, had had similar negative feelings when first hearing about this weekend. But she challenged me to do battle with my own fears and doubts, and not to be so judgmental. I realized that I was pissed off by her ability to call me on my own fears. That was when I decided to take on the challenge of the weekend. It would be another attempt to recreate my inner world and do something healthy for myself.

From that moment on, before even arriving at the workshop, I began what has been referred to as a descent within. I had no idea what was happening, but I felt an enormous rush of emotions trying to surface and escape through my voice and eye sockets. I hated crying. In my experience, it did no good. So I suppressed all the emotions and tears that I could.

It was a September evening and I was headed for Maryland. I was anxious when I arrived at the site in a secluded, wooded area. I had driven up with a friend and we chatted nervously on the three-hour drive. We arrived late and were greeted in a manner that would make anyone want to run. Our greeter was very plain and curt. "You're late," she said.

"We got stuck in traffic."

"Park your car over there and hurry up."

I said to my friend, "Can you believe we paid for this shit?"

"I hope we are not sleeping here. This looks like a campground."

This was a bad idea, I told myself. I was ready to leave. But, we parked the car, grabbed our luggage, and found the other participants. I wanted to run away so badly. I felt sick. Whining, sappy women all gathered to share? What was this crap anyway? I both hated these women and wanted to be close to them as well. I'd had strained relationships with the women in my family and longed for a place where women could get away from the clutches of men. In America it is thought that we are free. Women are not. We are slaves to the exploitation of our bodies, while our wisdom and strength are denounced. I was Amber—tough, cool, and composed—protecting my heart. Women were the competitors, the enemy. Somehow, we had been matched against our own gender, waging war over sex, fashion, men, and money.

My friend and I were invited to sit down in a totally different tone than we had been greeted with. So we sat and filled out a lot of paperwork.

I believed I had the ability to manipulate people while distracting them from my innermost fears and insecurities. And I did exactly that until one of the leaders of the weekend noticed my careful crying as I described myself to my audience. I did not know her, but she walked with intention directly toward me, "This isn't the place to act like a child. This is woman's work." I was stunned. What the hell was she talking about? I was already a woman.

I had no idea how deeply that comment would shape my future.

"This is woman's work."

Throughout the course of the experiential weekend I found my heart, which had been neatly stored in the basement of my soul. It ached just to breathe again, but it was beautiful. I found I was beautiful. I had softened and adopted a completely different view of people. There was hope. It had resided within me all along.

We were taught to ground our new feelings of joy by choosing a color or sound that would remind us of our experience. I chose white. I felt bright inside and never wanted to forget what I had discovered about myself as a woman. I would need this knowledge to face the upcoming challenges and many difficult memories that were surfacing in my mind, as they could affect my thoughts, choices, and behaviors. Joy was new to me, and I feared it as I drove home. The world moved swiftly, and I was afraid to be happy for too long. Something might happen to take it away. I simply did not trust it to last.

Living on my own was a nightmare. Depression and anxiety draped over me like wet, saggy curtains. I was consumed with darkness. I hated the daylight hours and feared the darkness of nightfall. I blocked out my feelings for my son, and cared little for myself. I felt inadequate and incapable as a mother. I had failed. The ugliness inside me was festering into a pit of despair and rage. I hated people, and yet my heart kept trying to love them. I attributed that softness to my femininity, and hated the fact that I was a woman. I hated the softness and felt that my only true value was my ability to be sexually satisfying to a man.

I resented being alone with a child and was furious with myself for thinking I could be a good mom. My son was innocent and my soul loved him powerfully. I pushed him away in my crazy thinking to protect him from my inadequacies. I did not feel I had been worthy to bring him into the world and I did not protect him. I had three marriages behind me and I was a deeply wounded woman. I was full of self-disgust, self-loathing, and a powerful rage. I lived in fear and did not trust anyone, not even myself. I projected all of this on my son. He created opportunities for me to grow, and it hurt.

I truly understood the amount of transformation I was undergoing. It cut me deeply. I was so afraid to admit my vulnerability in loving Ringer. Instead I blocked him out and only opened up in tears while I gazed upon him when he slept. In those moments, I poured out all of my inner little girl's love for him, my baby, my inner teenager's desire to be a good mom; and the love of the wounded woman who wished she had more to give from her heart and soul. I was deeply ashamed to call myself his mother. Yet, in the quietest of moments, I longed for him. My flesh and blood, how beautiful he was. I desperately believed he deserved someone better than me.

One night, as I lay sleeping, I was awakened by a loud sound. My son, who was sleeping in the same room, had heard the same sound. I was immobilized with fear. I had visions that a man had come into our garden-style apartment to hurt us. Frantically, I called the police. They were there within minutes. After searching the exterior of the property, they knocked on the door. Terror-stricken, I had no idea how to get safely to the door if someone was in the home. I hid my son in the closet and ran directly to the door as fast as I could. The police swarmed into my tiny space and quickly discovered a picture had fallen from the wall in the kitchen.

They were calm and soothing. They told me I had done the right thing and that I should not hesitate to call for any reason. One of the officers stayed with me until I calmed down. During our discussion he told me about self-defense classes and martial arts schools. He suggested this could add to my confidence and relieve some of my fears. The next day, I found a school very close to our home and enrolled my son and myself in tae kwon do classes.

I started off with learning basic self-defense techniques. The woman who owned the center was the mother of four sons, of whom two were instructors. After several classes, I asked for a private session and was assigned to study with one of the sons. This was how I met Cyrus.

It was a Friday evening when I met him. I walked in quietly and caught sight of him practicing his martial art. His every move was perfect. I could not hear a sound in the room as he practiced. He was so graceful. He released an enormous sound from deep within his being as he concluded. The sound was known as the voice of the chi, representing inner strength.

Ours was a sweet, distorted love at first sight. I felt Cyrus could protect me, and teach me to protect myself. He had a heart as bright as the sun, and I could open mine to him and shine at last.

A powerful chemistry bonded us almost immediately. I became incredibly shy and felt like a little girl. After class the first night, we were like two children excited about sharing our toys. Cyrus showed me his swords and his fourth-degree tae kwon do black belt. He was deliciously flirtatious and expressed an open admiration for my dedication in the classes. I shared some of my writing with him while he watched my every gesture. He noticed the way my hands moved and complimented my gracefulness. He noticed my hair fall across my face and the way my feet crossed over each other. Cyrus feasted his eyes on me as if he were visually touching every part of my body. I knew he was coming on to me. Under his gaze, I realized that I still had purity living in my heart.

Late that evening as he walked me to my car, he asked me out for coffee. We went to the local diner and shared stories from our lives as our souls played hide-and-seek with each other. He was nervous about being seen by anyone he knew. He told me that as my teacher he should not be out with me. He was twenty-eight years old and still had a curfew. Cyrus lived at home and having such restrictions was just the way it was with his culture. He was Iranian. I found that odd and nonetheless enjoyed being with him.

As we headed toward our cars, he wondered out loud why I was interested in him. This was a strange question, but I responded to it anyway. "What is not to love about Cyrus?" He did not think much of himself, but I could see a world of talent in him, and a pool of tenderness that opened me like a flower at dawn. I left feeling his energy all through me.

Cyrus was shorter than me, younger than me, and had little money. These were things my female friends avoided in a man, but I felt this man was something special and I did not care. I had been single for more than a year when we met. I wanted someone to love, but naturally shied away from committed relationships. I was still hurting inside and did not have the energy or desire to become involved. Cyrus' curfew and exotic culture seemed perfect for me, as I did not have to commit. He felt the same and would state as much the first time we made love. I am also generally attracted to those whom others would judge negatively or put aside for some reason, and I was very attracted to him.

Sometime within the first few weeks of knowing him, Cyrus came to my home for breakfast and sang a song for me from *The Godfather.* For someone with low self-esteem, like me, he was the most enchanting man ever. We sat on my sofa watching his tae kwon do performance videos. I was in awe as Cyrus moved gracefully across the floor in perfect motion and his *ki-op* yells were deep and passionate. This seemed to be a form of release from the emotional demons that troubled him. I wanted to love him immediately. As we watched the video, he asked me to sit closer.

For a man who looked so young, he did not act shy. He was graceful and courteous. As I moved next to Cyrus, I leaned my back against him. I could feel his nearness and the subtle gestures he made as he smelled my hair. I was intoxicated with his presence. Every move Cyrus made was akin to an art form. He stood up and laid me back on the sofa. He moved next to me and told me I had beautiful eyes. He picked up my hand, gently looked at each finger, and then placed my hand on my stomach. He asked permission to further touch me.

Cyrus touched my waistline and gently reached to touch the small of my back as he drew me closer to him. I looked into his dark eyes and saw his passion. He whispered, "May I kiss you?" I nodded and he slowly and gently placed his soft lips on mine. I felt tears release from within me as he expressed his love. He was truly a beautiful man to me despite his height, thin frame, and boyish looks. I guided Cyrus into my bedroom where we made love for the first time. I felt like a woman of beauty in his eyes and experienced no shame about my body. He loved every curve and every movement I made. His eyes lingered upon me as he stroked my waist, hips, and back as if he were bringing a painting to life with his passion. The intensity was overwhelming and I climaxed with him, in awe at the level of comfort I had with him.

After making love, we dressed and went into the living room for a snack. Cyrus told me about his family. His parents wanted him to be a doctor, but his real passion was photography. He had an artist's sensibility. When he mentioned his mother, the owner of the tae kwon do studio, whom I'd already met, his gentleness turned to a dark storm. He said, "Don't fall in love with me because my mother will never let it happen." Though I did not understand his turmoil, I felt it presumptuous to assume I would fall in love with him. I challenged him on this and Cyrus began to cry. Red flags went up in my mind at that, as if someone had marched them in for me to see, shouting,

"Run for your life!" By this time I had acquired communication skills that allowed me to control my side of a dialogue with a man.

Instead of telling Cyrus to get out, I steered the conversation to less emotional topics and learned more of his struggles with his family. I learned that Cyrus felt unworthy. He had a brother who seemed to do everything right. Cyrus had once had an American girlfriend, but his Middle Eastern family had pressured him to dump her and date someone who shared his roots. Cyrus reminded me that things could never work out between us. I was thankful that he realized this, because that would make it easier for me to maneuver my way around our friendship and possibly an ongoing sexual relationship. He did not want commitment and neither did I.

We became passionate lovers after that. Both of us were emotionally vulnerable. For my part, I was actually happy that he was tied to his family, which meant I was free from the burden of commitment. Sex and some quality sharing was enough for me. As a woman of the world, and three times divorced, I felt free to be sexual without the rigidity of religion or the organizational institution of marriage. Our connection was uplifting.

To see me, Cyrus would sneak away from the college classes where his parents thought he was spending his time. We would dance and seduce each other. We were always dancing, sometimes not touching each other for hours. I would dance for him, playing Middle Eastern music and wearing belly chains and ankle bracelets to tantalize him. I thoroughly enjoyed being looked at as a woman of beauty. I enjoyed the opening of my sensual soul.

I would take hour-long baths in Cyrus's favorite scent of musk. Sometimes I would hide in the candlelight waiting for him to find me. Cyrus would take his time. When he did find me, all of my eroticism burst forth as every part of my body yearned for his touch and the words he whispered in my ear. He would guide me to the middle of the room, ever so lightly touching my hands. Sometimes before I would dance for him he would kneel down and remove my sandals, commanding me to lift my skirts to show my feet and legs for him. Fire would pour from my soul as I felt him notice everything about me.

Cyrus would then sit like a king and allow his passion to heighten as he watched me. When he reached a certain point of desire, he would stand and reach out his hand for me to follow him, and I would surrender my heart, body, and soul to him. His body was smaller than mine, but I felt an enormous sense of security as he lay with me. Inside he was all man. He had a strength that could not be judged by his outward appearance. In the precious place of passion where we met, both of us were free.

As the nights passed by, Cyrus began to be uneasy earlier and earlier in the evening. He had pressure from his family to be home by 10:00 or 11:00 P.M., and they asked him repeatedly where he had been and what he had been doing. He was a man in his early-thirties so I couldn't understand this and urged him to stand up to his parents. I did not know at the time how much he lied to protect us. He went through hell with his father, who screamed at him and belittled him for his life's choices. Cyrus ultimately told his family about me and tried to get them to accept me as his girlfriend, but they would not because of their expectations on him.

One day after my tae kwon do lesson, Cyrus's father called me into the office for a meeting. Cyrus was present at first, but his father asked him to leave so he could speak to me in private. I saw Cyrus's suppressed rage as he walked out and closed the door. I had no fear of his father and was curious to hear what he had to say.

In accented English, he asked, "Are you seeing my son?"

"Yes," I said. Something was strange here.

"Cyrus is a little slow and not very worldly. He is not very bright about things, but you are a mature woman. Surely you must see that." He continued, "I want you to keep this between us and just drop Cyrus, because he doesn't know how to take care of himself. Just forget him. Act as though nothing ever happened and you can remain a student at our school."

I was startled to hear a father belittle his son so coldly, especially with the son right outside the door. I asked, "Are you finished?"

He said, "Yes, and I am glad you understand. Just ignore Cyrus on the way out and I'll see you in class."

"Excuse me. I have something to say to you," I said.

He raised his eyebrows and said, "Please, go ahead, Miss Amber." I knew this was a moment to stand up for the underdog, my beloved Cyrus.

I remembered a time when I was out dancing at a nightclub where a midget was asking women to dance. From across the room I watched a series of women ridicule and humiliate him. It infuriated me. I approached the midget and asked him to dance. His eyes were level with my breasts as he maneuvered me around the dance floor. He smiled triumphantly while others laughed at us. When the song ended I thanked him and left the club. People can be brutally cruel.

I had just heard a father's cruel description of a human being, and his son at that, who had treated me like a flower in his garden. Cyrus was a poet, an artist, a photographer, and full of creativity. His parents and family belittled these qualities. I knew about that from

Cyrus, but I had not known until now that his father judged his son to be slow and childlike. I could not believe he would ask me to dishonor his son by simply disposing of him as if he were nothing more than human waste.

I rose up and said to his father, "I won't be attending your school any longer. Furthermore, I will not ignore Cyrus and strip him of his dignity. I am shocked that you would ask me to dishonor and humiliate him. Cyrus is a man, not a boy, and I will not treat him as anything but a man."

"My son is young and needs his mother. What can you give him that we cannot?"

"The love of a powerful woman," I replied.

I walked out and in front of his father told Cyrus that I would see him later at my home. Thus began a cultural tug-of-war between his parents and me with the soul of Cyrus as the rope. I could not bear to witness his tortured and splintered heart. I would get angry with him for lying to his parents about me, and for lying to me about his parents. I could not discern truth from lie. As weeks passed, it put a strain on our relationship. Cyrus danced seductively between me and his dependency on his family. He lied in order to try and keep us both. He could not walk away from the financial and emotional bonds he had with his family, especially those related to the family's matriarch, his mother. On one hand, I provided a nurturing mother figure for him, one who accepted his artistic nature. On the other hand, I was a seductress who made him feel like the man he was.

I did not understand the deep cultural influences of his family and their values. They were wealthy and foreign and I knew I was not what the daughter-in-law they wanted in their family. Cyrus was well-educated and that was important to them. Artistry was nonsense, in their opinion, a hobby. Higher education would keep the family name intact and allow Cyrus to inherit his fortune, but they would only give his inheritance to him if he married the right woman. They knew he lied, but could not understand why. Their generational attitudes and value system clashed with the influences of the western world on their son. He behaved as he did to survive. I knew all of this and continued this experience with Cyrus. Cyrus was torn between what I represented to him and his lifelong connection to his family.

The powerful passion that had bonded us inevitably brought us together ever faster as his family pushed against us. I became a rescuer, preventing Cyrus from standing up for himself. My protective love expanded like the sun, and I wanted to help him, nurture him, and surrender to his loving embrace. I needed his love. Whenever I called for Cyrus, he would come. He told me that for the rest of our lives he would always find me. He breathed his love into my mouth. We held each other, wept in each other's arms, and supported each other through pain, sorrow, joy, and fear.

A few years prior to meeting Cyrus, I'd one day sought out and found my father. I was curious about the man that my mother still loved. The day I reunited with my father, he was like a child, very intent on behaving well in order to gain my forgiveness. He was a simple man, a painter. He had spent his life running from job to job and woman to woman. He was ill with cancer and dying. He was hungry for forgiveness as guilt and shame engulfed him. Death calling opened him to the unknown and unexplored depths of his soul. Psychologically he reminded me of Cyrus—smaller in stature, artistic, passionate and utterly lost. Neither were men who created a life. Both were men layered in self-doubt, deep loneliness and the inability to change it. To survive both men avoided, wandered, and lied. My attraction to Cyrus helped me to understand my own child-like need for a daddy's love.

In my confusion about Cyrus, I asked my father one day about what to do. He said to me, "Don't measure a man by his belongings, but by the measure of his love." Cyrus was my dearest friend, the only person I had ever just loved outside of Ringer. I would get mad and then forgive him. I just did. At times, the family pressure was more than I could handle. I would break up with him only to go back to him many times over a four-year period.

I continued to be confused about relationships. I was learning. Both of us were conflicted, but whether or not he was a life partner for me did not ultimately matter. For the time we were together, he was kind and tender with me. I deserved that and was willing to weather the tumultuous storms that blew upon the shore of our connection.

Almost four years after we met, a few days before Independence Day, Cyrus asked me to marry him. I had not seen him for a year and had become disconnected from the thought of being in relationship. I had no intentions of getting married again. Marriage was not a big deal to me any longer. I never envisioned this possibility, so I was stunned by his proposal. I had a panicky moment and then said, "Yes. What the hell." It was an honor for me to marry him. I wanted to stand up to the world and profess my love for this simplest of men, and become his queen. I wanted to help him use his wings to fly out into the world, filling his days with other passions than tae kwon do and me. We eloped on July 4, and were married in blue jeans, outdoors in the rain, by an alternative minister whom we'd found through the courthouse.

Cyrus was exhilarated and nervous. He was taking the biggest step of his life, and knowingly cutting himself off from his family from whom he had never been separated. But he told me he never wanted to lose me again. Our wedding day was a good day—for someone in love with the idea of love, like I was. This was my fourth wedding and I hoped it would be my last. Despite the rain and the hounding by his family to come home and give up this foolishness, Cyrus and I celebrated our bond like we actually understood what we were doing. He was running and I was enabling him to run, and we called it love and sealed it with a marriage contract. Perhaps we were fools, but humans often do foolish things to feel safe, loved, and in control.

Within weeks, the separation from his family began to eat at Cyrus. He was haunted by dreams of his father, and missed his younger brother very much. He tried to find comfort in our home with me and Ringer, but longed for the acceptance of his original family and their culture. Cyrus yearned to take me to his family's home to participate in their frequent gatherings and celebrations, of which they held many every year.

His family's hatred of me was partially due to cultural differences, and partially because of information they had dug up about my past. While we were dating off and on they had hired a private investigator in hopes of finding something dreadful they could use to lure Cyrus away. They also held the mental picture of me that had been presented to them by Cyrus each time we separated. In a letter to Cyrus that he received after our wedding, his father referred to me as a *whore* and his mother referred to me as a *sugar mommy*. She knew I was the primary earner in our household. His parents continued to refuse to get to know me. Over the years, there were threats, accusations, and verbal assaults made against me by them. His parents believed that I was evil and had placed a hex on their son. I can't blame them for being angry. We had ruffled their plans for their son's life. They felt they knew what was best for him.

Once we were married, Cyrus became forgetful and unmotivated. He began to lie about many small things and some larger ones. This was the same behavior he had demonstrated with his parents while he was living with them. Before he had met me, Cyrus had promised to marry a young woman from his country and bring her to America to live. Previously he had told me that his family was trying to force her upon him, that when he got engaged to her he was just trying to please his family. One day while I was organizing photographs, I came across pictures of them together and some letters from her. I realized then that he had lied to me about the nature of their relationship. It was serious. I was shocked. I had pictures.

He still denied it. "Those letters meant nothing to me," he said. "It's over." I could see how his hands perspired from the anxiety of telling me the lie. He had obviously pressed for us to marry quickly so he could get out of marrying her. Being that I had considered him my friend, my buddy, and my lover, I simply had not thought about my decision at all. I'd just said yes without thinking what had been going on while we were apart, or the implications to me.

I really wanted to believe what Cyrus was telling me, but I could not. I received a series of email messages from his sister-in-law that supported the evidence I had found. At first I did not trust her, and tried to discount her messages as invasive attempts at manipulation. Then we got into an argument one afternoon. Cyrus had been spending at least $60 dollars per month on pornographic computer sites. He tried to deny that also, but I could see the debits on his bank statements. Knowing his history of lying, I called the toll-free number to one of the sites. They told me that on one particular day when I had been out of town the site had been "hit" thirty-eight times from my home computer. Cyrus insisted that his brother had access to the same account and had used it. He swore he did not know the site was in use, even though he was still paying for the service.

I don't think I actually knew how to understand his behavior. Who would? I threw a statue across the room. Though our marriage was young, I was already weary of distrusting him and felt as if I had lost him. Sure, he cared about me, in a codependent way. But real-life responsibility made him anxious to run back to his parents. They had food, shelter, electricity, water, phone service, laundry service, cable television, a car, and auto insurance. All he had to do was perform, showing one face to them, another to me, playing us against each other.

I had no ability to comprehend this. Instead I had the idea that I could teach him how to be accountable, and that our being together would provide for him a place to grow up.

Overall our relationship was a good experience for me. What I learned from it was that he had a completely different cultural neurology than I did. I wasn't really in it for that romantic notion of love engrained in my head from social programming. I wasn't grounded enough to see that selecting a life partner meant that hard choices would have to be made, like recognizing that our relationship would not last if for no other reason than the fact that I was emotionally unstable and unavailable. We were separated within three months of our marriage. It was done gracefully with the help of a friend of his, who offered to let Cyrus live with him. Initially, we planned to get counseling. That never happened. We had a difficult time parting, as our behavior patterns fed each other's fear and anxiety. Cyrus decided he needed to find his own way. He said he would be ashamed if he went back to his family, and left, determined to make it on his own with help from his friends.

One day we were emailing and phoning each other, and the next day we were not. I tried to telephone his office, but his coworkers would not let me speak to him. Surprised, I called his supervisor and she told me not to call anymore, per Cyrus's request. Stunned, I knew then that he had gone back to his family. I don't know what he told them to get back in their good graces, but I knew that he would have been told to stop speaking to me. Cyrus needed the love and acceptance of his family. He needed their promise of the money they'd give him if he did as they preferred. The outside world and independence were not things he'd been taught to deal with. His doting parents had sheltered him from too much independence, in order to control the outcome of his life. They had plans for him. Most parents do.

Within weeks I was being sued for divorce. I was served papers accusing me of "spousal abuse." Cyrus had a fourth-degree black belt in tae kwon do, nonetheless he requested that I keep a 1,000-foot distance from him for at least two years. At first I was angry, but then I realized that he had to sell out his beloved American bride in order to be accepted back by his family. I cried. It was time to change and move on, but I did not understand. I felt hurt. I still had the Disney princess-like wedding dress, rings, and photos of our wedding, but I had lost my best friend and I missed him. He had listened to all of my life stories and never judged me. He had held me crying in his arms many times as I healed. He had helped me through therapy from my childhood, and however briefly, he was there when I called.

Cyrus frequently lied and had low self-esteem. I cared for him regardless. I was full of imperfections and so I accepted his. He appreciated the feminine part of me that I had been completely unaware of. He loved me passionately for my womanly ways. After our divorce, he ended up marrying the girl from Iran and inherited his support.

I felt enormous empathy for Cyrus's mother. In one conversation she had said to me, "You are a mother, so you know there is no greater love than that of a mother for her son." She also told me she had married when she was young and had no choice, and that she did not believe in true love. Her own beliefs and experiences had deprived her own son of possibility of true love.

I have grown since being married to Cyrus. I know how beautiful I am. I know the beauty of Amber and how lovely my hands are. I am not hidden any longer. How lovely are my eyes and how graceful is my walk. I have become a woman. I know of strengths and sorrows of loving, and would not change one minute of my life with Cyrus—possibly simply because I cannot. It took a while for me to sever the emotional dependency threads I had to him because he was my friend. We divorced from the fantasy of the love we vowed on a rainy day in July, but the experiences will remain forever. I still think about him from time to time, especially his graceful hands, and I know he will make a great father one day if he can gain some footing, build his confidence, and gain independence from his family. I will always love and respect him for his contributions to the uplifting of my self-esteem, and self-worth.

I can love. I can receive love now. Partly I can do so because Cyrus was willing to hear my pain and help me face it and get through it, because he saw me as beautiful and I could see myself as beautiful through his eyes. We were what we ultimately were for each other, neither right nor wrong. Our relationship was an experience that enhanced my life greatly. He faced the power and control of his family in order to help me evolve, and in doing so gained a taste of freedom and had an opportunity to choose his own life course and evolve in his own way. Despite our imperfections and challenges, we aided each other in the development of our individuality. To experience his gentle ways after experiencing so much violence transformed me forever.

Cyrus's love will forever strengthen me, for our experiences helped me release the essence of Amber hidden within my radiant soul.

PART TWO

THE FOREST

. . . into the dark nature of the mind we begin to see why people do what they do . . .

Worms, mud, snakes, and trees, creeks, twigs, and rocks, flowers in the spring, and dead leaves in the winter. This magical place once brought me a child's feast and fantasy as well as the gloomy and pervading darkness of the dangers in the density of a most beautiful haven of nature. As a little girl, I buried my treasures early on and deep within the earth to keep them safe for eternity. One day, the uprooting of the cherished playground within me propelled me to go back and retrieve what I had left behind. Writing has since empowered me to construct a map in my head that provides me understanding of the landscape of my behavior as an adult woman.

My very own buried beauty haunted me and lured me back through the days of my youth. I had to go back and find this great beauty within. It is a love so deep that it calls me to walk each haunting step through the words of my own being. And yes, my friend, I will tell you that it hurts. Horribly. I once feared to face my own intrinsic worth, measured by the value of the words that laid out a picture of who I am this day. I felt I must go back and see and free myself from suffering in hiding. It is the suffering that cycles through me which was calling me to new heights of passion and a deep desire to be free of horrible moments of my youth.

Learning that dignity is not on the distribution list of human attributes, I ask you to walk with me through the living memories of the place where I buried myself. Walk with me through the forest that shaped my thoughts, molded my character, and infected my mind and body. Breathe with me through the delicate waterways, the neural pathways that nudged me into this present moment. Each intoxicating experience is nothing more than a memoir of a human life. Let us not ask why any longer. Rather let us see what has shaped us so that we may have the wisdom and inner guidance to alter the course of the future for women, for children, for humanity.

CHAPTER 5
WILD GREEN ONIONS

 I have neither the will nor the desire to venture back into the trees, storms, and pathways that have led me here. Nonetheless, my green eyes will lead me back through the first twenty-two years of my life to shed light on the unspoken interpretations of my soul.

The earliest I can remember is around the age of three. Prior to that, my mother created my memories for me. She described a woman named Barbara who loved me dearly. My mother worked all day, so she would leave me with the warmth and tenderness of her dearest friend. My mother said that Barbara never left my side and always held and kissed me. She would play with me all day long as if I were her baby doll.

Barbara was younger than my mother and lived in pretty much the same set of circumstances. She was an impoverished woman in the early 1960s who had little self-esteem and little support from her family. She gave and received all her love from me. It was much less complicated with a newborn baby. I attribute this love as being the "protector of my will." It has sustained me throughout my life, in that I have passionately tried to rekindle its beauty within me.

In my quest to have such unconditional nurturing, I began my search at a very early age. The perception of love seems to vary from person to person, religion to religion, and community to community. For children, it simply means, "Don't hit me, don't leave me, kiss me, hug me, feed me, teach me, play with me," and most importantly, "Protect me."

As a child, I was completely blind to the warped cruelty and the twisted love that infects so many people. Sometimes people think that those who dress poorly or live in poor conditions are the abusers and derelicts of society by nature. *Misfits* may be a more appropriate name, as circumstances can impoverish people and disempower them. People like Mom, who abruptly had to change the environment in which her children were living, made the decision to charge the care of her children to people she trusted.

Barbara's life changed after she got a new job and was no longer able to care for me. At the time, my mother was twenty-two years old with six children already and pregnant with another when my father left her. (Of these, I was her fifth baby.) I do not know the circumstances, and the effect of his leaving did not seem that powerful to me at the time as I was so young and he had never been at home very often anyway. He was a Navy man, and my mother created for me most of my visual and emotional memories of him. She kept his football helmet and a handsome picture of him on her vanity table. I had seen it many times as a toddler and harbored only fond memories of him. I even imagined him a hero. My mother loved him, and I knew nothing of her emotional turmoil.

I was a green-eyed, blond little girl who loved to play house. Sticks, leaves, wild onions, and green grass were delicacies I served to my imaginary friends on my favorite toys: small metal and plastic dishes with flowers printed on them. Bugs and butterflies, birds, stray cats, and I played for hours, cooking and preparing feasts for our souls. I stayed away from people as much as possible because they frightened me. They were not as friendly as my insect and animal companions, or as Barbara. The sweet smell of the earth called me to run barefoot and sometimes play Double Dutch jump rope with some of the neighborhood children. My heart and spirit were always pulling me into the bigger world surrounding me. I had enormous curiosity and was equally bold.

The outdoors were beautiful and *mine,* but indoors was an entirely different experience. I spent much of my indoor time beneath the table, hiding and lying across the chairs to pick at crusty food that had slipped through the cracks. It was safe there, for a while. My mother's floor was white and immaculately clean. She said my father was meticulous and required that the floors be scuff-free and waxed. I stared at that floor sometimes for hours on rainy days, hiding from the people in my life. During the school day, life was different. My preschool and elementary schoolteachers adored me and gave me pretty dresses. Several times a week during naptime I would be called to the office and fawned over by the ladies. I was barely six and did not speak much. I was living in a fantasy world that consisted of Santa Claus, bugs, animals, flowers, and wild green onions. Some days, sunny or not, I was trapped inside the house with the deadbolt locked and out of my reach. Living in a housing project, my mother spent her days working toward getting her GED, as a first step toward obtaining a nurse's aide certificate. She was also active in the community, trying to improve the playgrounds for her children.

One summer, when I was five, my mother suddenly found herself in need of childcare for the four youngest. Because she was in a pinch, she trusted a reference and sent us to stay with an elderly woman named Elsie O'Toole. Elsie had big, flat, smacking lips that spewed saliva as she bellowed out her words. She babysat my two sisters, my younger brother, and me for the entire summer.

Typically, the parent checks out the caretaker and the children check out the yard and location of the nearest playground. Children do not have either the interest or the ability to even know if a person is good or bad. Their needs are simple. They arrive. They are innocent. They trust.

I would be happy not to remember how things began. Remembering as much as I am about to describe makes me sick with misery as each word pours forth from my memory.

You see, Miss O'Toole had an unusual way of dealing with small children who wet their pants. On occasions when any of us did, she would take away our underpants and send us out to play without them. That's not necessarily so bad for a kid, but she was a little weird about dealing with it. When it happened to me, she would watch me remove my underwear with her lips smacking and would comment about how nasty a child I was for doing such a thing.

Adults are strange sometimes. When a kid is swinging high on the swings in competition with a friend for who can swing the highest or the fastest, wetting your pants just doesn't seem to have any punishable relevance at that age.

I felt strange and weird feelings around Miss O'Toole, but did as she told me because I feared her. Wearing skirts or shorts felt uncomfortable to me because other children around the swing sets could see that I was naked beneath my clothing and I felt ashamed. However, I was afraid to go into her funky-smelling dark house to use the bathroom, and would wet myself even after she had taken away my underwear. She never knew that on these occasions I would run like the wind as fast as my five-year-old legs could carry me, trying to dry out my shorts before the miserable lunch hour. It was much easier to do with one less layer of clothing. I played until the very last minute before lunchtime to give me more time to dry.

On the first day she watched us, Elsie pulled the drapes to darken the afternoon. We were fed canned chicken noodle soup and milk for lunch. As she moved about placing our lunch before us, her lips smacked and her body smelled. Her hair was matted and her clothing was dark and ugly, hanging from her body. She wore slippers and her hosiery hung loosely on her elderly legs.

I swung my feet nervously as we ate, until she smacked my leg and bellowed, "Enough of that nonsense, child, be still," but minutes later my legs were swinging again in semi-conscious defiance. We learned about chores and what I call child slavery. I was to iron clothing and if I did a good job I would get Oreo cookies and milk. Elsie's home was dingy and filled with strange, musty odors. I wanted the draperies open so I could see the sun, but she kept them closed.

From the first day, while I did my chores, Elsie ran bath water for the little ones. My youngest two siblings would have a bath and prepare themselves for their nap. Elsie would then take the two youngest children into her bedroom and close the door. For the next hour or more I would hear nothing but screams and crying. I do not know what my older sister, Greta, was doing, because I kept my nose to my ironing and memorized the suffering sounds of my siblings.

I carried a piece of wild green onion with me, whether it was in my shoe, my pocket, or anywhere, as long as Elsie did not find it. I would smell the onion and feel the safety of the afternoons when I had played and dined on them.

Each day, sometime around two o'clock in the afternoon, I heard whimpering in the bedroom as Elsie returned to the living room. I sat on the sofa, having put everything back as I had found it. I waited, wondered, and listened with all of my strength for the sounds of my little brother and sister. Eventually they quieted down, and they stayed in that room for the remainder of the day. A little before 4:00 P.M., Elsie gave me my underwear and awakened my siblings to prepare us for our mother. Never in my life had I been so desperate to see my mom. She and the sun shone into the darkness of that house as she came through the doorway.

I am haunted by the sounds and smells of those fresh summer days and the distorted memory associations with the innocent and precious days of my youth.

No one said a word to my mother. What words could small children utilize to explain such sickness? We did not know or understand what was happening. It simply was not in our vocabulary. So we relished our freedom and slept with an eerie dread of the next day to come, and the sight of our mother leaving as she hugged us good-bye. Mom trusted Elsie and was comforted to believe her children were safe as she tried to earn a living and improve herself. For almost two weeks we remained with Elsie. My mother had begun to notice strange behavior and marks on my younger siblings. No one spoke. As it was, my mother would leave us there for another day, and another, because she had no real knowledge that things were not as they should be and she had no other place to take her children.

One afternoon while eating my cookies and ironing, I decided to get closer to the door because the tortured sounds from within that room were within hearing distance of my heart and soul. The moaning and anguish were more than my little body could bear.

I decided to go in. Greta looked at me, terror-stricken, warning me not to go near that door. Her eyes bugged out. Staring at me and holding my arm frantically, she pleaded with me to stay away. Despite my sister's warning, my concern for the suffering of my siblings, which aroused by the unbearable sounds from that room, moved me closer to the door. I had my green onions in my left pocket, and I squeezed them so hard that I felt the juice on my hand and could smell the freshness of their scent. I peeked through the keyhole. Slowly, I opened the door. The room was dark. There was a bathroom off to the left. The tub was filled with steaming bath water. I walked in further, with my right hand clutching the doorknob and my left the green onions. I stopped dead in my tracks when I saw my little brother and sister lying naked on the bed clinging to each other. The curtains were drawn, but a hint of sunshine forced its way into that room. Elsie was standing at the foot of the bed holding a hot towel she twisted over and over in her hands. She did not know I was there. Greta was hysterical by this time and had come closer to the doorway.

"Amber," she pleaded in a loud whisper, "get out of there." Elsie spotted me. I moved closer to the left side of the bed facing the children. Elsie was off to my right. She was frozen in mid-twist, for she had been preparing to strike again. She regained control of herself as I stared at her. She said to me, "They were bad. They wouldn't go to sleep." She did not move as I reached out for the sheet and covered my siblings. I had no intention of leaving that room. Although concerned for all of us, I remained. I began to pray for my mother to come early. It was almost three in the afternoon.

Looking back, I know it is the hero's role in family dynamics to defend and protect. I remember feeling nauseous about "selling out," so to speak, in that I had put a lot of energy into being good and had been rewarded with Oreo cookies while my siblings were being tortured. As my heart and mind write these sorrowful memories, I still hear the voice of the hero inside me saying, "I could have taken their place to spare them this cruelty." But this type of injustice cannot be undone. Only the ones that suffer can release this poison from their heart, body, spirit, and soul. I remained in the room until my siblings' shrill tones of fear and terror became whimpering sounds of misery. God was there with me. God was within me. God was streaming through the draperies even as Elsie tried to block the warmth of the sun.

My mother appeared, frantically knocking at the door. Elsie regrouped and told me to help dress the younger children. Greta was lost in her own gentle misery, crying softly on the sofa. As

Elsie opened the door for my mother it was a strange transition of events and timing. The full brilliance of the sun entered the hallway, and hushed little children scrambled swiftly to leave that monstrous place. My mother saw it. We were outside before she could greet us. She knew something was wrong. My mother was an angel charged with the care of her young.

I do not know what conversation she had with the old lady, or how Elsie justified her behavior. But we were free! It's strange and remarkably beautiful how children can shift so quickly. We were exhilarated, liberated, and we ran wildly into that summer afternoon. Our gatekeeper, our savior had come, our Mommy.

That night, my mother questioned Greta and me. I could not get the words out, but my sister managed to describe how mean and weird the old lady was. That, combined with my mother's intuition, was enough for her to promise never to take us back there. I can only begin to imagine my mother's mental and emotional state at that time. She was a strong and fearless woman, but particularly vulnerable when it came to her children. She could not protect us from the unseen enemy: the dark side of smiling people. The police were called, but Elsie remained in the neighborhood. My mother had no proof, and her babies had no words.

In my childhood I was taught that Jesus Christ said He was the image of God, as we all are, and we all had the strength within us to stand up and help one another. My mother was definitely the image of God, for she fought for us and loved us every day of her life. As a little girl, I believed all mommies were God.

From this point forward the four of us younger kids were to be together with our older siblings, and they were charged with our care. I felt like a butterfly, believing I had freed my younger siblings. In my imagination I began to create what I believed to be an invincibility that would carry me through childhood. It was a blind belief in love, and a sense of understanding its opposite nature, cruelty. But if the moth could be transformed by the mystery of nature, then so could I, for I also came from nature of a more complex sort. And besides, I was a hero: I had courage, and I had a mission to help my family.

Woodland tea parties filled most of my days, my imagination directing the cast of characters I conjured up to accompany me on each of life's many colorful days. Of the seven of us, my eldest sister never seemed to be around during the summers. By default, my older brothers became our caretakers. We lived next door to a boy named Max. He loved to play with Barbie dolls and G.I. Joe action figures. According to my mother, I was too young to play with Barbie dolls. I was glad because I found it strange that the dolls' bodies so overwhelmingly fascinated Max and my brothers.

Instead, I skipped off into a nearby wooded area to play house as often as I could sneak that far away from everyone. We lived in a red brick government housing apartment. All of the buildings were the same, aligned almost like a prison. Since no one paid much attention to what anyone else did, it was not difficult to slip away. I went into these woods to build a playhouse. I created my kitchen as most important because that is where I prepared wild berries, green onions, grass, roots, leaves, acorns, and other wonders to feed my forest friends. Of course, I had my toy dishes and spent a great deal of time arranging them on my table. I spent hours talking to my imaginary friends and sometimes longed for a real friend.

There is no telling how long he had been watching me over the days I had been playing in the woods. He was the man who brought me cookies. He had imaginary tea with me from water I had gathered from a nearby stream. He stayed for a long time and helped me build my playhouse. One afternoon he said I was missing a room, and explained that my imaginary friends and I needed a bathroom.

Innocently I agreed, and he assisted me in making something out of wood for me to sit on "like campers did." When our tea parties concluded, he would remind me that I needed to go to the bathroom. I would imitate such an act and simulate closing the lid and washing my hands. I felt nothing amiss. I trusted this kind man and was happy to have a playmate. After a few days passed, he simulated unzipping his pants and went through the same ritual I had created. Then he told me I should go ahead and use the toilet because it worked. He said he would come with me to the bathroom. I agreed to let him show me how to go to the bathroom. I pulled my pants down and sometimes he helped me.

His manner changed to a sense of excitement. He helped me go to the potty and wipe myself. Then it was his turn. I did not want to help him wipe and refused to look at him. Our days were focused on tea parties, the treats he brought, the bathroom, and me. He would wipe me to be sure I was clean. I did not like this man now because I knew how to wipe myself. He caressed my hair and often combed it for me. This led to the play bedroom and the suggestion of naptime. I already had a fear of naptime from my experience at Elsie's, and told him I was too old for naps.

One day I gathered my dishes and told the man I would bring different ones back the next day. I allowed him to pull down my pants that day because I feared him, but I had a plan. I told him I had to go to the dentist, and I would have to leave early. I cleaned my dishes and hugged him goodbye so he would believe me. I tricked him into thinking I would return the next day. I walked away and made sure he did not follow me. I never returned. Something was not right about this man. Besides, I was a big girl now and did not need help with my dishes, tea parties, or bathroom activities.

When Mom came home at the end of each day, seven children needed her attention and she had many things to do. There was no time to question her about the man in the woods, and so my secret forest friend lay concealed for most of my life. A seed of distrust was being fertilized as I found myself interacting with adults. On one hand, I was a teacher's doll baby and spoiled with treats and presents of new clothing. On the other, there always seemed to be empty and restless adults just waiting around to exploit me in some way or another.

On Saturday evenings, Mom would prepare a feast of soup and bologna sandwiches with American cheese and white bread. I would make dough balls and drop them into my soup. We would bring our pillows and blankets from upstairs and scatter ourselves on the floor, each of us trying for the seat closest to the television. Mom would perch herself on a torn-up, olive-green rocker and we children would spread out on the cold floor waiting for our two favorite programs, *The Tom Jones Show* and *Mannix.* Mom loved Tom Jones and Elvis Presley. She would sing and laugh and dance with her children on these nights and almost every Sunday after church. I loved her so much, and it always warmed my heart to see her happy. That would be my reason for not telling her the things that happened to me. She had enough to bear and I needed her to be happy and loving because that made me feel safe. Children do that.

During summer days, while Mom was working, games were played inside our house with curtains drawn and the door securely fastened. Somewhere my older brothers and their buddy Max had learned some peculiar behavior patterns that were not very pleasant. After the doors were locked, the "captain" or the "airline crew" lured my younger siblings and me into the boys' bedroom. Some may judge what happened in there to be normal behavior for young children, but I viewed it as disturbing. Someone had to have hurt my brothers for them to turn this evil behavior onto their own younger brothers and sisters. Max was simply not right either.

They had bunk beds. Their room smelled of rancid underwear and shoes were scattered on the floor. The boys gave us younger children no food until we had our "flights," for which we had to remove our clothing.

Don't touch me! Mommy, Mommy, help me! was my silent scream.

Anger filled Max in particular, as his bizarre obsession with these games possessed him. Sometimes our hands were tied to the bedpost, but I squirmed out of the restraint even though my brothers and Max said I would fall to my death from the airplane. One of my sisters simply gave in. She was too young to comprehend and too emotionally, spiritually, and physically immature to resist. I hated my older brothers. As time went by, I resisted more and more. I could not let this happen to us. I would be locked outside of the room for hours. I was powerless to help anyone but myself.

I found the laundry hamper; put a pillow on it to play "horsey," and dreamed about magical beings coming to carry all of us away. Where was Santa? Why did my brothers get so many presents at Christmas? Where were God and the angels that the adults spoke about in church? I looked everywhere for them. I searched behind the curtains, under the rugs, and in the cabinets. I dug deep into the earth. I looked on the rooftops, searched under cars and in street gutters. I looked everywhere, thinking they were hidden and waiting for me to call out to them. God had been with me before, but where was God now?

Eventually, I became a threat to Max and the boys because I was not playing their games. I did play the "secretary" game, but hated it when I had to sit on my brother's Danny's lap. I was not allowed to go to the bathroom unless I sat on his lap while on the toilet and bounced up and down without my bottoms on. *Mommy, Mommy, help me! I* screamed silently in my head.

One day I refused to sit on his lap and I defecated on the wooden floor instead. I was filled with tears and shame. Danny was furious and made me clean it up. He told me that either I would obey the rules, or else. I decided to take my chance with the "or else." I was not popular with the boys. I fought them. Since I was not the favorite one who surrendered, my brothers had to decide what to do with me because they feared that I would tell. Max offered a plan.

It was a rainy day, miserable outside and inside. I was in the hallway preparing to ride my "horsey" when the boys came out of their room. They went into the girls' bedroom and rearranged a few things. I stayed in the hall with my dolly, Marguerite, named after a school friend. I was calling for the angels because I could feel something bad was coming. I hated the darkness of a rainy day without sunshine. My brother Henry came into the hallway and told me to get down on the floor. He stood behind me as he ordered me into the bedroom. I had Marguerite in my hand, but no green onions that day. As I walked, Henry pushed me. I was afraid. I felt icky, eerie. I clung to Marguerite. My body could sense danger. In the room was a dark brown wooden chair with chipped paint showing bright blue paint underneath. It was not in its usual place. I watched over my back at one brother and continued into the room while Max stood behind the chair, waiting. He was smiling in a mean way. I was angry with them all. They were very cruel at times and I was afraid of them. Max was the ringleader, but no matter what evil possessed him, I could not believe he was a monster.

Why was he acting this way at such a young age? What was wrong with him?

He ordered me to sit in the chair and my favorite brother, Henry, jerked Marguerite from my hands as I clutched her to my heart. Where were the angels? Could they not hear my cries? I wanted my baby doll. Could they not feel my fear? Could they not see what was happening?

Something was about to happen and there was no way out. Anxiety is like an ice storm, it's slippery, cutting, and difficult to manage. With belts, my feet were tied to the chair and my legs were spread and attached to different chair legs. Danny stood behind me and tied my wrists with something. "Somebody, anybody, help me, please!" I silently, desperately cried. I was so afraid.

Someone stuck their finger in me. They seemed to actually hate me. Danny said that if I ever told Mom, the consequences to me would be far worse. My hands were clenched and aching with pain. Henry then tore Marguerite apart, limb by limb, in front of me. I felt that I could hear her screams for me to save her. I was the family hero, but could help neither of us. One of her legs and then the other was ripped off. Then he tore off her arms and her head faced away from me. We could not see each other.

Danny laughed. He was too young to understand his darkness. Max watched.

The boys left the room for me to stare at my beloved Marguerite baby. I could not help her as she lay disassembled in front of me, and she could not help me with her loving eyes and smile. My brothers had said, "If you open your mouth to Mom, it will be worse." What darkness had overtaken my brothers? They were so angry. Perhaps their age held more awareness than I could comprehend. I sat there for a very long time, whimpering for my baby doll. They came back from time to time to check on me.

One of my sisters had learned that giving them her body was the right thing to do and that my torture was what happened to those who did not comply. She was still a baby herself. They brought her to me.

She just stood there, tiny, and looked at me.

Surrendering to my own pain was easier than imagining the pain of my sisters. The boys had power, and we did not. I decided to accept the pain rather than to accept what was happening to my family.

These memories are disgusting. Human beings create misery. It's a virus passed from person to person since the beginning of time. It always seems to be in the name of God or in the act of some perverse sexual behavior that we create such devastation. What had happened to the childlike nature of my brothers? Who had robbed them of their joy, innocence, and love? Had they experienced their own version of Elsie O'Toole or met a man in the woods who violated them? What had turned them to be so destructive? They were not born that way. Someone was hurting them and no one protected them from the darkness that ate them. We were poor and lost in a world of starving, miserable souls. Pain was a way of life. Justice, well that was something we watched in a TV show.

After witnessing Marguerite dismantled on the floor, I decided the world was not a safe place to birth children. I rid myself of my love for Marguerite or any dolly from that time forward. I decided on that day to never bring a child into the world. It wasn't safe and I could never protect her. A fertilized seed of fear had been implanted in me. As a woman, my subsequent pregnancy in my adulthood reactivated every possible strand of the fear at my core, and it would grow in me right alongside the baby in my womb. Pregnancy activated a flow of anxious and depressive chemicals that battled with the overflow of estrogen's love. How do women endure?

Silence was not birthed by the torture, but by the fact that my own beloved mother had suffered enough. If my brothers had believed I would not tell, perhaps they would not have been so harsh. They believed that the torture ensured my silence. So silence became my savior and that of my mother's. She did not need to bear any more sorrow than she had already faced. I could never tell her. I needed to see her happy. I needed that happiness to know that the world was a better place than home.

The day would eventually come, fourteen years later, when I would finally tell my mother. She would simply refuse to believe me and would forbid me ever to discuss it with her again. Knowing might have made her feel powerless to protect her good memories of her children. Her need to deny fed into the power of the festering silence savagely eating my soul.

No one spoke, ever about the "things" that were going on.

Summer days were also filled with Grandma. She hated me. She told me I was too helpful. She thought I was manipulative. Perhaps I was, as I was trying desperately to win her love and to survive in the trenches of life. She loved the boys most of all, and my younger sister. She was cold, calculating, and insensitive. I was too loving and feeling oriented for her taste—most people are not comfortable with that. Sharing intimately was not popular in our family.

Sanity has to be in the spoken truth. Therefore, insanity is in the unspoken truth. My home life was insane, and I struggled with why people would not talk about it. As long as we did "normal" things that families do while others are present, everyone seemed happy. That's what people do, isn't it? Stay busy trying to be happy and look the other way when bad things happen. My childhood fantasy was to rescue my family from the insane suffering of silence. Even as a child, the simplicity of talking was real. Tears, sorrow, hugs, and forgiveness could make the bad things go away. But instead, the insanity of denial was nurtured as I continued on the path of my youth into the larger world outside our home.

The following year, we became eligible to attend a Catholic school that mostly served rich, white children. The school was forced to take on a certain number of "charity" cases each year. All seven of us were eligible and attended Saint Leo from first grade through eighth. We wore uniforms: blue and white plaid pleated skirts, white blouses, and knee-high socks. Marcy Chapman was my hero. She had straight, dirty blond hair and wore big, round glasses. She always wore long-sleeved shirts with puffy sleeves. That was the fashion. I copied everything she did. I would watch how she placed her feet, how she moved her hair from her shoulders, how she held her pencil, and which hand she would raise to answer questions.

My plan was to win over the mean nun who was our teacher. I was not always the cleanest child in the classroom, and my shoes were not the preferred blue and white saddles. Sister Agnes could find the simplest reasons to isolate me from the other children. She would announce to the whole class that I needed a shower or that I did not speak very well. She hated me because I was a welfare child. "Only the good kids whose parents can afford it send their children here," she revealed to me in a hostile manner with her spit spattering my face. Her goal was that I sit as far as possible from the other students, as I was different. It was my goal to be her best student, so I copied everything Marcy did, but without a victory. All the spunk and courage in the world could not change the seething hatred Sister Agnes had for me.

One day I went to school with an abscessed tooth. It was extremely painful and had a terrible odor. Going to the dentist was not much fun for my siblings or me as we were singled out and pushed aside by the doctor, who was required by law to treat welfare recipients. We had to wait until everyone else had been treated, and we were given less Novocain and other procedural care than a paying customer might receive. I had been to the dentist several times for this tooth, and he had sent me home untreated. I don't know exactly what he told my young mother or what guilt he thrust upon her, but somehow he got her to leave each time with my tooth untreated. So I endured the foul smell and pain of this tooth. It provoked Sister Agnes beyond her Christian composure to the point that she decided to make a spectacle out of me.

I was so miserable on this particular day that I wasn't even paying attention to Marcy Chapman. I had to stay in during lunch hour to repent for my "lack of cleanliness."

"Cleanliness is next to godliness," Sister Agnes would often remind me publicly. It was obvious to me that she and I knew completely different gods.

Sister Agnes was so disgusted with me that she decided to put me in front of the room to criticize my hair, my clothing, and my poor, suffering tooth. She held her handkerchief to her nose as I sat there, legs swinging to and fro, and she pointed out my flaws. Marcy Chapman, my hero and the most popular girl in the class, began to laugh hysterically, and so the others followed suit.

"Speak up child, speak up," Sister Agnes bellowed at me. "Why do you not brush your teeth like these children? This is God's punishment to you for your filthy ways." She then smacked each of my hands ten times with her ruler and sent me to the furthest corner of the room, where I was to remain each day until my tooth was finally removed.

I had no idea why my tooth was sore. I did brush my teeth and I did bathe. I felt like a wilting flower overexposed to the heat. I needed love. I remained silent and withdrawn for the rest of the year. I slipped into a fantasy world and brought home Ds and Fs, which meant that I had to stay indoors at recess every day and clean the chalkboard and classroom after school. When my mother inquired about the situation, Sister Agnes projected a sour sweetness in her effort to be polite, while still maintaining her god-like authority.

Nevertheless, she watched her boundaries with my mother, who was poor, but no fool. My mother could be quite demanding on behalf of her children. Sister Agnes must have said something convincing, because I continued to be her after-school servant. Instead of tutoring me to catch up, she enslaved me with shame. What was it about filth and poverty that provoked her to be so cruel to an innocent child? What God did she work for? I only knew that it wasn't the one my mom had told me about. Everyone seemed to have their own version of God.

I did manage to get out of my after-school servitude one day due to classes being dismissed early. It was mid-afternoon when the school bells chimed. Nuns were running through the hallways telling everyone to get ready for an early dismissal. There was panic and chaos about, and looking out the window I saw parents pulled up into the parking lots anxiously waiting for their children. My siblings and I walked to and from school, so there was no rush as far as my six-year-old mind knew. I had chores to do. So I was sitting around waiting for everyone to leave when Sister Agnes said, "Don't you understand English, you foolish child? Get out of here." Whoopee for me! I did not smell smoke and could not understand why everyone was rushing so much. On my way to meet my family at our usual spot, I noticed all of the nuns running to their sleeping quarters. I could hear my feet tapping on the floor in the emptied hallways.

When my older brother, Danny, saw me coming out of the school, he yelled at me to hurry. His face was filled with fear. All of my siblings were there. As we headed across the wide parking lot, Danny ran up ahead as if scouting the area. My youngest sister and I fell behind, squabbling over something. Danny ran out into the street, but immediately came running back. He ran to the nuns' quarters, banging on the door. We stopped in stunned silence to watch the mania. The priest opened the door and waved his hand at my brother as if to say, "Go away."

I was beginning to be afraid. Everyone sensed some danger lurking around the corner. Led by my brother, we all began to run toward the street. It was time to run as fast as we could, Danny in the lead. The other older children tried to help the little ones move swiftly. I was about twenty-five feet behind Danny when he screamed in fear and frustration for us to run faster.

As I arrived at the street, out of my left eye I saw an amazing sight. The streets were completely covered with screaming, angry black teenagers. They were yelling at each other, "Get that Whitey!" Realizing the danger, I dropped everything I carried and began to follow as fast as I could. We were forced to take the long way home, through the woods. We caught up with some classmates of ours, John and Kathy Sundry, and all of us ran for our lives up a very steep climb through the woods, trying to reach the top. I was crying and so were my siblings. My two eldest brothers, although fearful, diligently led all of us up that hill while we were being aggressively chased. What we did not know was that at the top of the hill, rage-filled black children were waiting for us "little Whities." There was no way to escape.

I will never forget Danny's courage in that moment, as he stepped out into the streets to defend us. After him followed Henry. Both my abusers now were my protectors. *This moment would be profoundly played out again and again in my choice of future life partners.*

I managed to get my little brother and sister hidden beneath a huge bush while my two eldest sisters met a different fate. I witnessed them being slapped and punched, hair pulled, as they were forced to lift their skirts for everyone to see the rest of their skin. Fear stricken, I had to do something. I told my preschool-aged brother and sister to stay under the bush and not make a sound. And then I ran. I ran as fast as I could. Hundreds of kids were pulling and pushing me to the ground and kicking me to the point of mental hysteria. Kids! Acting on what our parents or teachers or neighbors had taught us, we were engaged in violent acts toward one another. I managed to get up, wounded, but feeling no pain. Adrenaline protected me. I had a mission.

As I ran, my brothers continued fighting. Kathy had made it to her home. Her brother fought alongside mine. My brothers were surrounded and being beaten. The teenagers were singing an old song, "I'm so dizzy my head is spinnin'," as my brothers hit the ground. I ran faster and cut between buildings as kids hollered at me, "Where you goin', girl?"

I was going to get my mother, our protector. She worked not far from there, and I knew that she would kill to protect her own. I think I could have broken the world record for running the mile. I made it breathlessly to the door of where she worked. When she opened the door to let me in, she was dressed in white coveralls with a look of absolute confidence on her face. She was calm, quiet, and focused. There existed fearlessness within her, an indomitable determination to face the obstacles before her. She pulled me in the door while looking out at the streets, as her coworkers, both black and white women said, "Charlene, you can't go out there." She pushed me down to the floor with the other ladies as rocks flew through the windows. In between breaths I tried to tell her where her other children were.

She settled me by the window and told me to stay down. The kids outside had been throwing rocks at any movement they saw in the windows. I clearly remember her stepping out into the street as fearlessly as a mountain lion or a large eagle swooping down on its prey. I did not fear for her, but for anyone who crossed her path. Teenagers stepped out of her way as she swiftly made her way to find her children. Dressed in white, she seemed to be untouchable. Her would-be assailants stepped back in her presence. She had a mission, and it was to find her babies.

I saw my mother sometime later. In her arms lay my brother Danny. With courage and phenomenal resolve, she led her other children to safety and prepared to take my brother to the hospital. He had fought alongside Henry until he was beaten down while trying to protect all of us.

I have no idea what challenges my brothers faced in their youths. I was lost in my childlike world. But looking back, I can tell they had much more to deal with than any nine- and ten-year-old should have to face. Someone had gotten to them. Someone had taken away their safety, their joy, their innocence.

It is moments like these in my life, when those who have harmed me show amazing acts of courage, which wipe out my resentment toward them. I can only feel my love for them. I developed a sense that mean people really didn't mean it, and that love always lurked just beneath the surface, though it rarely showed itself except at such a primal level known as survival. This basic instinct seemed to bring out the heroes in my family. The environment of cyclical violence and love I was raised within would later lead to my selection of these same types of people as my lovers, friends, husbands, and protectors. These experiences laid down behavioral tracks, like railroad tracks, creating a map for how I would choose people to be in my life. I would end up desperate for any scrap of love a man had to offer even if I was depressed or anxious about it, just like in my childhood. Love and violence would become a neurological drug, something I could not understand and always found myself attracted to. Some folks like to call this behavior "passion." How seductive we humans can be.

My brothers had tried to protect us in the face of hundreds of angry black teenagers looking for any white person they could find to harm. My mother, a young woman not more than twenty-five-years-old, showed a mother's courage in the face of danger. Love was once again born within me as those I loved and hated now stood and fought for my life and would for a long time attract me to people that would hurt me and then do something nice.

The strange and overwhelming traumas in those days of living in English Woods in Cincinnati, Ohio, created distorted emotions within my being and fragmented my young mind for a long, long time. I was unable to compartmentalize such things. My thoughts were jumbled and tossed like a salad. Understanding was simply not possible. That night, after the riots, my mother had made up her mind that we were moving. She had no idea as to how or where, but the decision had been made.

Fear, anger, and sadness filled all of our hearts, for some of the children that had terrorized my family had formerly been our friends. My mother sat us down to tell us what was happening. She explained that the riots had mostly been brought on by adults who passed on their anger to their children, like a baton passed in a race for life. Most kids fought because of their parents' anger about the social injustices endured by the black American. "It was a brotherhood, sort of like our family sticking up for one another," she said. She told us about racism and other such things we had known nothing about, as we lived in a predominately black neighborhood where racism had not existed. We had played with our black neighbors as they had played with their white neighbors. Without adult interpretation or interference, kids go beyond the fact that skin and hair are different. We just played day and night, our initial differences already calculated and dismissed. The formula for happiness was laughter, competition, hide-and-go-seek, Double Dutch jump rope, hopscotch, and hot dogs on a summer day.

My mother taught us not to fight because of the color of our skin, but only to save our skin. We were to protect our lives, and fight back in defense of them. She gave each of us a toy she'd picked up in preparation for the remainder of our stay in the neighborhood. The toys were called knockers. They were made of two glass balls tied to two separate ropes that were attached to a ring at the top. You put your finger through the ring so that when you moved the toy up and down the glass balls clanked together. She showed us another use for them: Hold one of the balls in your hand and swing the toy like a weapon at anyone who tries to hurt you. We were to carry these to school and everywhere we went.

For the remaining two weeks that we lived at 2001 G, Westwood Northern Boulevard, phone number 5-1-3-6-2-2-0-4-3-9 (all of which I remember to this day), she drove us to and from school. Then, one day we moved from that neighborhood into an entirely different world.

It's important to mention that as powerful as my mother's protective nature was, her need to teach right and wrong oftentimes was based on the limited knowledge of a young mother. On one such occasion and at Christmas, believing I'd lied to her about candy, she simply drove me to an orphanage and left me there for a weekend. I had no idea I was headed for that lonely, desolate place, because on the way she had told me we were going to a grocery mart.

Before she dropped me off, she told me that my father had been a compulsive liar and that she would not raise one of her children to be one as well. Even if I were not lying, she felt that I needed to learn this lesson to prevent me from lying in the future. She handed me over to a nun without telling me that she would ever be back for me.

Life as a youngster meant chaos, confusion, fear, and survival. Nature and Santa Claus filled my heart with hope as the dark and unpredictable events of life raped my mind of innocence, and left me naive, vulnerable, fearful, and in a constant state of shame.

When my mother came for me, I was simply too bashful to run and hold her. The pain was unbearable for my little body. She was tough and did not smile when she saw me. Scraps of warmth and tenderness from her were rare, and the fact that she came back for me at all was desperately enough. When I share this story with my mother today, she has to deny that she left me for an entire weekend. I get a little satisfaction simply in that she at least has the courage to admit that she took me there at all.

After returning home that weekend, I'd gone to school. Everything was decorated Christmas. Santa was coming to lunch that day to give the good children a present and the bad children coal. I sat at my table filled with cafeteria smells, my legs swinging nervously as Santa called up the children to give them gifts. I was breathless as one by one, names were called. Sounds of delighted children echoed in the room.

And then, the event was over.

My name had not been called.

I thought that Santa and God thought I was a bad girl after being in an orphanage for lying. As we started to get up, my heart dripping with sadness, my green eyes flooded with warm, little girl tears, they asked us all to sit back down. Then the school secretary said they had one more gift for a very special person. I held my breath. Santa was handed a large gift and the secretary called out my name, "Amber." I very shyly stared at my feet as I almost ran to the stage. Santa and that secretary both smiled at me warmly as they handed me the present. It was so big I could barely hold it. I walked back to the table and ripped open my gift. It was a beautiful set of dishes.

Santa and God loved me even if no one else did. That one, solitary act of human kindness filled me with hope that someone was watching over me. I was a good girl.

When my family left English Woods, the Saturday nights watching *Mannix* and *Tom Jones,* eating feasts of lunchmeat and cheese sandwiches, chips, and soup, and camping out on those white spit-shined floors were ended forever. So were the Christmases. Charities flooded us with gifts and candy. Our new lives awaited us, and with anticipation I left not only my home, but also my woodland friends and my favorite summer meal of choice: wild green onions.

CHAPTER 6
PURPLE SECRETS

 From boys in elementary school, to middle school, our new, middle-class white neighborhood, and puberty, change seemed to hit me all at once. Even so, I still possessed the same burning torch of hope as I moved into my new world.

Summer grass, fragrant autumn leaves, and crisp white winters remained the same. Something about the change of seasons—it had a rhythm, a pulse, and offered a guarantee that new days were ahead of me. And with my burning curiosity in the midst of chaos, I managed my way through a reality no one spoke of.

I became a fighter: bold, curious, and courageous. I possessed as much wisdom as a young lady can manage in the wake of hormonal mania. However, and most importantly, when I had the chance to actually look at my body, I felt ugly, shameful, and uncomfortable with my female parts. Not only did I want to fight back, I also wanted to hide my body from the world. I never wore skirts, but instead wore my brothers' clothing. I was damaged, and in my mind the new odors, scents, and the presence of my youthful blood flow were a constant reminder that I was somehow prey to the unknown predators that lingered on the edges of my existence.

It was time to defend myself, so with a compassionate love and a dreadful anger, I embarked upon an open rebellion against everything and everyone. The offense had advantages. I was exhausted from defending myself, and I needed a more proactive strategy. Standing on the sidelines of the senseless battlefield of life, I was constantly a victim of human error. If people were not going to do something about it, then I was. Life was ugly. I was seriously depressed, with no idea how I would survive the next day. Misery is like a strong current. If I allowed it to carry me as swiftly as possible, it seemed more bearable at times. New days were on the horizon, and small precious things—like Bazooka bubble gum and pop bottles worth a nickel—nourished me and strengthened my mind to keep going.

I truly hated people. I thought often of death, and wrote in the privacy of my blue-covered diary that I wanted to come home to God and leave this miserable place. No response, and to my amazement people just kept getting worse.

In that summer before seventh grade, my mother considered marrying my step-uncle.

My grandfather was actually my mother's stepfather, and Ted was his son. We were used to seeing him only at our grandparents' house, where he had always been a jovial, playful, and friendly man. But one Saturday he appeared unexpectedly at our home. Curious, some of us kids left our rooms to greet him.

Something was up.

"Hi, Uncle Ted."

"Hi, kids. Hello, Charlene." A brief hug was exchanged with my mother.

I had a weird feeling.

My mom started calling all of the kids to come to the dining room. Everyone was home, as we had been instructed to be this Saturday morning. Everyone straggled to the dining room and eventually got situated. Uncle Ted joked with my brothers.

I thought maybe we were taking a trip or something. My mother began to speak, cleared her nicotine throat, and casually announced, "Uncle Ted and I may be getting married."

"What?"

"Really, when?" came the responses from around the table.

"We'll see," she exhaled along with the smoke from her cigarette. "In the meantime, he has something he wants to talk about." She had a way of squinting her eyes while smoke encircled her. She would sit with one varicose-veined leg hiked up on her chair; while she either chewed Wrigley's Doublemint Gum or stuck it on her pinkie fingernail so she would not lose it. She sipped black coffee and sucked up fresh air as her throat gurgled with the exchange of oxygen for smoke. With a slight cough and a cool demeanor, she acknowledged my step-uncle as she attempted to find yet another solution to help her with her plight.

What was going on and what could he possibly say?

It would soon become apparent that these two adults, my mother and my step-uncle, had joined forces in a naïve strategy to inflict strict and unexpected punishment on us in order to create well-behaved children. As if discipline alone could sort out our problems.

My mother, still a young woman in her mid-thirties, meant well.

Uncle Ted wore glasses. He was built firm and tall. He drank Pepsi-Cola like an alcoholic drinks liquor. He had a bushy mustache, and that's all I really knew about him. Oh, except that he crossed his legs like a girl.

"You kids have gone far too long without discipline," he said with a slight grin on his face. I don't believe he was evil, just a bit nervous.

Uh oh, here it comes, I thought.

"You kids take advantage of your mother and I am here to help her in any way I can," he stated.

Well, it was about time someone was stepping up to help Mom. Maybe she wouldn't have to work so damned hard and she could see what was going on in the nice, new neighborhood and in our home. But something was not right about the manner in which he spoke. He spoke nothing of getting a job and providing for her and her children.

"You kids live like pigs," he interrupted my thoughts. *Did he say pigs? What is he talking about?* I looked up at my siblings for a brief moment before my eyes dropped back down to the crusted food left between the cracks on the table. My mind started to conjure up a cleaning fantasy, allowing me a second's reprieve from the wisdom of my intuition warning me that a storm was underway.

"You are going to learn some lessons about how to take care of your rooms," he continued.

Mom lit another cigarette and drank her coffee. Her lungs expelled as much smoke as possible in preparation for the next cigarette assault.

"Your mother needs help and I am going to help her. We will start today. You will have one hour to pick up all of your clothing and put it neatly in your drawers. I will show you how to fold your tee-shirts like I learned in the Marine Corps." That meant the tee-shirts would be folded in a square, six inches by six inches. It looked cool, but it did not make sense to me as long as I could find my things.

From then on, it was chaos. Everyone was pissed off. Uncle Ted had turned into potential stepfather and a drill sergeant in less than an hour.

Defiantly, I decided to take him up on his challenge. I was going to clean my room perfectly. This was something I was good at. I had always maintained my sanity through domesticity. I could not fix the people in my life, so I fixed furniture and cleaned the dirt away from the things I could control. Cleaning was the avenue to the heart of my mother's grace. I just knew I would receive the small drops of the love I so desired when Mom saw the artistry of my cleaning our home.

My uncle wanted a challenge, and I was up for it. I ran up the stairs determined to outsmart the bastard.

Within an hour it was inspection time. My uncle's heavy foot-steps echoed as he came up the wooden stairway. We were told to stand next to our dressers while the inspections took place. I took my place as directed. He inspected the boys' room first. I could hear him open their dresser drawers. I could hear things hit the floor. Then I heard him talking, but could not make out his words.

The next thing I heard was the crack of something that sounded like lightning. I heard one of my brothers cry. This noise repeated at least seven or eight times. I was in a state of panic and fear for my brothers, and for myself.

I glanced around my room to make one final check. Anxiety slammed against the edges of my thoughts. Then I heard my uncle bark, "You kids are going to learn to listen when you are told to do something." I was glad that I had done what I was told.

I heard his footsteps as he crossed the hall to the room I shared with my sisters. He entered our room. My mother was with him. I looked at her. She seemed troubled, but did not say a word. I noticed my uncle carrying a long, thick leather strap. His feet shuffled as he began the inspection. I was first. He rummaged through my drawers. Why was he messing up my neatly folded clothing?

I felt sick to my stomach.

Feelings of hatred churned within me. My heart was pounding. What was he doing and where did he get this idea? I did not really know him other than our encounters on visits to my grandmother's. He and my grandmother had always harassed my mother about getting a man in her life to discipline her children. (As if my mother hadn't been raising seven children on her own that far without a man). I watched him finish his inspection.

He looked at me and said, "I found several things wrong with your clothing. You will receive eight swats for this, so the next time, do a better job."

I saw the leather razor strap in his hands. I panicked and looked at my mother. She was astonished, but otherwise expressionless.

He told me, "Bend over and hold your ankles. If you move, you will get another."

Bastard! I hated him. I wanted to kill him. What the hell was going on? What was this going to teach me? In shame, rage, and fear I bent over. I felt so exposed wearing shorts. Had I known I would be damned near baring my ass for some idiot to get his jollies by beating me, I would have at least worn pants—if not an entire roll of toilet tissue in my underwear.

After the first crack I swore I would not holler or cry out. The strikes were brutal.

I gritted my teeth and winced hard. Like a soft drizzle, tears dropped from my eyes. I closed my eyes against their warmth on my face. The cracking sounds—like lighting—erupted over and over. My tears pushed harder and harder to release the fury held in by the heat of the summer's moment.

My mother stopped him at six strikes.

I had welts all over my legs where the straps had fanned out. I could feel the sting and burn from the whipping.

"Get up," he ordered.

Did they actually believe this would teach me anything? I turned around and stared directly into him with hatred. I had always taken pride in cleanliness and order. It was the only way for me to cleanse the ugliness in my life. I routinely spent laborious hours rearranging furniture, organizing silverware, and making curtains and chair covers out of cheap fabric my mother had. My cleaning brought joy to my mother. I organized out of love. I had just received a senseless punishment for doing something I loved, though not up to someone else's standard.

"Don't look at me that way." His eyes were magnified behind his glasses. He must have learned this macho bullshit in the Marine Corp. It really takes gall for someone to use this type of ignorant brutality on a kid. Today, I've long since let go of the perfection of folding underwear and tee-shirts. Looking back, I am constantly and proudly reminded of the strength and will of my teenage self to defiantly and boldly look him in the eye. He was a product of patriarchal ignorance and childrearing, and my mother was a product of feminine submission against her own maternal instincts.

While defiantly glaring at him, he grabbed my arm and ordered me to bend over again. Before I completely did, he struck me and I fell to the ground. I had nerve. He didn't like it.

I sat up right on the ground so filled with hatred that it almost consumed my sorrow. He walked past me to defend his violent behavior to my mother, who I knew suffered in a strange way from what he was doing to her kids. If not for the overwhelming sorrow I felt for her and my brothers, the hatred would have consumed me.

They finally left the room.

What were my sisters thinking? I can't imagine. In silence, I cried out my agony. My tormented heart was pounding through my chest as I lay on the floor. Tears melted the poison that raced through my veins. Crying shifted the misery overflowing in my heart. Kids are not born with misery. Adults pour it into them.

My older brother Henry came to my rescue. His straight hair stringy across his face, I could see the pain cut through his eyes. This teenage boy was tough. He had an easygoing laugh and a quiet strength, and watched over me in the neighborhood when he was around. He was also crying, but fought to hold back his tears. Our legs welted, our minds splintered, we managed to make it through the experience. He told me to stay in my room and I did.

I heard him as he escaped out of the house with my mother yelling at him to come back. He was gone. This was one of his first steps toward the world of drugs and alcohol that would eventually consume him. He was my favorite brother and, strangely, my hero. Something tortured his mind and haunted him. At night he would scream out in terror from his dreams and wake the entire family. I felt enormous compassion for him. What was so powerful within him that it would emerge only while his mind made its way to the depths of sleep? His toughness had no strength in this place. His only escape was in the dark screams of his soul. One night he reached up to the ceiling and with a powerful force yanked the light fixture out of the ceiling. What was it that tortured him so badly? What adult had hurt him, too? What had they done to my brothers?

I watched him from my window as he crossed the street and headed toward a direction that would feed his pain and provide escape. He was gone, and somehow I knew he was lost to this world forever. I felt an overwhelming sense of loss as he disappeared. I was alone with my scars, and I desperately needed someone to love me.

In my family, *love* was a word no one spoke. Hugs were quick pats on the back and very casual if at all. I felt icky and too emotional around my family. I really needed the safety of a warm hug until my nerves calmed. No such thing would ever occur in my youth. My nervous system's anxiety course would develop untamed like weeds in a garden. And if anxiety were the weeds then depression was the hardened earth—for in this place joy, bliss, and love could not blossom. My inner garden, my soul and heart, would become dependent on hard environments where anxiety grew wildly.

My mother decided that Uncle Ted was not the man for her. She had seen enough distorted adult behavior exercised on her children under the guise of parenting. After my uncle's departure, we resumed one of my mother's favorite Sunday rituals. Church, Elvis Presley, and Johnny Cash filled the day while Mom let her spirit free as she sang and danced for us. Standing with her arms stretched wide, her fingers snapped to the rhythm and mood of the song. She held her head high and smiled with pleasure as she moved her hips and feet, trying to bring the family together.

She loved us. And I absorbed every manifestation of her love: her hair brushing across her face, her closed-mouthed smile, and her thick feet swishing back and forth. I longed to dance in her arms.

To make the transition from welfare and government housing to residing in a middle-class neighborhood, my mother managed to overcome obstacles for the sake of her family. And it wore her down. Still a young woman, living without the tenderness of a loving touch from a man or someone to share her parental burdens often left her weary. We were too young to appreciate her tireless efforts to provide for us.

Years later, when I met my father, I asked him why he left. He said, "I was afraid I could not support all of you."

My mother: one woman, no education, no money, and seven children.

She stayed.

He left.

In the absence of social accountability, men have stripped themselves of honor, like a dirty shirt. Left to their own devices and socially unregulated, men have been impregnating women for a very long time and leaving both the woman and the children behind. Why stay? Being a man throughout history has had its perks: more sex and more money. Women and children simply get in the way. Only in recent history has our government enforced support for women and children.

Spending the day without Mom was always a scary experience for me. Things were still happening. I anxiously needed to see her smiling strength. I tried to bring joy into her life to cover up the creepy things that were going on in our household. She did not need to know. She had too much to bear already. Almost every week I would clean and organize the house. I rearranged the furniture in hopes of changing the environment to cover what was happening while she was away. I cleaned, organized, and rearranged the furniture. I rearranged memories and neatly organized them inside of me.

A couch was anger. I moved it several times per week. Both the floors and I were dirty. They were scrubbed—daily. I cleaned often so no one would notice the ugliness in our home. I ended up doing the same thing as a grown woman. It was at one time almost an obsession.

Mom would arrive home completely exhausted. Sometimes she did not notice the changes. By 6:00 P.M. on a summer's eve she would have drifted into a heavy sleep. I missed her while she was out at work and did not truly understand how tired she was. Sometimes I lay in bed next to her and cried. She was still "Mommy" to me and this was the easiest way to get close to her, to touch her, and smell her hair. I needed love.

I shielded my need for love by talking people to death. "Chatterbox," my grandfather used to call me. Talking was my revenge, my refuge, my body's way of engaging. My brain was active and full of life. Talking seemed to be something people were not afraid of. Underneath, as a frail, fighting young girl, I believed the world was a battleground between good things and bad things. Goodness struggled with the restlessness of chaos.

My heart ached. Laughter hurt.

Things were also happening at school that I did not know how to handle. I'd left a window open to my soul through which unsettling things crept in from the neighborhood that seemed to be hunting me and my unprotected siblings.

Some things were worse than others. They were things no one spoke about, as if they simply did not exist. I could feel it wasn't quite right somehow. Anxiety shrilled its high-pitched warning of danger. This behavior felt weird, ugly, and out of tune. It was poignantly cutting and gross. It was like the extra layer of clothing I wore to hide my tender sexuality. Reeking of pain, I failed over and over again at protecting my sister from spoiled schoolboys and others. Alcohol and drugs protected her from the emotional aftermath of her predators. Many adults spent their time ensuring we obeyed the rules to keep order. Order was the final curtain of the day. Anything out of place was edited quickly. And that was that.

My mother managed to buy a home. She got a Federal Housing Association loan. The house came with an above-ground pool, a yard, a basement, and a second floor. Pride was the salary for her effort. She loved to swim. As a young girl, she had done synchronized swimming. I could imagine her floating on the water, free and beautiful. She smiled when she swam.

When my sisters and I would swim, one of my brothers enjoyed sneaking up on us while we were under the water. Before a breath could fill me, he'd grab me and push me back under the water. There I would remain until I went limp. He hated. He tried to torture his hatred out of him by preying on weaker, smaller people like me. Cruelty was his secret drug. After his attacks, Greta would drag me to the side of the pool, hang my arms over the side, and pat me on the back while I hacked.

No one fought him. He would wake us when we slept. He was a shape shifter orchestrating shifts in environments from safety to fear—unannounced, unprovoked, and unexplainable.

We had a tree house in our neighborhood for boys only. Girls had things to do if they wanted in. I did not like the feelings I got around the boys and chose to play alone in the woods, thus shaping my interior neurology for a path of loneliness and neediness. I was a loner. Groups usually came with a leader doomed eventually to be eaten by the sheer power of it.

I was different. I was *Podist,* a childhood nickname. I hated it. I was learning how to hate myself. I was learning how important sexual things were in the world. I was learning that as a female I would have to be alone or let others have their way with me.

No one else to play with, I teamed up with another outcast. We were rejects. Her name was Karen Diamond. She lived in the other direction from the tree house. She had polio and walked with a limp. Her face had acne all over it and she wore big, thick glasses. The neighborhood kids, especially the boys, made fun of her. She was an easy target for angry, bored kids. I liked her.

We used to hang out in the woods behind Karen's house. We would hide in the woods, as sort of a game, in hopes of seeing a mentally impaired, seventeen-year-old boy who lived in the area so we could run screaming all the way back to her house. It gave us a chill on a warm summer day. We were advised to stay away from him, as he was supposed to be dangerous. We never really saw him except for a glance at his figure as he moved in and out of the trees and bushes. We were intrigued.

I was a total tomboy. I felt free in boys' clothes. I was adventurous, and danger gave me a rush of excitement. Boys were tough, and girls were wimpy. So I had to be tough. Karen was also tough. She didn't have other friends, so whether or not she agreed with whatever we got into, she went along with it.

One afternoon, as we made our way to the back of the woods, Karen and I stumbled upon an underground camp. Karen could not lift her right leg completely, so it dragged on the ground, which caused her to stumble over this gigantic hole mysteriously covered with a large piece of plywood and some shrubbery to conceal it. We decided to check out what was underneath. We were intrigued at the thought of finding the retarded guy inside.

We tore at the board, which was in several pieces and threw the branches aside. We peeked in to see if anyone was hiding inside. Hearts racing and sweat spewing, we discovered it was empty. Relieved, we removed the final boards and saw a ladder that led into the hole. It was at least five-feet deep and it could hold five or six kids. This was somebody's hideout. We decided to climb inside. The dirt walls were clammy and cool. We were sweaty and hot, and this felt wonderful after all we had to do to get inside. We were laughing at something when we heard someone coming. I was scared. If someone were to catch us in here we would be trapped.

I told Karen to get out first and helped her with the ladder. It took a lot of time for her to climb because of her leg, and I was panicking as the voice came closer. I gave her a push on her butt and she dropped her glasses. The voice was getting closer and it sounded like more than one.

Suddenly someone yelled, "Hey, someone is in our camp. Get 'em!"

I could hear their feet running fast. Underground it sounded like a stampede. Karen started crying and I was scared to death and irritated with her.

"Get up there, Karen! Forget your glasses!" I screamed.

The first boy arrived. He had blond hair and was older than we were. These boys lived in the housing complex at the back of the woods. This was their secret hideout. We were girls and we had invaded their turf.

"Oh, my God! We are in trouble," was all I could say. We were stuck. We didn't even manage to get out.

"Look who we caught," said the blond kid. He was the leader.

"Get back in there," another boy ordered. There were at least four or five of them. I helped Karen down and we leaned against the muddy, cool wall of the boys' clubhouse. We were doomed. What could these idiots possibly do anyway? One thing I had learned from adults was that if they used curse words they seemed tougher. So I said, "Leave us the hell alone, you bastards."

"Wow, we have a big shot down there. Is it a boy or a girl?" someone laughed.

"Let's go and find out," said the leader of the group.

I was panicking, and Karen was bawling her eyes out. She was annoying me as I tried to figure my way out of this. I had only been in one fight with a boy before, and I had beaten his butt. This was entirely different. There were too many of them.

"Leave us alone, you moron," I said.

All of the boys were now in the clubhouse, and they began to tease me about whether I was a girl or a boy. Karen was clearly a girl, as she had full breasts. I did not.

"Look at her ugly face," came out of the mouth of one of the idiots.

"Look at her goofy leg," some other stupid boy said.

"Hey, shut up, you punk," I said. At least I could stand up for her even if she couldn't do it herself.

Then, "Hey, let's make her show us her boobs," one of them said. Karen, like a wild animal already wounded, cried out a loud, whiny noise. I hoped someone would come and help us. Fat chance, as we were pretty far into the woods.

The biggest slob of the group, who was filthy and stunk up the place, had a look of greed in his eyes as if he were about to suck down a bunch of candy to add to the fat that dripped from his face, fingers, and stomach. Yuck, he made me sick. He reached out to grab Karen's breasts, and she let out another of those whiny screams. If nothing else, the birds were scattering. Then the spoiled, overzealous, cocky boys began grabbing at her breasts and pulling my hair. We were done for.

All of a sudden, out of the forest came the sounds of running feet.

Everyone froze.

Karen was still crying and I was barely breathing I was so angry. We heard a noise above our heads and within seconds a big guy appeared and gaped inside the hole.

I do not know what the gentle, disfigured young man above us saw, but his face contorted after taking in the scene. I was so thankful; because in that moment I heard bratty boys turn into wimpy, sappy, little, fearful idiots. I was relieved, but had no clue what was happening.

"It's him! Run for your life!"

"Let me out of here!"

Who was hollering? I had never seen boys scramble so quickly. Some did not even use the ladder, but clawed their way out of that hole. Karen and I were astonished, as was the stranger.

We heard the sounds of the boys as they ran screaming and hollering through the woods back toward their homes.

"Look out! Get out of my way!"

"Let's get Dad!"

The three of us remained in place. Where had this stranger come from? Karen's face softened as she looked at the man-boy. I could not really see his face because his back was to the sun and I was facing it. He then lay down on the ground and reached his hand into the hole to help us out. He and I helped Karen climb out of this chamber of girlish fears. As I ascended the ladder, the stranger reached out his hand to help me.

It came to me all at once. He was the boy we had been running from and looking for all summer. He was the supposed "psycho." I knew a little about kids that were mentally impaired from school. I could tell he was challenged. He could not speak clearly, but whatever he mumbled it was clear that he was especially fond of Karen.

It was kind of cool and sweet. For two young, imperfect people, they were a perfect fit. He walked us to the edge of the woods close to Karen's house, and along the way he stopped to look at the wondrous beauty of the woods. Karen was enchanted and I was humbled. This boy's disability made him a hero, and his heart made us safe. What others judged to be dangerous was an illusion. He had no idea that those boys feared him. He simply responded to the cries of what to him may have been a wounded animal in the woods where he spent most of his time. He didn't even have to say a word to frighten those macho boys. He reminded me of what I worked so hard at being, a protector of the innocent.

Finally, someone had come to protect me.

Finally.

Someone had come.

To protect me.

At the other end of the street, at my house, I was Podist, the weirdo. That self-image had rooted itself in my teenage skin as I entered the seventh grade.

I was a target.

In the neurological chaos of my youth, there remained in me a highly spirited spunkiness that just kept thriving. It wasn't a weed. It was more like a rose: thorny, fragrant, and sturdy, pushing through even the barren and toxic soil.

My genetic strength and evolutionary perseverance provided some very unusual paths for my survival. My bold and brave behavior championed the environmental turmoil in which I was living. Creative behavior led the charge as my being maneuvered its way through the fields of insanity.

I needed a cover, a mask to wear on this playing field where kids were clever, where kids sat on cruelty's bench and let their cutting words have a respite, as they'd found in mocking us, the outcasts, a place to rid themselves of the weight of their own pain.

My armor to defend myself had to have a presence of power, so I decided to become a star. I was thirteen and it was my first year in middle school. The seventh grade rules were dramatically different from what I was used to. I was now in the presence of kids who experienced the power of being in a group. I and others like me were the ones needed for jokes and other emotional viruses that infected our teenage years with stark loneliness, electric-knifelike pain, and intolerable sadness. I was a guinea pig for trickery. Boys accosted me in the hallways, grabbing at my crotch while cornering me against a wall with no way to escape. They poked and prodded me with their innocent, youthful bodies and darkness in their eyes. "Don't tell, or else," as they knocked me to the floor, fingers jabbing and poking me.

Guilt was not present. Shame was. She draped over me like a friend. She kept her voice soft and whispery as she invited me into her womb. I developed a longing for the safe watery darkness there. I was in a place of misery where space and time disappeared and swallowed me.

School sucked. It was only the first quarter of middle school.

My eldest sister, Grace, loved Elton John. She was an artist and a fashion designer, and quite talented. She had made a black blazer with shiny speckles and a pair of rust-colored satin overalls. My eyes gleamed when I looked at her clothing. Only movie stars and rock stars had clothing like that. Ideas brewed off in the distance as I pondered the beauty and power of the clothing. That's how I decided to become a star.

My creative, high-spirited mind conjured up an idea for protective power and attention of a different kind. I was going to make a statement. I was going to make my mark at my new school. I would become Elton John. Goodbye Norma Jean and hello Amber Blossom! I'd had enough hassling and abuse from people. If I was going to survive, I needed an image.

I very decidedly rose to my potential as a famous person cloaked in my sister's handmade fashions and transformed myself into a famous star. I stole lipstick from my mom and put it on my cheeks to make them rosy. I stabbed at my eyes with black mascara.

I hated being female. Yuck, I hated it. I was a tomboy. I was Elton John!

My grand début happened on a Monday after a long weekend of planning. I walked to school with my siblings. The plan was, "Oh no, I forgot my schoolbooks!" Then, dramatically, I raced toward home to transform myself. The clothes were hidden in my room, ready to grab and go. Quickly I filled a bag and was out the door again, gliding on my winded wings.

I had only a few minutes left until homeroom class when I ran into the bathroom with my boyish clothes on. When I came out, I was dressed as a star. Elton John had arrived.

I brazenly paraded through the halls, daring wannabes to challenge me on my outfit or touch my crotch. The first kids to get a glimpse of me stopped in mid-walk to openly gape. *Humph!* I strutted along. I had succeeded, and it wasn't even first period. As I entered homeroom, my teacher did a double take. She looked once, looked twice, and then simply stared at me while she mumbled, "Take your seats."

I had succeeded. Fame was mine. I was the center of attention. I had power.

Shocked kids pointed and laughed. "What is she doing?" mumbled some.

"Hey, freak," said one of the boys.

They were jealous and I was victorious. Clothing had transformed me. This trick is one I would end up using as an adult woman to hide my authentic self. It was easy to ignore them because I was transformed by the mere texture of the fabric. The satin of the clothing Grace had made was soft and silken. The sequined blazer still had the scent of new material. It had never been worn. It scratched my skin. I felt exhilarated and famous, and the fame occupied my mind. A thunderous day of reckoning would arrive later that week. But for now, in my bright state of fantasy I could not see the illumination of anything other than my precious wounded self.

Teachers had an entirely different reaction to my wardrobe. They were simply shocked.

My home economics teacher was very kind. She helped me get a lipstick smear off my face. I was breaking out horribly. She asked me, "Amber, where did you get your outfit?"

"I made it," I lied.

"Oh my, you did an amazing job. I am looking forward to our sewing class next semester so you can show me your work." That was a long way away. No need to worry about that now. I was too busy enjoying my imagined popularity and fame while feeling the luxury of the clothing I wore.

Reality began to wrestle with me. Outside events became animated as people began to participate in my fantasy. I continued my strut around the school in my Elton John clothes. I felt so cool wearing them. Costumes provided a reprieve from the madness of teenage reality. The blazer had pockets and I kept my hands in them all day long. It looked cool. I was important. The misfits agreed. They loved my coolness. I had succeeded in being their hero. After all, who else had enough nerve to pull this off? I had put our name in the game. I had established my presence in middle school.

Within a week of the beginning of my charade, my sister Greta told Grace that I was stealing her clothing. She had no idea. She attended a Catholic school and wore a uniform. She never even noticed. My illusion was shattered in one clean gesture. An all-out attack was underway.

Outraged and furious, she screeched, "Whaaat? She did what? Where are my clothes? Where is she?"

I heard this and a tidal wave of panic wrapped its palms around me. "Oh, my God, look at her face," I thought. I began to tremble. I was victorious at school, but not at home.

"Where are my clothes, you snot?" she roared. Her bitch nature sliced the air.

I shriveled in terror.

"I am going to kill you," she screamed.

Cornered, I could not move.

"Where are my clothes, you little bitch?" Her red-painted claws came out.

The clothes were hidden under my bed. I kept them neatly laid out there each day until I had the chance to put them back at night. Fortunately, I wanted to look good so I had been taking care of them, except for a few lunchroom spots here and there.

Swiftly and with precision, fear invaded me. There was dust on the floor under the bed. I snorted it up my nose as I reached for the outfit. Then I hit my head on the springs of the bed. The metal scratched the back of my neck. I could feel Grace's breath on my skin as her hatred hissed out with each exhalation. I reluctantly hand- ed Grace the outfit. My fame and my identity fizzled. I whimpered. I needed kindness. I needed empathy. Outfit in hand, her adrenaline slithering; she raced to the household mediator, our mother, to tell on me. Breathing was not easy. Reality was back to normal. Pain awaited me.

"Amber Blossom. Get down here." The powerful voice of my mother reverberated through the house.

In that moment, I hated walking, breathing, laughing, eating, and everything that reminded me I was alive. I crept down the stairway, one step at a time. My bare feet hit the turquoise carpet as I chatted with myself about how I needed to clean it. I guess I was already working on my strategy to get back in my mother's good graces.

I wish I could have seen my own face. Sitting at the dining room table, my mother laughed almost uncontrollably. I wondered, "Was I still in trouble?"

Grace was furious.

"This is not funny, Mom," she barked.

My mother was in that particular sitting pose, chewing her Doublemint chewing gum and smoking her Benson and Hedges cigarettes. Left foot propped up on the seat of her chair, she rested her left arm on her knee while she smoked, installed in her standard position of ease and authority. With slow words and a restrained, humorous tone she said, "Amber Blossom, you have stolen your sisters clothing that she spent a lot of time sewing. Is this true?"

"Yes," I replied.

"Well then, since the clothing belongs to your sister, I leave it to her to decide your punishment."

I panicked. Grace could be ruthless about her belongings. She already hated having to share a room with me. Her territorial possessiveness was energy, a fuel needed for her survival.

A tight grimace on her face, Grace then, ever-so-patiently, said to me, "You will wear dirty clothing all mixed up and mismatched for one week. Your top will be plaid and so will your pants. You can wash your hair once during this time."

"Mom, I can't go to school that way," I squeaked.

My mother was red in the face as she tried hard not to laugh.

Grace noticed and added, "And your shoes and socks cannot match either."

She was wicked.

I like to believe that this was one of the highlights of my mother's life watching me grow up. I certainly was brazen if nothing else. I had to have attention. I had to have someone's attention. I was starving for acceptance and love. What was a young girl supposed to do?

"Noooooooooo!" I screamed. I was a star. I could not go to school that way. I would be crucified. "Noooooooooooooooooooo!" I screamed again.

Maliciously, Grace licked her chops as she said, "I am going to get her clothing right now!"

The alcohol of hysteria flooded my veins. I slumped into an adrenaline hangover. My head was swirled, my brain intoxicated with fear. Hyperventilation tried to protect me. My mother was lost in her own hysteria. Comedy danced in the dining room and captured my mother's attention, caging her in an uncontrollable amount of laughter. Laughter burst through her. She just couldn't take it any longer.

What the hell was wrong with her? Couldn't she see I was about to have a heart attack? Meanwhile, my evil sister concocted an outfit that not even a homeless person would wear. At the sight of the outfit, my brain stopped functioning. I was lost in a swirl of angles, patterns, shapes, and icky colors that made up the next outfit for Elton John. Plaid on plaid! Layered waves of destruction came over me as my brain registered the upcoming events to come.

I do not remember going to bed that evening. My poor brain raced around and around all night long. My outfit of hideous plaid pants and a yucky plaid top sat in my room. I hated and feared this collection of threads and patterns that combined actually to be called clothing. Who in their right mind could even think of creating these hideous things? *Ahhhhhhhhhhh!* The front of my brain felt like a freight train. I didn't even know we had these clothes in the house. Where had they come from? I didn't care about the socks and the shoes. After everyone saw my outfit, they wouldn't notice my accessories.

I was doomed. Stardom was about to take a whole new twist. What would Elton John do? After an entire night of mind-racing mania, morning presented itself to me.

Skip school? Maybe a car would hit me!

My mother anticipated my mood and made sure I made it to school. She drove us. I was in MEGA trouble now. I was a lamb being led to the slaughter. I could already hear the roars and jeering remarks as I watched my demise on the screen of my eyelids. I tried to shut out the upcoming dramatic events. All the kids who'd been shocked by my grand entrance just a week earlier, adorned in sparkles and satin, were really in for a treat this morning.

There was only one thing to do. Elton John could wear whatever he wanted. I would act like a star. I was a star. Head high, nose tilted upward, I burst forth from the car with my shoulders back, eyes straight ahead, to face my fans. Call it mania, judge it mental, or see it for the courageous heart of a teenage girl lost during a playing field misfortune.

The students did not like the outfit! Chris Parker provided me with the most memorable moment from that week. On the second day of my popularity fashion exposition, he stopped dead in the hallway, hit the floor, and laughed like a madman. He simply could not believe it was me, the one and only Elton John.

With nothing more than a façade of persnickety wit and a thrashing tongue, I endured that humiliating week. I completely redesigned the imagination circuitry in my brain. One day would have done the trick, but five really reinforced my beliefs about the cruelty of human beings. I am glad it was me, not someone else, because I could handle it—I told myself. But I did learn lifelong, valuable lessons about true friendship, for the misfits still honored me as their friend and hero even as I endured the humiliation. My charade gave the other "prey" a reprieve for the week. A short break from pain. Much simpler reasons usually set them up for their own plights. Maybe glasses, acne, poverty, or brains—all were obvious socially granted targets for the packs that hid behind the leader of a group. Groups were made of up the wealthy, the beautiful ones, those with athletic ability and skill, and those with powerful parents. Those that had learned they were better or that it was important to be better, to fit in, to go along, to hide their voices, and to bury their authentic self were merciless to me and my band of outcasts.

Outcasts were at least afforded one opportunity, thrust on them by very bad circumstances, but an opportunity nonetheless. They could not hide from who they were. They could not hide from imperfection. I think this was gift for me, forever releasing my attachment to perfection. I know. I was stuck with myself and somehow learned to love it.

I chose to remain alone in seventh grade. No group felt like home. I had no idea that I was forcing myself into a much deeper relationship—a relationship with myself. All good moments and all sad moments shared were the same.

During the summer before my fourteenth birthday, I met a girl named Tracy Edwards. She lived in the upper part of the Edwards' residence with her mother. This white house was the biggest and prettiest on our street. Her mother wore her hair high on her head, as if she had whipped it up each morning like fresh cream. To me though, it looked like a hive, a place for bugs to hang out. She did not have eyebrows made of hair, but used a cosmetic pencil to compensate for what was lacking. She was petite and always wore a proper dress or pantsuit. She fascinated me as I waited for her to leave each summer morning on her way to the bank where she was a teller. She liked to drink Coca-Cola and chain smoke. Like my mom, she was a single mother.

Tracy, on the other hand, was taller, bigger, and sloppier. Her hair was straight, light, and a totally different texture from her mother's. They did not seem even to be related.

I was intrigued. Who were they?

Tracy had everything: Barbie dolls, great clothes, and a banana bike with a high bar in the back and a colorful flag that hung still until it was time to ride. That blue-seated banana bike could fly. When it cruised you never felt a bump on the sidewalk, just a smooth ride. I loved that bike, but more than that, I loved Coca-Cola. And she had plenty of it. The best part about the Coke we drank at her house was the cash value of the bottles. I spent hours persuading Tracy to take all her mother's Coke bottles and cash them in for the nickel they were worth. I wanted candy, and Tracy was the target of my plan to get it. Utilizing the art of persuasion, and motivated by the vision of candy and my favorite gum, I always seemed to win.

When there weren't any Coke bottles to be had, I convinced her to collect the loose change in her house for our venture to The Pony Keg across the street. This store sold my favorite bubble gum in the world, Bazooka. We could get three pieces for a nickel. Chewing Bazooka bubble gum and cracking it as loudly as I could, made me feel like one of the older girls. I felt cool as I rode Tracy's bicycle, popped my gum, and raced through the humidity of summer.

Privately, I began to discover another way of looking at boys. When a car drove by with the high school boys in the car, if I was lucky enough to be noticed, they would yell out, "Hey doll, you look gooooood." I got the biggest rush and flush at being noticed. I began to look more carefully at my hair and outfits, and to wash the mud off my tomboy face after a day splashing in muddy puddles while cruising on Tracy's blue banana bike.

Summer nights were altogether different. I did not have many privileges. I had to be in before dark and I felt the misery of watching fireflies from a distance without having the chance to capture them. Sorrow and a deep yearning to play with the neighborhood kids filled my heart and soul with agony, as the loneliness of the darkness in our home surrounded me, bidding me into its abyss of silence and emptiness. I sat, watched, and listened to the squeals of the kids outdoors who were caught up in a game of hide-and-seek just beyond my screen door. So much desire to feel the joy of summer made it impossible for me to sleep when I finally went to bed.

By that time, Mom would be either already asleep or reading in her favorite chair. So, when I snuck out at night, which I began to do with some regularity, I'd have to slide down the slanted roof from the bathroom, hold on to the gutter, and lower myself onto the kitchen windowsill where I could see her sitting in her chair in the living room reading, and sometimes sleeping, in that chair, oblivious to my exit from home and entry into the mysteries of the night.

The bathroom window was my doorway to freedoms that only existed at night. Solitude was one of them. In the quiet of the evening, perched on the rooftop, I would stare at the stars and dream. During many confusing teenage nights, I dreamed of love. I wanted to be married to my favorite brother. One summer evening before I had to come in the house for the night, I proposed. "Henry, will you marry me when I grow up?" I asked innocently.

He smiled at me with a surly sort of grimace and said, "Amber, I would love to, but I've found my wife already." He put his arm around his girlfriend who was seated next to him on the itchy grass. "Don't worry though, Sis. I'll always be there for you."

Henry was my hero, but as he had been released from my list as a possible husband, I instead began dreaming of a mystery man to love and protect me. If love was anything like it was in the movies, I wanted it. But more importantly, I dreamed of the future with my eyes wide open, as I could see the glow of the city off in the distance. Life was out there, somewhere, and I knew that one day I would be a part of something much larger than I could conjure up in my own mind. I also dreamed of writing and telling a story that would talk about my family and me. I had no idea why, but I felt it so strongly that I wrote about it in my diary.

Each time I wrote my little secrets in the safety of my key-locked blue diary, I felt a release of compressed air as if I were a balloon popping. Clutching the diary, I would lie slanted on the grainy rooftop, which was still warm from the summer sun, and write without light unless the moon offered some. I had found a resting place, a safe place to be something else: someone I knew I would be one day, who could smile in the freedom I had created for myself.

I had no idea of the obstacles that awaited me out in the world and in my marriages, and I am glad. Now, as a grown woman with both feet on the ground, it is bittersweet to remember those summer days of my tender youth spent in awe of the possibility of a life that awaited me. I was afflicted with the confusion of vaginal mania. I was hot with hormones. I would be going along and out of nowhere it felt like warm tea was brewing between my legs. I barely looked at my private parts. Even so, I experienced the pleasure they brought me.

I had strange fantasies about doctors, nurses, cheerleaders, and teachers. Where had these thoughts come from? It is funny that when I imagined myself with my dream man I dreamed only of being kissed. But these men, women, boys, and girls of my fantasies were different. The sexual pleasure I was experiencing in the lower half of my body had nothing to do with the ideas of love I had in my head. In the movies, the nice guys only kissed their girls. Only the bad guys ripped at their clothing and made the women scream and cry.

None of it made sense to me.

My body odors seemed to change. I could tell and frantically tried to stay clean. I did not want anyone else to smell these flavors, these scents that aroused me. Sex was everywhere. There is a song called "Summer Time" by Mungo Jerry that was popular that year and was constantly playing on the radio. I used to walk around humming the lyrics to myself, which were about rich girls and poor girls, and how a boy could do whatever he wanted with a poor girl.

And I was poor.

Television was worse. I used to watch *Hee Haw*, a country and western variety show with comedy sketches and music, at my grandmother's house. The buxom women on the show, who were scantly clothed, always seemed to be poised and exposed for the male audience. I had a crush on Elton John and Peter Frampton, but other than displaying their chest hair they always had their clothes on. Look at The Beatles. They were always fully dressed and look how successful they were. Women, on the other hand, always seemed to have to show their breasts (which I did not possess) or some other part of the female anatomy, and I was angry about it. I was shrouded in guilt and shame about my body. My shame felt like an oversized coat, drenched in rain and too heavy to carry, as it really did not serve a purpose. I was already soaked in the confusion of my sexuality and I felt weighted down by it.. Why did everyone look at the body, sing about sex, write about sex, but not tell kids about it?

Odors, moods, and strange and unplanned emotions and pleasures began to dominate my life, until one day I'd had enough. Thinking I was going crazy and that I must be the only one who was experiencing this madness, the decision was made to ask my new friend, Tracy. One afternoon miserable and determined I made my way to her house to get some answers. She seemed to be smart and talked to her mom a lot. Maybe she could help me figure this stuff out.

"Tracy, I've got to tell you something. You promise you won't tell anyone?" I asked.

"Sure, what is it?" she said.

"Well, do you ever get these feelings, you know, down there?"

Tracy always fidgeted with her hair when she felt uncomfortable, and now her index finger began to make curlicues. She shifted her weight and asked, "What are you talking about?"

"You know, down there!" I pointed.

Both of her hands began to twirl and swirl hair faster now.

"Tracy, stop it. You look stupid." I said.

No reply.

"What is wrong with you?" I asked, starting to feel embarrassed for asking. "Do you ever touch yourself down there?" I demanded more directly.

I knew absolutely nothing about sex or the word *masturbation*. I was curious as hell to know what this was all about. She was my friend and I trusted her. Everything I had been through in my life so far that had dealt with my body had been bad. I had had these sensations for a long time by that point, but had never let anyone share them with me. If someone touched me that I did not like, I would not give them my pleasure. My arousal and pleasure was my secret, and I wanted to find out if my best friend felt it, too.

Tracy's body was more mature than mine. She had a much closer relationship with her mother than I did, so I figured she had already talked to her mom about this sexual stuff. But I guess I was mistaken. The situation went from bad to worse. I'll never know what she thought because the only words she said to me were, "You should go home now."

I was shocked. I felt like I was weird or something for even asking.

Tracy stood up and opened the kitchen door for me, sending me down the stairs and back into the big world full of questions that no one seemed particularly interested in answering.

"What's wrong with you?" I asked, trying quickly to make her seem like the weird one.

Nothing. Not a word did she utter.

I left, and she simply closed the door as I walked down the steps.

We never spoke about sexual feelings again, and I certainly wasn't going to ask anyone else. Hormones ran like movies in my head, sending little pleasure directors to that spot between my legs that girls my age referred to as down there. Summer had too much free time for me to build up a cesspool of guilt for what brought me so much pleasure.

Eighth grade was just as confusing, if not worse, than seventh.

One of the girls at school, Danielle Glover, was a major player in the daily humiliation I endured. She had really big boobs, which made her popular with the boys. She had a thin nose, short hair, a tight smile, and I thought her breasts made her frumpy. In eighth grade, any boobs were amazing to boys. So if you had them, you were popular. These girls knew why they were popular, but were too desperate to notice that they were actually the object of the sick jokes and fantasies of horny little boys. So Danielle was popular, and all the girls wanted to be her friend. Everyone, especially the boys, was constantly around her. Her friends were so prissy and clingy that I wanted to vomit when I looked at them. I thought they were stupid, brainless, and cruel.

One day, Danielle decided to talk to me. Immediately, all my negative thoughts disappeared as I thought I was finally about to fit in. I was at my locker. Surrounded by her groupies, she walked over to me. She said, "I like your hair." My hair sucked, but since this comment came from her I figured I was about to become popular.

I said, "You have a pretty blouse on."

I just didn't see it coming. She responded with a surly smile, "Flattery will get you nowhere," as she pointed at my chest.

The other girls laughed hysterically. At first I didn't get it. What was flattery? Realizing I did not get it, someone shouted, "Carpenter's dream, flat as a board."

They laughed. I died.

Why didn't I have breasts? My sisters didn't either. I had no idea what made them grow.

I fought back. I don't know why I didn't think anyone would notice the sudden appearance of breasts, but I ended up wearing four bras to give myself the appearance of having them. Well, I tried other things first. I stuffed my bra with toilet tissue. That looked stupid and way too bumpy. I had a terrible fear of getting them wet and sinking like the Titanic in front of everyone. I tried socks, but they kept moving, especially in gym class. One day, on the parallel bars I flipped over and noticed a sock coming out of my exercise clothing. Quickly, I doubled over the bar and shoved the sucker back in. It was crooked. I begged to go to the bathroom, pleading my menstrual cycle. I ran in hysteria out of the gym with a flushed face.

Life was cruel. I could never use socks again. I knew the others had seen, but what was a flat-chested, eighth-grade girl to do?

Bras, however, do not move. Layered, they added volume to my chest. I decided to wear them four at a time. The first day I wore two.

The next day I added the third. Finally, I added my last bra. Suddenly I had breasts! Adding bras was an acceptable way of increasing my bust line because it wasn't really like stuffing. The day of the addition of my fourth brassiere, I did a bit of prancing, thrusting my breasts made of polyester in front of Danielle Glover and her groupies. I did not pay attention to their laughter because I felt a new sense of self-esteem.

I was truly a character, a survivor and a wonderful, confused teenager in desperate need of love and guidance.

There was one major problem with wearing four bras. Changing in the locker room was a bit difficult. Every time I had to change my top I needed to escape to the toilet and act like I was on my period. That meant I pretended to be bleeding all the time. I had no idea how ridiculous this seemed even to the girls who did like me.

"What are you doing in there?" my only (sort of) friend asked me. I had no reply.

Somehow, my mother got wind of my layering of the bras. Number one, they were beginning to stink. You see, I did not want to wash them because the first time I did it changed their shape. Secondly, people were talking about seeing all of these bras under some of my more formfitting tops. Can you imagine? I was still in eighth grade. I was a star. Well, a spectacle. Nonetheless, I had attention and that's exactly what I wanted.

The day my mother confronted me wasn't long after the incident with my sister's clothing. I had my mother's attention, again, but I was delicately embarrassed. My sister Greta had quietly brought my new breasts to my mother's attention. Greta felt bad for me as she knew what I was going through at school. My mother took my bras away and thus caused my deepest humiliation of eighth grade. She wasn't trying to humiliate me, but going to school the next day without breasts (even if they were layers of polyester) after having them was truly devastating.

I suffocated emotionally until the end of the school year, further developing neurological patterns for the depression and loneliness I would feel for decades to come.

Other lost and confused teenagers engaged in back and forth verbal volleys with me. Cruelty was like a virus infecting all of us. I suffered. Others watched. For everyone, this cruelty destroyed the innocence of kindness that had once existed within our young hearts. It captured our voices and darkened our souls.

School ended and new things began happening.

Summer came. My mother met a man named Leroy T. Johnson. What a charmer! He was tall, with reptilian eyes and suave manners. His hair was bushy and tinted in tones of gray. He was a country boy from Kentucky. He had a pudgy stomach and wore overalls and work boots almost every day. He lived down the street among some of our friendlier neighbors, people who thought it a good idea to introduce him to my poor, lonely mother, the woman "with all those kids." He was disgusting to me.

My mother was beautiful, classier than Leroy, and intelligent. She was wonderful. I thought she would never go for him.

My grandmother was a major player in the seduction of my mother into marrying this shyster. She felt burdened by the continued need to give assistance to her daughter and her grandchildren. My grandfather, on the other hand, loved my mother and enjoyed the time he spent with his grandchildren. He had money, and generously gave as much as my grandmother would allow him to. It was very little. Grandma constantly needed to buy new things to keep her own miserable inner negativity tame. With Leroy, she figured out how to get rid of my mother.

It is strange for me to tell you the following story about my mother. It seems bizarre to me that she would be so blinded by her beliefs that she would allow herself to be manipulated into yet another horrific and costly decision in her life. But it happened.

The reason I am telling you this is that as her daughter, my behavioral neurology was patterned directly from hers, even though my mind could clearly see her mistakes.

A young Catholic woman, my mother believed wholeheartedly in God and Jesus Christ. One day, in a desperate cry for a mate, she had devised a plan and presented it to her God. She had created a list of three things a man would do for her if he were destined to be her husband and father to her children. She sincerely believed that at the time she found a man who would do these three things, she would clearly recognize it as a sign from God to marry him. She kept this secret between her and God until one day she decided to share the details with her mother.

My mom revealed her naiveté when she expressed to her mother an idea that the man who loved her would do the following three things: one, pick a rose from her garden; two, present it to her while he professed his love; and three, ask her to dinner where he would propose marriage and offer his undying love and support for her and her children.

What was so bad about that? Nothing really, except if someone found a way to use the information to trick her into making a decision she might regret.

Mr. Johnson was making his own greedy moves toward capturing my mother's heart. His first objective was to win over her children by any means necessary. His methods of seducing us were hidden from my mother. For my brothers, he bought beer and pornographic magazines. For my sisters, he bought candy and argued with my mother to grant extra privileges—especially for my elder sisters. For me, however, he could do nothing. I refused his candy and his sickening, smiling ways. I hated the son of a bitch. Instinctively, I knew he was bad.

I would lose that skill of discernment as a grown woman.

My mother took great comfort in the idea that most of her children really liked this man. He seemed to bring harmony to the family and he certainly gave a spark to my mother, as she was experiencing the love of a man for the first time in over a decade.

When my grandmother met this man she was ecstatic. She cooked for him and wooed him for my mother's sake. I recall overhearing a conversation she had with my mother. "Charlene," she said, "You need a man in your life to help raise these kids. This man is a country boy who has a heart of gold. Stop waiting around and get on with it."

My mother was under a tremendous amount of pressure. I did not believe she loved Leroy. I remember lying on the floor in the back hallway eavesdropping. That is when I first found out about her secret. My mother shared her three wishes with her mother. Upon hearing her secret, I was comforted and went to bed. I knew this man was not smart enough or romantic enough to do such things for my mom. I slept well. I was the only one who actually despised this dreadful man.

Within a few weeks, it was announced that my mother was going to marry Leroy. What had happened to the secret? Had God whispered it to this man? It just wasn't possible. Shortly before the marriage he moved into our home. He started making changes to our lives, such as earlier bedtimes, very limited phone privileges, and no playing outside after dark. The niceties he once gave to us children stopped and he denied ever having given such things to us, boldly lying about it to my mother. He started to get resistance from the other kids. They were beginning to see this man for who he was. It was evident that he was mooching off my mother and grandparents. He had fights with my mother and cursed at her openly in front of me and my siblings. He was always badmouthing her children to her. He used her exhaustion to make her a victim and effectively causing her one bad day after another.

For her part, Mom trusted in her decision, for God had led her to it. In that trust, she was blind.

Accustomed to fighting and surviving, I had become even more of a risk taker than I always was. I so desperately needed love. The world seemed to suck. I felt love and joy move within me, but as a teenager I felt ashamed at their presence. No one else seemed to see or feel things the way I did. No one fought for anything that I believed was worth fighting for. I pushed for truth. I pushed for reality. I pushed for everyone to wake up. I pushed for love.

"What is your problem? Why do you have to be so different?" my youngest brother said to me one day.

"Why don't you just leave things alone?" my sister Greta barked at me. Resignation was a safe haven, a temporary taming of my heart's anxious fluttering.

I did not have the answers to their questions. I had a powerful force within me pushing me to speak up, which I did or I would have exploded. I hated myself for speaking out so much, yet I was compelled to do so. I felt different, odd somehow, and everyone around me seemed to feel the same.

Not long before Leroy was to marry my mother they had a big fight. I heard them arguing and came running downstairs. As usual, I was ready to defend my mother. When I arrived, I found Leroy sitting in the dining room at the head of the table, playing Solitaire and drinking coffee. Everyone was provoked when he drank coffee. He would pour himself a cupful, add sugar and milk, and then clank the sides of the cup over and over and over with the spoon while he stirred them in. You could see everyone cringe each time he did this. He was a big, overgrown boy with the privileges of an adult male. Couldn't anyone else see that he was sucking the milk out of my mother's life?

It seemed to me that my mother was about to marry a child younger than any of her own. Leroy was selfish, greedy, and manipulative, and in his arrogance he gave himself authority and power over our lives. He used that power to irritate and annoy the hell out of everyone in our household, especially me. He was a bully with blue eyes and a smile on his face.

There he was, sitting at the table, clanking away at his coffee cup, when he noticed me staring at him. Hate-filled, I looked directly at him. I did have a way of scaring him and I felt a sense of enjoyment and power over him. "Where is Mom?" I demanded.

"I don't have to put up with this shit," he mumbled.

I heard Mom in the basement, where she had been sewing our bridesmaid dresses for the wedding. I went down to her. "What's going on, Mom?" I asked.

"Amber Blossom, go back upstairs and mind your own business."

"Mom," I pleaded, but she wouldn't listen.

Frustrated, I went back upstairs as Leroy screamed down the basement stairs at my mother, "You fucking bitch. I am not going to marry you."

In a murderous rage, I ran into the dining room and yelled, "Shut up, you bastard. You don't talk to my mom that way."

My mother had overheard our fighting and quickly came upstairs.

"Mom, did you hear what he said? Why are you marrying this prick?" I held back my thunderous tears.

"Amber Blossom, come with me," she said.

I stomped my feet as I followed her back into the basement, where she lit a cigarette and went back to her sewing. On edge and very sad, I said, "Mom, you can't marry him. Do you hear how he talks about you? He doesn't love you, and he doesn't love us either."

"Amber, this is none of your business," she said, as she paused her sewing, concluding, "and you had better stay out of it." Calmly, she then went back to her sewing.

I could tell she knew he was an asshole. I could tell she was going to marry him anyway. Another pattern I would pick up from her.

Angrily, I stormed upstairs, shouting, "I hate this house! I hate it here!" This seemed to bring some satisfaction to the prick, Leroy, but at a quick glance I also saw fear in his eyes. For an instant I thought I had succeeded in making him think I was taking his mommy away.

I cried myself to sleep that night, wishing I were dead.

Closer to the wedding date, life changed. We used to have Saturday family nights together watching television shows. Not anymore. Leroy was jealous of our family nights so he restricted us from watching television for any reason he could find. He wanted my mother all to himself.

In addition to hoarding all of my mother's time, he also had a knack for lying and blamed things on the kids to make himself look better. Lying was his way of maintaining power and control. It worked because he knew my mother would side with him. My mother's solution, "Respect your elders," was her only way of combating the tension between her children and her fiancé. This man was enjoying the power he had over my family. He wanted the older kids running the streets and the rest of us in bed so he could separate us from our mother. At this time in our lives, we needed reliable parents more than ever. Taking the television privileges away was a mechanism of control over us and suppression. My mother trusted him and expected us to oblige. And so we did.

Leroy consumed whatever time and energy my mother had left after working all day long. I had to be very crafty just to get in a few words with her. We were not allowed to talk with her in the evening because he said that she needed her rest. She needed her children! Worn out after the workday, the traffic, and the constant fighting at home, she simply gave in to his demands out of sheer exhaustion.

Whenever I had the opportunity to defy Leroy, I did—especially when it came to talking with my mother. No one was going to stop that from happening. So when she was awake I would walk in on her conversations with my stepfather and brazenly interrupt just to tell her about my school day. She would smile, recognizing what I was doing, give me a few minutes, and then send me away. I felt triumphant on those occasions.

My mother, being somewhat, and surprisingly, submissive, did not argue with the new arrangements, and this led to the next privilege that was to be restricted. Telephone calls were now limited to one minute, and the younger five children were not allowed to receive any calls—that is, except my sister Greta. Her devotion to the Southern Baptist church made her acceptable to him. Men were superior in the church setting and he needed to maintain his status there. He held a position of importance in the Christian community. He had a penis. That was that.

My sister's chosen method of escapism, coping, and survival met with Leroy's approval. Most Sundays we children were hauled off to church to get a weekly dose of humiliation regarding our evil ways. Leroy had a way of charming the minister and the other members of the congregation with his blue eyes, charisma, and calculated platitudes. The right words made them feel safe, relieving them of the responsibility of the truth. He clearly knew how to get what he wanted from people. He was praised as a self-sacrificing parishioner, charitably trying to raise seven children that were not his own. He wore the Sunday church clothing of a pitifully overworked man who was about to do my mother a huge favor: overalls!

Sitting in church was emotionally choppy. The stand-up-sit-down routine nauseated me. By the time I was able to personally connect with the "Spirit of God," it was time to stand up and sing, or to kneel down and pray. There wasn't a moment's peace without interruption in that house of the Spirit. Instead, we performed.

Every week, I sat in a pew with the man who had infiltrated our lives, and was causing us enormous strife, a churchgoing man who seemed to get a lot of respect. In front of the congregation, he would proclaim the futility of his efforts to make his future stepchildren into better Christians. He pleaded for the prayers of the congregation and support for his hard work and dedication to this troubled family.

They loved him.

I fantasized about ways to get rid of him. He must have known. I guess I got what was coming to me because he would call my name in particular to go up to the front of the church so that he could criticize and condemn my defiant ways in front of the rapt audience. The fact that I was a cheerleader at school gave the church members a focus for the exorcism of my evil ways. Women in the Southern Baptist community were not permitted to wear skirts above the calf, blouses had to be elbow length and high collared, shoes were to be modest with low heels, and absolutely no makeup was to be worn under any circumstances. People would snarl at me as I walked up the aisle. My mother's face was distraught, but unmoving.

What were they trying to save me from?

"You are a sinner, child. Your filthy ways will be judged in the eyes of our Lord Jesus. You must cleanse yourself and be saved before it's too late," bellowed the minister.

"Amen, brother! Amen!" someone cried out.

I hated Leroy. I wasn't jumping into that pool for anything. I was a good kid. Besides, would God not accept me if I was wearing a short cheerleading skirt? Who had decided that was a sin?

"Repent! Repent and redeem your soul. Be saved and accepted unto our Lord Jesus Christ."

"No, I am not ready," I would whisper.

"Speak up, child."

I could see my mother in the congregation. What was she thinking? I was speechless for a moment. I had no intention of becoming like these people. I had no idea whom to follow, but it was not these fanatics. "I am not ready," I spoke out in an audible voice this time. Nor will I ever be, I hissed in the silence of my mind. I hated all of them.

"Let us sing from our hymn book 'Holy, Holy, Holy,' and pray for this sinner."

I struggled to remain standing as the judgments of the staring faces scrubbed over me. I felt them seep deep into my skin. I shamefully wondered if they were judging the clothing I had worn in order to fit in at church. My shame was my only protection, and I blanketed myself with it as I walked back to my seat.

I loved cheerleading. It was one of the few joyful activities I had in my life. I had worked very hard to be good at this thing I was receiving so much criticism for. I therefore sat in fury and nurtured my hatred. Murder was not far from my thoughts.

As my life continued, so did the wedding plans. My grandmother loved Leroy. Maybe it was his country mannerisms and schoolboy charm, or maybe she was just frustrated with my mother. Grandma felt that Mom needed a man at her side to help raise us kids. She had pushed hard for this the marriage. She believed in Leroy so much that she convinced Grandpa to lend him $7,000 to buy a dump truck. Whatever magic he had spun with Grandma, it worked, for she was head over heels in love with the idea of him marrying her daughter.

I, however, was not in her good graces. No matter how much work I did for her, it never seemed to make a difference. I spent my time trying to win her affections through hard work. I scrubbed floors and rugs; washed ceilings, walls, dust boards, and windows; cleaned dishes, clothes, and her car. I picked bushels of apples and garden vegetables, helped can vegetables, made jellies, froze foods, baked, and cooked meals. None of it mattered, for she expected me to work as part of my keep for visiting. Grandma simply was annoyed by my kindness and eagerness to please her. How could the manipulative ways of Leroy sway her after all my futile attempts to receive kindness from her had failed? I would make this same mistake as an adult woman—trying to get a coldhearted person to love me.

After a brief courtship with this man, my mother began receiving even more pressure from my grandmother. Leroy had smooth-talked my grandmother about his home in Kentucky, and how his parents had left him as a small boy. He had blue eyes, long eyelashes, and curly hair. When he went to visit my grandparents, he was spit-shined and starched stiff as a board. But he wore his blue jeans, cowboy hat, and boots. They were quite the pair: greedy, manipulative, and basically unkind—unless of course it suited them.

Inside, fury exploded. I felt intense rage that my mother would marry such a schmuck. My mother, like any other woman in her position, not only relied on her own mother and God, but her children as well. I was the only one who so viciously despised this guy. With my reputation as the family rebel, my mother concluded that the reason for my sentiment was that I just didn't want to share her with anyone. That was the story she told herself. My attempts to expose Leroy's original bribery and seduction of her children didn't work. She was in denial that my siblings had been bought or would have sold out for newfound freedoms and luxuries as they had. Innocent as they were, they had been bamboozled. What a nightmare!

After he moved in, I spent my days fighting with everyone in the family, and mostly having moments of bold eye-to-eye contact with Leroy. The more he despised me, the more he seduced my siblings to build up his alliances. My heart ached daily. Life smothered me. I fought beneath the suffocation of the truth I was aware of.

Within weeks, a big wedding had been planned. It was to be held on the lawn of my grandparents' twenty-six acres. They owned a lovely piece of land with a thirty-foot deep lake to catch the phases of the sun and moon and a big catfish or two. My grandfather was a silent man, and my grandmother had a way of wearing him down. He loved me. He kept quiet most of the time and would do special things for me without my Grandma knowing. Thus, he was my solace. I could just look at him and be comforted.

I must admit the lawn and the large tent were a spectacular sight to see. Grandma had done a fantastic job with the decorations, food, cake, music, cameras, and my dear mother's wedding gown. She was adorned in a chiffon peach dress, with flowers in her hair. She was lovely, and looked so young. Dressed as she was, the strong woman I knew her to be seemed to disappear into a soft and naive woman. This marriage touched her heart, for she still believed that God had made it happen. She was in love with the idea of love and thought it was ordained by God himself.

These things don't happen for a reason. They happen because we create them. We support each other in the stories and use concepts like "God" as a backup plan if something goes wrong. "It was meant to be" is a particular "favorite" aphorism of mine. After all, why take responsibility when we can blame God, karma, or other fantastic stories to soothe our conscious? My mother married this man because she wanted to believe that God had sent him to her. Of course, in reality, my grandmother, a Christian woman herself, intentionally manipulated the situation.

God's plan? Do you really think so?

My mother's surrender to irrational choices led her to the altar to wed a man she believed God had chosen for her. She felt supported in her choice by everything she told herself she knew. Furthermore, she laid the neural network for her daughters to be in relationships that would later not make sense. I could not wrap my head around "God." I had a drive to protect the family. God certainly wasn't doing it. Neither was my grandmother. I had stood up to my soon-to-be stepfather any chance I could get. I had waited for him to step out of line: to curse at my mother, to give pornography to my brothers, or to tell my eldest sister she could do something when my mother said no. My plan had simply been to tell, as if the truth would bring Mom clarity.

The day of the wedding, I stood up with my siblings to take part in the wedding ceremony. When I fidgeted my grandmother grabbed me from the sidelines and tried to choke me. Her perfectionist nature made her anxious and I had caused a ripple in her vision of order, her need for approval, and her management of the marriage agreement.

Defending the family started sooner than I could have imagined. My Uncle Felix was the minister for the ceremony. As he started the welcome, I remember being invaded by butterflies in my stomach, fluttering, darting anticipating a release through my mouth. I hated the cunning, smiling, two-faced Leroy who escorted my beautiful mother down the aisle. My uncle asked, "If anyone here thinks this man and woman should not be together, speak now or forever hold your peace."

I remember shyly looking around to see if someone else would stand up for my mother's honor. And then it happened: My hand went up very slowly until it was as high as it could be with the full length of my arm to support it.

The guests were stunned and flabbergasted, and some chuckled nervously. I think they thought it was cute. But my hand boldly re-mained high above me as my siblings loudly whispered verbal threats to me. Uncle Felix was a good man, and he took his religious vows seriously. So he kindly asked if he could have a few moments with me, and asked my mother to join us. I started to walk away, and my eyes met those of my almost-stepfather. His eyes were cold, piercing, blue, and full of nauseating fear. I felt nervous, but victorious.

As it turned out, Uncle Felix also ascribed to the theory that I just did not want to let go of my mother. My mom was sympathetic, but impatient with my nerve in boldly interrupting this elaborate ceremo-ny that my grandmother had arranged to marry her off with her sev-en dependent children. My mother loved to please my grandmother, but her children just seemed to get in the way. After the ceremony, my grandmother grabbed my ear in between her fingers. Furious at me for my daring behavior, she put me to work, insisting I clean up after all the guests.

I was swimming in fear and ecstasy. When the emotions spiral, it's like planetary movement, emotional gas being released through the body. Toxic if you try to contain it, hide it, or deny it. Through self-expression, I had let my stepfather know that I was on to him and that I would always be there to challenge him. I picked up trash and dishes and ate delicious food while cleaning up. Some people hugged me under the assumption that I was just afraid and did not want to lose my mommy. I was so blond and cute that people saw what they wanted to see. Beauty has a way of blinding people from seeing the entire picture.

For the next two weeks, my grandmother beat my rear end for any reason she could think of. She made it clear that she despised me.

Later that summer, I ran away from home. I went to Aurora, Indiana, where I stayed with a family who lived in the middle of 200 acres, with cows, pigs, and chickens. The family a included a horny sixteen-year-old boy named Fred. My mother, who worked hard all week, had decided out of sheer frustration to lock us out of the house until she came home from work. For two weeks, we were locked out of the home the entire day. She was frustrated that the house was a mess when she would come home. That's when I ran away.

My decision to run away seemed reasonable to me as a young person. Home sucked. People lied. People did things and never spoke about them. One day, I snuck into the house, grabbed a sheet, and tossed as much as I could into it. Then I slid out the bathroom window, down the rooftop, and was off to the unknown. I picked up a ride from a neighbor who had family that lived on a farm. They had a small pickup truck, and I climbed in the back and hid beneath a canvas tarp. I could smell gasoline. I was free and afraid, but it felt good.

It took a while to get out there, but we finally arrived, at which point I shyly, but fearlessly, greeted my caretakers. They had no idea what was going on, but welcomed me and said I could stay as long as I kept up with my chores.

At the farm, I worked my heart away at sorting out a very cluttered home. I reorganized rooms, and the lady of the house's salt and pepper shaker collection. I had no plans to return to my own home. I remember spending an entire Saturday organizing a room filled with dust, junk, and a beautiful antique bedroom set. By the evening meal I was ready to show off my artistry. They were very pleased with me and subsequently made that room my bedroom.

The farmhouse did not have indoor plumbing for the toilet, so I had to use an outhouse. Thankfully, I'd had some training in this at my grandparents' house, but at this time of my life I had started menstruating. I had to cross a small yard that bypassed the bulls. The first time I did this, I caused quite a stir amongst the animals. I did not know that they could tell from my scent that I was menstruating. I was so embarrassed, and Fred, who had developed a thirst for me, laughed me into a very deep shame about my natural feminine process. He referred to me as being "on the rag," which is literally what they had me use to handle my period, as they did not have money to spare for such luxuries as sanitary products.

In my humiliation, I decided to bathe. I had to carry water for the tub, so I only filled it halfway. There were holes in the door to the bathroom, and Fred had also made holes from his bedroom to the bathroom to watch me. His parents barked at him to leave me alone, but he persisted like a raging bull. He was horny and cocky. Out of modesty I had poked tissues into the holes, but he stuck his fingers through them and laughingly stared at me. Frightened and angry, all I could see was his eyeball. One particular day, his father came up the stairs and chased him out of the house for the evening. I was so relieved. During his absence, I scrubbed the dirt from cleaning all day out of my nose and scrubbed my hair. I put on clean shorts and a little summer top, as it was almost 100 degrees outside and 110 inside.

We had sat down in the TV room to watch a movie when the phone rang. It was a call from Indianapolis for the family to pick up feed for their stock. This family did not have much money, so this had to be done whenever the call came in—day or night. I was happy because I could then watch whatever I wanted on television and fall asleep early.

As they readied themselves for their two-hour drive, they told me that Fred would be gone until tomorrow and that I should not have any problems with him. After they left, I lounged on the couch, flipping the channels to find a good, non-scary movie to watch. It was totally dark outside, and the next house was at least a mile or more away. As I lay there, I heard the back door to the kitchen open, and then Fred and his friend Billy came into the living room. Fred had come back to get something that he had forgotten, and figured that his parents must have gone to Indianapolis because they were not usually gone at that hour.

Fred told his friend to go into the kitchen and wait. My heart was racing incredibly fast at the prospect of being alone with him. I was irritated that I only had shorts on because I didn't want him to see my body. Within moments, he had jumped on the couch and began trying to force himself upon me. As I fought him, he turned me over his knee to rip my shorts off, and spanked me for not cooperating. In response, I grabbed an ashtray and swung it up over his head and whacked him hard. He released me.

As I ran from him I heard Fred cursing and telling Billy to grab a gun. I was out the door and into the black night in no time. Barefoot, I found the grass damp and I feared stepping on a snake or something creepy. There was a huge tree in the front yard; it took four people holding hands to encircle it. That's where I headed, as it was the closest thing to hide behind. I heard the back screen door slam and the weapon cock. Billy was trying to persuade Fred to leave me alone, but with rage in his eyes Fred told his friend to go one way as he headed directly my way.

Fred came directly up to that tree, and as he walked around one side, I crept around the other. I was breathing so hard that he had to have heard me, and twigs were painfully breaking beneath my feet. After he'd made a full circle, he stopped and did not move. I froze. It seemed like forever before he turned and walked away, hollering at his friend to get the car.

I took the opportunity and low-crawled my way to a nearby one-lane bridge. I was grass-covered, itchy, and cut up by the time I reached it. I hid underneath. I was shivering when Fred finally came to the bridge in the car. He paused before crossing. The moon was full and I knew he could see me, but he drove on. I then followed the creek and ran the way to the house of the nearest neighbor, Fred's older sister. She listened as I breathlessly told her the story. She'd heard I was staying with her family, and knew her brother was an idiot, so she laughingly took me in.

The next morning I walked back to the farmhouse. Fred's family had told me I could stay as long as I needed, as they had grown fond of me, but on this particular morning a police car was parked in the driveway. I had been away from my mother's home for al-most two months by then. The family was well known throughout the county because the land had been in the family for generations. They were kind, humble folks and well-liked.

I hid outside until the police car left. When I went inside, they tearfully handed me five dollars and told me to run. They said the police had been on my trail for some time due to a homesick call I'd made to my grandmother, the only one with a working phone at the time, who had reversed the charges. I'd promised my sister Grace I'd phone and let her know I was safe. I was a county away from home, but now the word was out because that friendly police officer had just happened to be in the neighborhood having some homemade cooking when a neighbor mentioned what a good worker I was. She was bragging about me, which had started the police officer asking questions.

Quickly, I packed what I could in the sheet I had originally brought with me. Without hesitation, I was then out the door and headed through the back pasture to an old oak tree at the top of the hill. Breathlessly, I collapsed beneath the huge tree. Supported by the massive trunk, I caught my breath and anxiously watched the scene below to see what was happening.

I saw my grandparents drive up to the farmhouse in Grandpa's new pickup truck. The heat of the end of summer suffocated me. My breathing raced against the pounding of my heart, and I could not catch enough air as I saw my rather large, authoritative grandmother step out of the truck. I longed to slip into a death-filled sleep.

A lazy breeze bent the tall grasses and blew on the leaves above me. I cried as I memorized the details of this beautiful unpeopled place. I felt safe at the farm, but if I did not leave its sanctity behind, it would be tarnished by the angry people who were hunting me. Soundlessly, I cried. It was time to go. I got up and walked down the hill, glancing back only once, and in the process locked a door within me protecting this memory forever.

The lady of the house had grown to love me. When I drew near the group on the front lawn I could see her desperate visual attempts to guide me away from their direction. I kept walking. I loved her also, but knew she would be in trouble trying to harbor a fifteen-year-old runaway.

I placed my belongings on the ground, looked up, and saw the sheriff. He had a large gut and smiling lips. He was trying to make things easy. And then I saw her, my angry grandmother, who obviously felt triumphant in her quest to find me. No torment appeared on her face and no relief either. Just stern, frustrated indifference. She reminded me of a fat, frozen mug bubbling over with root beer: way too frosty to actually be enjoyed.

I glanced at the truck and felt a cool breeze ease my suffering as I rested my eyes on my youngest sister who was seated inside it. She was smiling. I felt better already. How was she? Why was she there? I had not realized I missed her so much. And then, Grandpa, with his firm, large belly, walked slowly around the front of the truck and gave me an "I'm trying hard not to smile" look. My heart warmed. I missed home. This had never occurred to me.

My caretakers hugged me. I had a pebble from the driveway in my shoe and consciously used its irritation on my foot to forever anchor in the memory of the scent of these two simple and kind people. They smelled like the farm: animally. What I had once feared, being found, now brought me great comfort, and I said goodbye.

"You be good," the farmer said to me as he slipped another five-dollar bill into my hand. "That's all I have, young lady, and you deserve it. We loved havin' you here." His eyes teared then and he walked away.

Sadness and sorrow are the heaviest of my emotions. They painfully stretch me beyond what I can only fathom. Even the sunny day turned rainy as we drove the almost-three hours home. The small joy I had felt at seeing my sister turned into an intense, dark depression as we drove. I had many things ahead of me to face. I missed my new family more and more with each passing mile. Grandpa winked at me in the rear view mirror. Fortunately, he was happy to see me.

Grandma scolded me for as long as she could manage, using every hateful word she could think of. She did not want to understand that I was hurting and angry at living in a troubled and unstable environment. How could she? All she knew was that I had run away from home, and that was wrong. To me, running away had seemed like the right thing to do, though I still don't believe it was running. I had simply decided to take a chance at a better life and leave the misery of our household to those seeking its company.

People say you should not run from your problems. As an adult, I agree, but for kids it's different. Most of the time, kids have no power to stay and face the problem and bring about a positive change. They are widely disrespected by any adult who likes to control and suppress. Running usually comes after crying out for help. It becomes an exercise in justice.

Not one person at the police station, juvenile division, my school, or family would ever ask me why I had run. What mattered was only that I had done something wrong: gone away without permission. My mother grounded me to my room with no social interaction, and when she subsequently found out that I was communicating through the window with my little sister and my best friend, Tracy, she grounded me to the cubbyhole in my room.

In the darkness of that room and the depths of my soul, I believed that I was dying. I wanted to die. I could not bear the pain breeding within me. Good energy and beauty emerged from my exile in the cubbyhole of my room. I began to write. Words became my friend, and somehow gave life to the strange and disturbing feelings I had inside of me. Once written, rereading became my enemy, because the manuscript reminded me of the reality of my life. I struggled to write about new things, though without much imagination due to a lack of belief in humanity.

Scrambled thoughts raced through my brain constantly as I also began scribbling numbers and mathematical formulas. Numbers, symbols, and dots raced from my brain and through my hands onto the gray-green walls of the bathroom. I escaped to this approved area outside of my cubby. I would linger and use the light of that small room and the wall for space to let go, to release, until pressed back into the darkness of the cubby. I was serving as a teacher to myself. Being grounded had served another purpose: birthing a fountain of knowledge in me along with a deep, yearning desire to live and discover. To accompany my words and numbers, masturbation seemed to preoccupy my body. I spent hours imagining myself as a professor without panties on. As I reached up high to write my equations, my skirt would lift and I would talk to my imaginary students, fantasizing about their hands and bodies caressing my naked skin. I could orgasm simply by touching myself. What a feeling!

How did my mind learn such a thing? And why did I feel so damn bad about it? The pleasure was the only good thing I had going for me. Orgasm was an explosive sensation fed by images conjured up in my mind. One day, after I had been liberated from my grounding, I decided to ask my sisters if they ever had this feeling. Uneasily, they admitted to having similar feelings. This deepened the mystery. But instead of feeling better, I felt lonelier. None of us understood what was wrong with our bodies. We all felt bad about it. We swore each other to secrecy. We could not explain the inner explosions erupting in our youthful bodies, and so we felt afraid and powerless.

What is wrong with society to leave young people trapped in a guilt that is not real?

Out of puberty came complications and mysteries that created misery. What felt good seemed to be bad, and what seemed to be bad was a way of life. The gray-green bathroom walls and the wild green onions symbolized something about growth. I managed to maneuver my way through the forest of my youth only to become a fighter, convinced that I was creating hope and love.

CHAPTER 7
YELLOW —
IN SUNLIGHT

Shortly after my return home from Indiana, we moved. It had been planned while I was away. My stepfather had settled quite nicely into our new eighty-six-acre farm. Grandma helped them secure the property. Far away and removed from any sign of culture, we were further secluded from possibility, from hope that things might ever get better. It was a farm, and there were many beautiful moments discovered while bolting from reality and bumping into nature. The trees whispered to me and beckoned me to climb as high as the branches could reach. One tree in particular seemed to call out to me. When the wild rains came pouring from the sky, they sometimes whipped its branches and made loud cracking noises. Unlike me, it was old, but like me, it had seen a lot of life. We were companions. There were days when I stormed from the house, tears pouring from my eyes as I headed straight for that big, old oak tree. I would climb and cry and stumble, and sometimes scrape up my legs, as I climbed her ferociously.

The warm glow of the city lights in the distance once again haunted me with a teenage hope that there might be something out there for me. College seemed to be out there in the luminous mystery that awaited me. Someone finally believed in me my senior year in high school: my guidance counselor, who helped me apply for financial aid to go to college.

"Amber, you are a very smart girl," she said. "You just need a break and a chance to make something of yourself." I never knew what to say to her in reply.

I had no idea what *college* was. I thought of cauliflower every time I heard the word.

I was the only working person in our household the final year before my departure. My stepfather had unbelievable excuses for not having work or money. My mother lost her job as she had birthed my half-brother, Benjamin, and my half-sister, Holly. I can only speculate why my mother added two more children to her lot. But I know she loved babies. It was less complicated to love and be loved by babies. They just love their mommies. Unfortunately for them, and for all of us, my stepfather was a tyrant. Instead of working, he spent his time brewing trouble every miserable day of my life. He was a powerful force. He murdered moments. He decapitated ideas. It did not matter who paid the price. His house rules consisted of: no laughing, dancing, singing, talking, or arm movements that could be construed as cheerleading. He also felt that disconnecting the electricity for the better part of the year would teach us something. I heard him say, "These kids are nothing more than a waste. I'm not gonna spend my money on them. They can do without." Little did I know that one day I would marry a "country boy" just like him.

Showers were ice-cold and timed. Leroy would stand outside the bathroom door, which we were not allowed to lock, and after three minutes he would pound on the door. Maybe I got four minutes. Hate warmed me. I mentally dared him to come in. I knew my mother would have killed him if he'd done the same thing to her. Many times I'd have to get out of the shower with soap still in my hair. God, it was awful at seventeen to go to school menstruating and not feeling clean. I was miserable and barely surviving. Clean clothes were a privilege. Laundry from a house of six kids (the eldest three had already moved out) would pile waist high before we were allowed to wash our clothing. Winters were miserable. We were only allowed the use of one oil lantern for the entire house. Winter's darkness layered itself upon us.

Leroy lit a wood stove in the kitchen area for heat. Heat rises, but not up those stairs. He purposely blocked the stairwell with heavy curtains so the heat would not circulate in our bedrooms. God, I was freezing. Sleeping was not a pleasant experience. It was so cold that my cheap Miss Kitty cologne sat frozen on my dresser. For warmth, I would sleep with all of my clothing piled on top of the one thin quilt I owned. I hated Leroy with a seething passion.

My siblings were miserable, too. I could not stand to watch them suffer.

One snowy school night around 12:45 A.M., I awoke to hear Leroy hollering at me. My bare feet hit the hardwood floor and I screamed out because of the icy feeling.

"Stop your damn yelling and get your ass down here! Wake up your sister!"

I only had on a cotton nightgown. I woke Nicole. "What? What is it?" She was a miserable little thing, so frail and beautiful. She reminded me of a bird that had lost its sound. She hardly spoke. Where she went in her mind, I never understood, but I ached miserably as I watched her struggle to survive. I could never kill myself and leave her behind. She was my favorite sister. She was precious to me and yet I could not protect her from the cruelties life had brought her. I was tormented by the details of my rage. It stretched me senseless at times. I could feel love's burning presence call me to keep living, as much as I hungered for death.

We crept downstairs, as the house was quiet. It was smoky as usual from the burning wood.

I walked the edge between love and rage. I had nerve. "What do you want with us?" I asked. "It's late and it's freezing. We've got school tomorrow." I had really begun to lash out at Leroy verbally during my senior year. I'd had enough of him and hated the fact that the entire school and neighborhood knew how miserably we lived and yet no one spoke a word. They looked the other way. Who had taught people to be such cowards?

"Take the trash out back and burn it!" Burning trash was an ordeal. First, because the place we did the burning was around 3,000 feet away from the back door, out behind the farthest barn. Second, because the snow was more than foot deep.

"Are you out of your mind, you creep?" Oh yes, I had a lot of nerve.

Nicole had an event she wanted to attend. A high school dance or something was at stake. Leroy knew I did not care if I went, so her desire was why he made me drag her along. "If you don't do it, then Nicole will not go out on Friday evening," he said. That sweet child was so miserable. I couldn't fight him on this and he knew it. I gritted my teeth so hard I had an instant headache. It felt as if I'd been clubbed on the head.

"Let's get a coat, Nicole."

"You don't have time for that. Now, do as you're told."

Like a snake, I darted across the floor so quickly I successfully struck him with icy fear. "She will wear a coat and we both will wear our boots!" I said. I never flinched when in this mode. It was how I learned to defy the malicious drill instructors I would encounter later, after I joined the Army. My rage was too powerful to let me back down. I didn't want to wear a coat just to prove to the bastard that I didn't need one. But Nicole needed one.

Booted, coat-clad, and loaded with the trash, we headed out the door. It was slippery and the moon was full. Housed in the barns were chickens, guinea fowl, cows, and a white workhorse. I had a special relationship with all these magnificent creatures. I knew they hated my stepfather as much as I did. However, they were defenseless to fight back when he kicked one of them. He beat the poor horse when it didn't work hard enough. *Can you possibly imagine living in defense of so many living things?* This cruel man hated everything and everyone.

Along the way, I greeted the animals, which stirred with their awareness of our presence. My favorite tree loomed close to our destination and made very pleasant passage for us. I knew this was my fantasy world, and I wished my sister could share in it with me. Finally arriving at our destination, we dropped the trash. Misery was no competition for the brilliance and mystery of the moon. In my mind, it said to me, "Thank you for waking up and visiting me." As crazy as that sounds, my incredible imagination never left my side and provided me with a tapestry of undeniable beauty. I decided to act like the moon was my spotlight and cheerfully began to sing the Stevie Nicks song "Landslide" at the top of my lungs. I actually wanted to wake the whole neighborhood to the wicked ways of my stepfather. But we were too far out to be heard.

"Sing, Nicole, sing! What's the bastard going to do? We're burning the fuckin' trash aren't we? He's too lazy to actually walk out here and tell us to stop singing."

God, she smiled! I felt it in my heart. It was a tight smile that tried to spread its way across her face. Her mind knew all too well about settling into happiness. It wouldn't last, so why enjoy it in the first place? As she held back her smile, she came closer to the fire. She was cold and I was freezing, but I had a strange free feeling to be naked beneath my thin cotton pajamas. I was spunky, and still fighting merely to keep alive the desire to live. Black ashes whirled out of the barrel and fell upon white snow. As we burned the trash, soot was smudged on my hands and my nightgown. Nicole never spoke a word the entire time.

"Come on, let's get going. I'm freezing." I began to laugh gleeful-ly and tried to run back. The crunch of the snow was playful and icy on my legs. I loved the sight of my summer trees naked with winter. Branches were stripped for cleansing and purification by the white of the season. In their nudity, I could see the branches, the curves and bends of the elegant ladies. Cherry trees, apple trees, and my tall oak stood naked to the fierceness of the night air. The season of sun was not far away. They were beautiful and I loved them.

We did not have much food in the house.

I can remember eating only six slices of white bread for break-fast. That's what we had. I would catch the bus and head into a part of my day that I hardly remember. I felt invisible at school even though I was a cheerleader. I was poor. Popular kids had a hard time with that, and the poor kids felt me to be a snob because I was a cheerleader and had to spend time with the "rich kids." Most of the cheerleaders came from affluent families. They could afford to buy all the outfits needed to cheer.

One eventful evening full of homecoming activities I finally realized that I actually was visible. My mother had allowed me to go to the homecoming bonfire after the football game. Janet Haley, a friend of mine, was our hostess. Her stepfather was very weird about her. She had the blackest straight hair, blue eyes, and a very developed bust line. She was not popular, but she had money. She and I sort of hung out together. Guys, including some of the male teachers, made it obvious that they were looking at her breasts. She had very pale skin and would blush profusely when this happened. Sometimes she would run and hide in shame in the bathroom stall. I did not know what to say to her; I had enough people in my life to look after.

At her party, all the popular kids gathered around the bonfire. The game was that everyone was to run and hide while someone counted to sixty. That person was then responsible to find everyone. I followed the crowd. Almost everyone ran into the barn. Maggie and Scott, Cindy and Seth were couples. I'd heard the girls saying to each other that they wanted to switch partners in the dark. What did I know? I just followed. So up a ladder and into the hayloft I found myself going. Low crawling between haystacks, I was following somebody through a narrow passage in the loft. When I reached one particular spot, someone pulled me up and into his arms and proceeded to kiss me.

I had never been kissed before.

Fire sizzled throughout my body. I was shocked by the sensation. My lips were barely parted and the boy's lips were moist and very tender.

I froze.

He stopped kissing me.

"Cindy, is that you?"

I was speechless. I did not move.

He pulled me closer.

I held my breath.

He kissed me again, ever so softly.

"Maggie?"

I could not reply.

"This can't be Amber Blossom?"

I nodded. It was so dark we could not see each other, but I could smell the sweat on the skin of his neck. He chuckled.

"Amber, I can't believe it!"

I could not utter a word. It was Seth Glover, the most popular boy in school. I was terrified to move. He pulled me in closer to him and hugged me. Hardly breathing, I rested my head on his shoulder.

"Oooooooh, I got you," we heard one of the girls get caught. Someone was coming this way. He put a finger over my lips. My breathing was so heavy, trying to keep up with my heart. As they were about four-feet away, we heard, "I got Scott and Maggie!"

"What about got Cindy and Seth?" No one imagined I'd be up there at all. It was assumed that since they had Cindy also Seth was caught, so whoever was looking for us turned and went back down the ladder.

Seth released me just a little, but did not let me out of his arms. I still could not move. "Do you know who this is?" he asked. "It's me, Seth Glover."

I barely uttered, "I know."

"What are you doing up here?"

"I was following everybody."

"I didn't even know you were here. You never go out anywhere after the games."

"My mom let me out until eleven tonight. Carol Ann gave me a ride."

"Can I kiss you again? You kiss so softly."

I nodded my head. I was thirsty for all the new sensations I felt in his presence. This time I let him open my lips with his tongue. For a moment I remembered thinking how gross this would be. Why did the French bring kissing to America? But now, I began to find out why. Wow! I was exhilarated. Nothing so sweet had ever filled my body before. I never wanted it to end.

We could hear kids screaming, "I got you" and "Run, you've almost made it," as some tried to make it to the bonfire before being caught. The autumn air was crisp and I was shivering a little bit. "Are you cold?" He held me closer. After that keen observation, I decided it was good to be cold for the entire time I spent with him. This was a magical moment. Things like this just did not happen.

"You know, I've always thought you were the prettiest girl in school. You have pretty eyes," he remarked.

"Where is Amber?" someone shouted.

"Seth is missing, too," we heard off in the distance.

"Oohhh! Sethy, where are you? We know who you're with."

God, don't let them find us. I wondered what time it was.

My butt was killing me, so I had to shift. When I sat up, Seth pulled me back to lean against him and put his arms around me. I could smell the hay. I could see the moonlight. I felt beautiful. I had not been touched so lovingly in a very long time.

"Can I call you? I heard your stepfather wouldn't let you get phone calls?"

Breathlessly, I said, "Yes, just act like you are a kid in my class calling about homework."

"I am a kid in your class. At least he can't say I'm lying." We laughed.

"They're up in the loft," someone shouted.

"Let's go!" said Seth.

It was so much fun being caught then. When we got downstairs everyone circled around us, teasing Seth. Carol Ann was looking for me. She had a crush on Seth. Every girl in the school did, and I was with him.

"What were you doing up there?" she teased. But she never waited for a response. "Hey, we gotta go. You're late. It's ten till." She was stoned. I could smell it. She didn't believe anything could happen between Seth and me.

Dreamily, on the way home, I shared a fantasy with her. I asked her if she thought Seth would go to the prom with me.

"Dream on, girl. I want to go to the prom with him, too, and so does every girl in the school. Don't mess around with that idea. He's dating Cindy."

I decided to keep his kisses all to myself.

Sunday, Seth called. My brother Adam answered the phone. I heard him say, "Yeah right, you're Seth Glover and you want to speak to my sister."

My stepfather took the phone. "Who is this?" he demanded.

My heart was beating fast. I could not believe Seth had called.

"She can have five minutes," Leroy told Seth, "but you'd better be doin' homework." He gave me the phone. I was so nervous.

"Hello," I said.

"Seth Glover is on the phone with you?" my brother teased me.

"Get lost, you punk," I whispered dangerously.

"Hello, are you there? Amber?"

"Yes, I'm here."

"Listen, it's me Seth. Just go and get your English book and act like you are telling me what the homework is."

"Okay, I have my books right here."

My stepfather lingered close by. "Page 268 and we are supposed to . . ." While I spoke he said to me, "We only have a few minutes and I wanted to ask you to go to the prom with me. Will you go?"

Stunned. I was simply stunned. "Pages 268 to 297. Read all of them by tomorrow."

"Amber, listen to what you are saying," Seth laughed.

"It's about time you got off the phone," said my ill-bred stepfather. God, I hated him.

"Yes, I'll go," I told Seth.

"Great. Meet me at the front ticket stand by the student council table in the morning. Got to go! And hey, don't worry about your stepdad. I'm good with parents."

"Okay, Seth, I gotta go. See you in English class," I said for show.

I must have been beaming, and my stepfather couldn't stand it.

"Amber. Was that really Seth Glover?" asked Adam.

"Yes."

"Why did he call you?"

"Because he asked me to the prom," I whispered, and ran up to my room. I felt hysterical. Joy radiated from within me. I meticulously laid out my outfit on the floor for the following morning. I could not sleep. My heart raced the entire night. The next day, Seth met me after each class and carried my books. By first period, the entire school knew we were a couple. We were like newlyweds. Blushing and shy, we walked side by side.

I almost missed that prom. I had made an emerald green dress on our sewing machine and my mom had told me I could stay out all night. *Wow!* I was so excited. My stepdad decided one hour before Seth was to arrive that I could not go, and I had to wage a war with him. I tried not to cry so I would not mess up my face. Seth showed up on time and anxiously waited for me in the dining room. Adam tried to fill him in without being heard. I waited breathlessly at the top of the stairs. Seth had never seen where I lived. That was shameful enough, but my stepfather's behavior was so embarrassing.

"Amber Blossom, come down here," I finally heard my mother say.

Shyly, I crept down the stairs, remembering everything I'd ever learned from the grand ladies on TV at Grandma's house. Walking with books on my head I had practiced poise. I wanted to be a lady. I loved romance and long evening gowns. Seth saw me as I descended the stairwell.

"Wow, Amber, you look beautiful," he said.

My face was burning and so was my body. My mother smiled at me and told us to get out of the house and go have a good time.

My stepfather was indignant. My brother smiled as Nicole crept to the top of the stairs in her own white dress. She was also going. We smiled at each other before breathlessly I was swept away into the most memorable night of my youth. Seth was a perfect gentleman and we were the sweethearts of the dance. He won the title of Prom King. I was so thrilled by being with him that I barely knew how to behave. He never left my side.

Our relationship faded away soon after that night. I wasn't allowed to go out with him or accept phone calls. I started to pull back from him because I was embarrassed. My rejection hurt him, but I felt I would have hurt him more if he knew about my family. So one day during school lunch, the year almost over, I told him I never wanted to see him again. He did not understand, but I knew it could be no other way.

My memory of Seth has long blessed me with something sweet to remember about my youth. Something sweet to remember about me.

There had been rumors in the house that Leroy was married to another woman. Mom simply would not listen when the woman to whom he was also supposed to be married called and told her that he had been visiting with her while away on weekends. These were the weekends he was supposedly working, and would have a flat tire and had to spend all his money to fix it so he could get home penniless.

One day, I answered the phone when this lady called. She told me her name. My blood boiled. "Who are you?" I asked.

"I have been married to your stepdaddy for the past twelve years. We were married before he married your mother."

Shame sizzled through my body. It burns when it goes as deep down as the vagina. I had taken another hit on my femininity. Was I not worthy of having a decent family that actually loved and cared for one another? This was my lot in life and every new horror story just made it worse for me.

"Why don't you tell my mother?" I screamed.

"Child, I have tried, but she won't listen to me and I want that bastard to take care of his babies here," she screeched back at me with a heavy country accent.

I hung up the phone. This was just too much for me.

My mother and stepfather walked in with my two youngest siblings.

"Amber, what's the matter with you?" my mother asked.

I simply charged over to my stepdad and landed a punch on his face so hard that he fell back. "I hate you," I hissed. "I hate you." Then I told her the news. "He's married, Mom." Tears spilled from my eyes.

"Charlene, you'd better get a hold of that girl or I'm gonna . . ."

"What, you bastard? You're gonna what?" I shouted.

He was such a wimp. He quickly picked up his son, Benjamin, as if to hide behind him.

"Amber, calm down. That woman is a fraud," my mom said.

"Mom, you actually believe him? This rumor has been around for a long time and this woman is now calling our house. Why would a stranger do such a thing?"

"She has been trying to get back at Leroy for a long time. Yes, she has his children, but they never married." Leroy was still nervously twitching. I think he saw the fury in my eyes and the power that accompanied it.

"I don't believe it, Mom. I think you are stupid to believe him."

She walked directly over to me and slapped me hard across the face. This was good because it helped calm me, then I quietly walked upstairs to my room. Months went by with continuous calls from this lady. One night I heard the truth come out. My mother had made some inquiries and found out that Leroy was indeed married to another woman. A bigamist! I thought she was going to kill him. The next day he was still there, but I decided he would not be for long.

That night I made chili and heavily accented it with cinnamon, cumin, pepper, and chili powder. It was the perfect meal to hide one other special ingredient for Leroy: rat poisoning. For the first time in a long time I felt euphoric. I was going to end some of the suffering in our house.

I set the table.

The old saltine crackers were four little crackers still attached to make one big cracker. I put out six bowls of chili (one was the special bowl I'd prepared just for Leroy), saltines, spoons, paper napkins, milk, glasses, butter, and the sugar for the coffee. It was just about dark.

Everyone came to the table.

My mother sat at one end of the table and my stepfather at the other. I sat to the left of my stepfather, with a sibling on my left and one across from me. Leroy had this habit of grabbing his genitals and picking at his butt. I remember him standing up and doing this very thing while he waited for the coffee to finish percolating. I grinned because I knew that would all be over with soon.

He and my mother were talking, as we kids were not allowed to talk at the table. Everyone was starving. We buttered our crackers. Leroy came over with his coffee and a teaspoon. He sat down. I was seething with hatred. It dripped from me like hot, melted butter.

The clanking of his coffee cup began. My mother finished her cigarette. "Amber, say the evening prayer," she directed. I was unprepared for this. Why me? Why tonight? Wasn't it somebody else's turn?

"Bless us, O Lord, in these thy gifts which we are about to receive, and from thy body and through thy mouth . . ." I droned. I was sweating. I had loaded Leroy's bowl of chili with the rat poisoning. I used so much I had emptied the container and put a fresh coat of chili on top so he would not notice.

Leroy sat next to me, clanking away at his coffee. His coffee cup was spring green. I couldn't eat a thing as I waited. Then he began the tedious and arduous task of simply buttering his crackers. No, he did not butter one, but all four pieces individually. As he started buttering the fourth piece, I took a moment to look around the table at my family with such love, desperately wanting to rid them of this crumb of a man.

All in an instant, I felt a presence. It was so powerful. Enormous compassion seemed to flood the room and I was swimming in it. I surrendered to that softness, and reluctantly, I simply put my arm on the table and swooped away his bowl of chili.

Everyone froze.

Tears slid down my face. Leroy's eyes misted over. He was startled by my sudden action. My continual confident confrontations unsettled him. *I made him very nervous.* Though he didn't know it, however, I had just saved him. I couldn't go through with my plan. Defeated by the stinging warmth of compassion, I rose to my feet.

My mother broke the stunned silence. "What the hell is wrong with you?" That question seemed to bring everyone back to life. Chili was strewn all over the floor and the wall, and Leroy's plastic bowl lay silent on the floor.

"Charlene, I told you she is crazy," Leroy said. "She's obviously got the Devil 'n her."

I had no words. God was still there with me. Peace bathed me as I stood. Life would tend to the needs of my family. I was now charged with my own care.

I was ordered to clean up the mess and go to bed without supper. I was humbly aware of the impact I'd had on my family. I loved them. I did not have to hurt someone to preserve that. It was time for me to let go, to step out into the world, and I was scared. I lacked the experience needed to move into the swift current of humanity.

The weekend of my high school graduation, I found myself living on the street. I had to move out of my home, since I had graduated. That was the rule imposed on my mother's children by my stepfather. My mother never objected. I guess they had figured out that I was trouble. I hated the man, and they knew it. Unfortunately for me, I had no place to live until college began. As shameful as it still is, I remember sleeping and hiding in a nasty, grimy dumpster as I tried to outrun some punks chasing me late at night. I was drunk. There was no place else to go. I made up my mind that night to ask one of my older sisters if I could live with her for the summer.

That was a miserable experience. My sister's live-in boyfriend sold marijuana, cocaine, and speed. I was handed a bag a couple of times a week by him and told to get a certain amount of money in exchange for the package or else I'd be on the street again. I hated him. He had a bad temper, and he turned it on my sister. She never fought back when he yelled at her or hit her, and she never said a word. She was miserable.

Finally, that long summer ended and it was time for college. In my high hopes for a new life, I had a long fall ahead of me. I was totally unprepared for the dark side of the smiling faces I would meet. Extremely naïve, nothing could have prepared me for any of it. It began with a girl named Sharon.

Registering late, I lived in efficiency apartment off campus in a small Kentucky town. It belonged to an older woman who'd rented this space out for years to the kids in school. It was a small place. The bed, refrigerator, and stove were all in the same room. But it was my very own and I loved it.

I went to the campus the first night I was at school and saw a group of kids gathered. I approached. Some of the kids thought I was German, so I slipped into an accent and said I was, even though I had no foreign exposure at all. Instantly popular, as this façade protected the ugliness I thought I was hiding, I had charmed the entire group.

"Hi, I'm Sharon McKulsky. I live here and go to school here. Where are you from?"

"Cincinnati, Ohio." I told her.

"So you are not German."

"Well my family background is, but I have no accent. I was just having fun."

"You've got to watch out for these college kids. They come from rich, yuppie families and they only like their own kind."

I had no idea what to say. I had just made my way into the crowd successfully.

"Do you want to go have a soda or something?" she asked.

"I don't have a lot of money. I am waiting on my money for school."

"My treat, I'll show you around." Sharon was a character. Her hair had black roots at least two-inches long while the rest of her hair was bleached blond. Her black eyes were unusual and strange. I felt uneasy with her, but blew off my intuitive twinges as "new friend jitters." Besides, I was lonely and therfor happy to have a friend.

Sharon was skinny, but had extra-large boobs. Her skin had bumps on it. I can't remember what her skin problem was, but it was something weird. She wore a short, red and white striped turtleneck that bared her entire stomach. She also wore skin-tight jeans and smiled a wicked sort of smile whenever boys passed by.

"This is my car. I'll drive you to the Family Dog. It's a local hangout."

"Okay. Are there good-looking boys there?"

Her El Camino stalled as Sharon said, "Yeah, but stay away from boys. Are you a virgin?"

"Of course. Aren't you?"

The car started, "You are so sweet, Amber. I am going to like you."

I had started college with a bang, and I had a friend.

The drill team captured my interest. I wanted to wear those white boots and that little purple uniform. My tryouts were successful and I was in. I enjoyed writing and won a poetry contest. I loved my class-es and was fascinated with boys. I was a college student.

Lonely in my tiny efficiency apartment, I spent a lot of time on campus. One boy in particular was very nice to me. Geoff Durbin,

Jr., was tall and liked to carry my books. I enjoyed the attention. But it seemed that every time I was around Geoff, Sharon popped up. It was strange that this kept happening.

I also made friends with a football player named Chad Arnold. His jersey number was 86. I had a huge crush on him. He was a junior and lived not far from me at the Theta Kappa Epsilon fraternity house. I went to my first fraternity party at TKE one Friday evening. The object of the party was to get drunk and then pair up with someone. I felt alone as people were drinking from hoses down their throats. The people I met were not really my friends, but I tried to latch on to them because I was nervous. I started doing shots of tequila. The best part of the evening from my perspective was that the booze was free. After a while, I loosened up and followed a cute guy to another part of the house where there was a room with three or four beds in it. People were making out, giggling, and moving around quite a bit on the beds. I got scared. I asked where the bathroom was and then made my way out the door instead. I was high, and walked back to my place to sleep and munch. I was so glad I got out of TKE.

There were two entrances to my place. One from the landlady's back porch and the other was an entrance that I left open except for the latched screen door; I had no air conditioning and it was scorching. Sometime later that night, I remember seeing my doorway open and a big guy stumble into my apartment. He had ripped open the screen door and busted the latch. I got up. He was ten feet from me. It was Chad, the football player, who was obviously drunk.

"What are you doing here?" I asked.

"I saw you at the frat party and wanted to talk to you."

I was flattered. He was a jock, a popular guy. I guessed he was going to be like Seth.

"Are you hungry? Do you want some food? I have some pizza in the refrigerator."

He advanced toward me, and knocked me over onto my bed. It was an old bed with squeaky springs. I thought it was going to break because he must have weighed at least 195 pounds.

"Chad, get off of me."

"Don't play hard to get with me, you bitch."

Wow. I was too shocked to be scared. He ripped my shorts off and tried to stick his large penis in me. I started screaming like a wild animal until he collapsed on me. I could not breathe. He was so heavy. He put his hand over my mouth and told me, "If you don't want me to stick it in you, then grab it with your hand and don't make another sound."

He almost fell off the bed when he rolled over, but he got right back up and grabbed my hand. I had never actually seen a penis before and did not want to look at his. He grabbed my hand and tried to get me to move it up and down, faster and faster, until I thought my arm would drop off. I didn't know what I was supposed to do or for how long, but when I heard him snoring, I quietly got dressed and left my apartment. I wandered the streets until dawn, sneaking up to the back window to see if he had left. I remember watching him leave. He slammed the door on the way out as he boldly left my apartment. I hoped no one else had seen him leave.

I slept most of that afternoon, and then called my friend Sharon. I told her what had happened and she freaked.

"Did you have sex?"

"Sharon, I don't think so. He didn't get it in me. He was too big for me."

"That creep! I am going to kill him. Are you sure he never got any of his penis in you?" I really believed she cared for me.

"No, he didn't. I am still a virgin."

That night was the first of many fear-filled nights. I had a hard time sleeping. I would wander onto the campus and bump into Sharon at weird hours of the night.

"Hi," she would say, appearing suddenly and smiling at me.

"What are you doing out here, Sharon? Why am I always running into you?"

"Just watching over you, sweetie."

One night in particular, a strange sequence of events occurred at around 10:30 P.M. For some reason, I was hanging outside of the Christian Community Center in the middle of campus. Three people came up to me and said, "Amber, we have been waiting to talk to you."

"Who are you?"

"We work in the Christian Community Center."

"What do you want?"

"Do you know that girl you hang out with named Sharon?"

"Yeah, she's my friend. Why?"

"Amber, she is dangerous."

"How do you know my name?"

"Because we have been watching over you. That girl is a witch."

"What are you talking about?"

And there she was, out of nowhere, her piercing black eyes staring at all of us. This was one of the weirder moments in my life, for in that very moment I knew that Sharon was dangerous, if not evil.

"She is coming with us, Sharon. Leave her alone."

What the hell was going on? I wasn't going anywhere with anyone, especially not those Christian freaks.

"Amber, remember what I told you about boys. This guy just has a crush on you. Come on, sweetie. We can spend the night at my house."

"Sharon, what are you doing here?"

"I was studying late with a friend of mine and I am crossing over campus because my car is on the other side."

"Amber, come with us and don't listen to her."

"I am outta here. I am not going with any of you. No offense, Sharon, I just have to go home. I have a lot of homework to do." She knew I was lying.

"Amber, you know where we are when you need us. My name is Michael," one boy said.

I turned to walk away, and then looked over my shoulder. All of them were already gone. I thought, *I have been drinking a lot lately. Maybe I am hallucinating.* My thoughts remained troubled as I kept looking back over my shoulder and still could not see them. Something had awakened within me that I had not been aware of before: the understanding that Sharon was not a good person. I had felt it, and now could see it in her eyes.

On my way home, I walked past a phone booth that I had been using to call home when I could. I longed to call home that night, but it was late and I did not have enough money. As I was walking, I came upon a white German shepherd just sitting on the side of the road. It was after midnight.

"Hi, puppy, what are you doing here?" I scratched his ears.

He looked happy and not very hungry. He wasn't wearing a collar. He licked my face and hands and I sat with him for a while. "Listen, buddy, I have to go home now and it's starting to rain. You stay here. I love you, sweetie," I said. Despite my instruction, the dog followed me. I kept trying to get him to go back. My landlady would kill me. But he still followed me.

"Are you hungry, boy? I'll try to sneak you in the house and get you some food. Come on and *shhhh.* You've got to be quiet so we don't get caught."

I went to the side door, and as I was unlocking it the dog started to growl. "Hey it's all right boy. What's wrong?" I started to become afraid, wondering if someone was in my house. As I looked up, I saw Sharon's face reflected in the door glass. I screamed. The dog growled a low and deep growl. I turned to look at him and saw Sharon staring at the dog. She had been right behind me.

"Jesus, you scared me." The dog never moved, even when I said, "It's alright boy. It's alright." I did not want her to know I was afraid.

Sharon removed her eyes from the dog only long enough to say, "I see you've found a guardian. I drove here to make sure you made it home okay. I have been waiting for you."

"Listen, I've got to go. I am really tired. I found this dog on the way home and he followed me." As an afterthought I said, "And I am going to keep him."

The dog was still tense. He had not budged. Sharon smiled and said, "See you tomorrow, Amber. Sweet dreams."

I took the dog inside and we raided the refrigerator. If my landlord found out I had him, she'd throw me out for sure.

That night we both slept on the floor. I put all my blankets down and made a bed. In the middle of the night I had a terrible dream, and awoke to the sounds of my dog growling viciously at the door. God, I was terrified. I had woken from a dream and felt like I was still in it. Yes, I could see the dog growling, but I could also see something else that simply was not there. It was a figure—black, all black. It had the shape of a person. I could see it in the mirror on the dresser. I panicked. The worst part about the experience was the dog growling at the door when what I was looking at was four feet to his left. I thought I was going out of my mind. I found myself drawn to the darkness. I was moving toward it. I found a Bible. It was lying on the floor between the figure and me. All I could say out loud was, "Fear not, for I am always with you." My mother had said that to me at least a thousand times.

Tears were running down my face, and the dog's growls were even more pronounced than his teeth as he made his way toward me. Had he turned on me? Between him, the dark figure, and the Bible, I knew something was happening here that words would never explain. I turned and reached toward the dark figure, only to hit the floor.

Was I losing my mind?

As I clutched the Bible, the darkness faded into nothing. The dog began to yelp as he ran around my apartment as though searching for something. He then put his paws on the window and nudged at the blinds. And I saw Sharon. The dog barked so loudly that the landlady came banging on my door.

"What in tarnation are you doin' in there, young lady?"

I opened the back door and the dog went tearing out of the house. He scared both of us to death. I ran to her arms and cried so hard that I could not control it. I was still clutching my mother's Bible.

We went into her house and she turned on the kitchen lights. I was so happy for the lights. She began to heat up water and said to me, "Are you all right, child?"

I didn't speak. I had no idea what to say. That night, after she calmed me, she told me that bad things had been said about Sharon. She had tried to warn me to be careful about my friends once before, but I had believed that she was talking about Chad Arnold and the frat boys. I told her the story about my dog and she said I could keep him if I wanted. We went outside, but he was gone. Fortunately, the next morning he was outside my door waiting for me.

I started thinking back about my relationship with Sharon. I remembered one night when I had gone out dancing with her and a really cute boy I liked was trying to dance with me. We finally got together, but Sharon used her boobs to seduce the guy away from me. She started dancing solo to the slow music. She was a seductress, and the naïve, horny college boys were easy to manipulate. I couldn't understand why she was trying to keep people away from me.

Shortly after I got the dog, Sharon told me her mom wanted me to come over for dinner. I wanted to bring the dog with me, but she said her mom wouldn't go for that. I needed to find out about her, and if her mom was there I figured it would be safe. I couldn't believe she was a witch of the Black Arts. In fact, I didn't even know what that was when someone tried to tell me.

She picked me up with the rock group Blondie's "Rapture" playing on her eight-track player. She loved Blondie. I met her mom on the way into the house, and she looked at me real funny. Am I paranoid? I asked myself. Sharon had a younger brother and no father living at home.

"Sharon, none of that crazy shit. You hear me, girl?" her mother said to us.

"Shut up, Mom. Let's go, Amber." We went into her room.

"Do you think I am a witch like everybody else, Amber?" she asked.

I was shocked as I hadn't expected her to say that. I didn't know what to say. "Why would you say that, Sharon?" I asked. "Are you?"

She laughed hysterically and changed the subject. "Let's get some food. I want to take you to a party tonight. Since I have you here, you can't say no, and I won't have to pick you up."

Sharon loaned me a dress to wear. It was pretty, and not something I would usually see her in. She told me we would go to this party and then to The Family Dog for a drink afterwards. I went along with her plan.

We drove down the highway to a long, dirt back road until we eventually came upon a lot of people standing around outside a big barn with a hexagon on the top. Some of the people, both men and women, were wearing clothes that seemed like gowns. Everyone was outside. There were a few fires here and there. I got out of the car and followed Sharon. Everyone smiled in a sinister way. Something was not right. People were touching my hair and my body as we walked further into the crowd. It was almost dark.

I was very uneasy. And then I saw something that sliced me in half with a rush of adrenaline. I felt my feet running and hands trying to grab me. Silence filled my head except for the sounds of my breathing and the mind-disturbing mania that signaled terror throughout my being. Off in the distance, I could hear people shouting, "Get her!"

I could see the forest. I stormed the edge of the trees and tore through them like a rabid animal. I could hear people following me as I ran, and I could hear a car that sounded like Sharon's revving up and spinning its wheels in the dirt. I could sense her parallel to me on my left. Her car raced down the road as I was racing through the woods. Tree limbs grabbed at me and twigs snapped beneath my feet. I could see the end of the woods and I darted from within it. I ran directly into the side of a car and hit the ground. Dazed, I scrambled to my feet. Someone was approaching me, "Oh, my God! Amber, is that you?"

I was hysterical. I screamed and clawed at my assailant, but when I finally looked at him, it was Geoff. Breathlessly, I begged, "Geoff, Geoff, let's get out of here. Hurry!"

In shock, he picked me up, put me in his open-top jeep, and sped away. "What the hell is going on, Amber? What are you doing way out here?"

I looked over my shoulder and could see Sharon's El Camino tailing us.

"Hurry!" I screamed.

Geoff floored it, and we crossed the train tracks just ahead of a train. We made it across, but Sharon did not.

Geoff drove me to the campus. He lived there. I asked him to swear that he would not leave me alone that night. He promised he wouldn't. As we got out of his jeep, Sharon pulled up. "Hey, good looking," she said, as if nothing had happened. "What's going on? Hi, Amber. What are you guys up to?"

I said nothing.

Sharon purred her way up to Geoff and rubbed her breasts on him. He was taken aback. Sharon had hardly ever shown him any attention. I was inching away, toward the car. Sharon asked Geoff to come with her for a moment as I saw three boys coming out of a dorm. I took the opportunity and ran over to them for security. I recognized one of the boys. His name was Sander. He was a freshman in my music appreciation class. We usually just stared at each other, smiled, blushed, and then turned away. He seemed sweet.

"Hey, where are you guys going? Can I come with you?" I asked the boys. I looked over my shoulder to see Sharon and Geoff talking and laughing. She was watching me.

"Sure, baby. I'm here from Cincinnati playing baseball for a few weeks and I'd like to have some fun," one of the two older boys said as we got into his car and drove away together. I was nervous and felt nauseous, and when we were out of sight of Sharon, I asked if they wouldn't mind dropping me off.

"Sure, we'll drop you off, won't we?" said Cincinnati, "but we were on our way to take Sander on a little fraternity initiation, and you've just made things easier for us." I began to get more nervous.

Sander was sitting in the back. "Hey guys, not this way. No way." The driver pulled the car off the main road and drove down some dirt road off campus. That seemed to be all Kentucky was made of.

I was told to get out of the car. I did. I was then pushed into the front seat, which was a bucket seat. Across the front seat of that car, I was raped of my virginity. When Sander's turn came, he was crying a little. They called him a pussy. I just cried without a sound. I guessed this was better than what Sharon had had in store for me. The boy from Cincinnati was the oldest and the roughest. He was totally wasted as he slobbered all over my face. It hurt. My back ached.

On the way back, they stopped the car near campus and the baseball player told me to get out. He then threw a bottle of beer at me and slammed the door.

I found my way to the nearest pine tree, where I lay down in the fetal position wrapped around the trunk of the tree. I cried, I moaned, and I could tell the fall season was changing more rapidly. I could smell its sweetness in the air. That night, tucked safely in my own bed in my bedroom, I dreamed that I awoke, freezing cold, and was blessed with the most amazing sight: The branches from that tree seemed to hover close around me. I slipped back into a deep sleep.

The following Monday I went to some friends' dorm room to hang out. These two girls were from the same hometown as each other. They were usually very sweet to me. While I was there, the phone rang.

"Yes, I told you she'd be here with us. Amber, it's for you."

"Who is it?"

"It's that cute guy you like in music class, Sander." Oh, my God, I was going to puke. I had not told anyone what had happened; I had just started skipping classes to avoid seeing the boys.

"Go on. Don't be shy. Talk to him."

"Hello."

"Hi, baby. Let me see, how did it go? Faster, baby, faster. *Uh! Uh! Uh!*" the boys were all there and laughed into the phone. "We had a great time fucking you the other night. Wanna do it again?"

I was petrified. "No, thank you," I said, "I am seeing someone else," and hung up the phone, smiling. To my girlfriends I said, "You guys, you are so nice, trying to fix me up with him. But I don't like him. I like someone else."

"*Woooh.* Who is it? Who is it?" they teased. These were really sweet girls. But I was about to burst with emotion. I had to get out of there.

"Hey, guys, I gotta go. Thanks anyway."

"Okay, sweetie," they said and both hugged me.

I ran out the door. That night I started drinking more heavily. I started writing checks for liquor and pizza. I bought a bottle of sangria, a six-pack of beer, and a bottle of peach vodka. I called and ordered a large pizza. When I opened the door for my pizza delivery, the dog was there. I let him in. "Where have you been, little buddy?" I cried, and hugged him. "Want some pizza?"

I got drunk, and about 8 P.M. started looking for coins to make a call home. My stepfather would not accept collect calls. I needed eighty-five cents. It took me a few hours to bum the money and find some on the street. I took my dog to the phone booth from which I could call home. I needed to talk to my mother badly. I put the money in. It was late. I hoped she wasn't sleeping.

"Hello," I heard a male voice say.

"Leroy, it's me. I need to talk to Mom."

"You ain't gonna talk to her."

"Please, I only have a few minutes."

"Now you need your momma, but you ain't gonna talk to her. You are on your own, kid." And he hung up.

The emptiness slapped me across the face. Miserable, I sank to the floor of the phone booth. My dog and I slept there for a long time. It was small. It was safe. I can still remember that dog's face on my shoulder. He never left my side.

At daybreak, I went to my apartment to sleep. I had nowhere else to go. I was miserable, and I did not know how to live *life*. I was filled with shame and self-disgust.

Sometime before Thanksgiving, the cops came looking for me. My landlady told me, "I don't know what you did, child, but you better stay out of sight. You are in big trouble." It was a Saturday afternoon. As we spoke, the cops were pounding on the front door. She slipped me out the back. The dog was sleeping in the driveway. I knew they would come to my apartment and I could hear them coming. So I ran and hid in one of the window wells on the side of the house. I covered myself with leaves. Fortunately for me, it was an old house and this was a rather large window well. I had a healthy fear of the law. I had no idea why they were after me. I hoped it had nothing to do with that night in the woods with Sharon and her friends.

I heard the police officers shuffling around in the leaves and talking to the dog. "What a nice dog you are, boy. Look here at this dog."

"Yep, he's a nice dog," said the policeman who was headed straight for me. I was breathing so hard I knew the leaves were shaking. He stood directly above me and never made a move to come and get me.

"Sheriff, did you find her? That's such a nice girl." I heard the old lady holler.

He stood in place. "No, ma'am. I haven't found her yet, but you tell her to report to the District Attorney's office by 10 A.M. sharp on Monday morning."

The next thing I knew, the dog was sniffing at me. I was so afraid that the police were close by that I did not want to move. He just kept nudging at me until I came out. Then I snuck up to the back door to see if the cops had left and the lady came out looking for me.

"Child, I was scared to death, worried about you." She hugged me. She fed me dinner. It was good, and I was starving.

The following Monday I went into the courthouse. I spoke to the DA. He was a very nice man. He told me that I had written about two thousand dollars in bounced checks, and that this was a felony. I did not know what a felony was, but he told me I had until the following morning at 10 A.M. to come up with the money.

"Can you call someone in your family to help you pay for this?"

"No."

"A friend?"

"No."

"Young lady, I suggest you call someone because if you don't you are going to jail. You will have to appear in court and have the money by tomorrow morning at 10 A.M."

I left. Jail seemed safe to me. Really, I had nowhere else to go. I had simply stopped going to classes. I could not face the guys on campus. Rumors in the TKE fraternity had started and now all kinds of guys were making cracks at me. That night, I drank all the remaining alcohol I had in the house, including an entire bottle of peach vodka. I passed out. I awoke to my own vomit bubbling out of my throat and all over my Bible. I did not see the dog, but I knew he was there.

I reeked of alcohol and wondered why I was still alive. I had drunk several beers and half a bottle of the sangria on top of the vodka. I had heard that if I drank too much, it would kill me. Basically, I was trying to kill myself.

The following morning, I made my way to the DA's office, and was sitting outside when a lady went rushing in and closed the door. When she came out, she said, "You are one special little lady, my dear." She smiled and walked away.

The DA came to his door, directed me in, and I sat down. He said to me, "Who'd you call?"

"Sir, I don't have anyone to call."

"Well, you called someone, because at nine o'clock sharp this morning, a man walked into the bank with your account number and asked the teller how much it would take to clear up your account."

"To all our surprise, she accepted the money. She was not supposed to do that. She said that the man was so loving and so nice to her that she couldn't say no. Because of this, you are free to go. Do you have family?"

"Yes, but I never told anyone about this." I didn't tell him I had tried to drink myself to death the night before, although he should have been able to smell it.

"Don't write any more bad checks or you will go to jail, young lady. Go on and get out of here."

I got up, said, "Thank you," and left. I went home to sleep, where I remained for the next several days. I never saw my dog again. One day he just disappeared.

I did have one more visit from Sharon before I left college. On that occasion she warned me, "We will find you. You cannot escape us." That remark remained a powerful fear in my life until I had the courage to begin to heal. In those healing moments, I learned of a power as great as hers, but far more beautiful and life enriching to me: the power of love, the power of the peace within me, and the power of light in the presence of darkness.

After I returned to my hometown, I slept most of my days shrouded in a darkness I created. Light continually punched at me through cracks in the dark curtains bursting into the black hole I existed in. I'd rented a tiny room infested with bedbugs. It was dirty, but cheap. I worked part time at a convenience store on the third shift—the same convenience store where I ultimately met my first husband, Sam. I also danced in a bar with my sister, clothes on, and experienced being robbed, being followed home by strangers, and other incidents that contributed to a continuous internal nurturing of the fireworks of anxiety. I trained my neurology to run wild, as I continually ended up in unsafe and even dangerous situations. Instead of blossoming into a butterfly, my cocoon collapsed. I was buried deep within my own psyche with no desire to be released.

I hated the sunlight. It was just too darned revealing.

One night after many months of deep introversion, I decided to attend a party several blocks away from my apartment. I needed to get out. I met a nice, clean-cut guy there who lived out of town and was visiting his friends. He walked me home. We sat outside and talked until dawn. He asked to hug me goodbye. We did. I watched him start to walk away. He turned and called out to me and asked for a drink of water. Of course, I said yes, and he walked up the stairs with me to my one-room efficiency. When I opened the door, the sink was right there. My neighbor was only ten feet away in her room. He stepped in behind me and closed the door. Then he raped me right there on the floor. When he was finished, he stood up and, towering over me, commented, "You thought I was different, didn't you?"

To answer his question: Yes, I truly did.

Sex is an "energy" of its own. It's the ultimate predator. If you don't see it coming you are that much more appetizing to the hunter.

I simply had not seen it coming.

CHAPTER 8
BLACK VELVET CURTAINS

 I started writing this book in 2001 and finished it twelve years later. When I began, I had a hard time liking myself. I felt strongly that I needed to write my story, but I hated doing it. Writing brought back all the loss, all the darkness, and all the memories of things I blamed myself for.

In fall 2003, when I finished writing the initial draft of the story of the rape in my apartment, I told the guy I was dating then, and temporarily living with, what had happened to me. In his powerlessness to protect me from my past, his response to me was to blame me, the victim. "Well, it wasn't his fault," he said. "You should never have let him in your home." My greatest fear was realized in that instant: judgment. Shame gripped me. My vagina actually sizzled with the stickiness of it. Grief opened its mouth and consumed me. I could taste the puke of an eerie death. It welcomed me.

The next day, I found my way to a graveyard and sat among the dead, longing to be released from the hell in my head. I despised breathing. It infected my lungs with the filth of judgment. Each grueling breath kept me alive in the absence of my own will to live. I sat there for hours until I could bear it no longer. In my pocket, I had a prepaid cell phone. I used it to call my sister in Oregon. Through $12 worth of minutes, she soothed me—just enough to keep me going. Among other things she said, she invited me to keep living.

I did.

I was really living in an emotional abyss at that time—had been for two years. How did I get there? Well, within ten months of the 9/11 disaster, I'd lost my ten-year-old business. Clients simply stopped spending money. My investor disappeared. The terrorists had destroyed the economy. Soon my former staff, bill collectors, and federal, state, and local tax agents were coming after me, thirsting for money. But I had nothing to give them.

In my quest for employment, I went out interviewing and was turned down thirty-nine times over a period of thirteen months, often being told that I was "too talented" to be hired for a position, or "overqualified." My ego withered in the face of these useless compliments. Though I was smart, I had no money.

I owed back rent on my apartment. I was facing eviction.

Despite being in serious financial trouble, I didn't qualify for government assistance. The $625 monthly child support payments I was supposed to receive from Jeremy for the care of Ringer—although he often didn't pay anything—prevented me from receiving welfare benefits. The "income" cut off for a single mother with one child was $500 per month.

The pity of the situation was that Ringer's father had never been involved in his life and owed over $70,000 in back child support. Even though Jeremy and his family had money, they managed it in such a way that we were not rewarded with the benefits of it. They hid it. Jeremy knew that I was unemployed and broke. He knew this would impact Ringer. Yet hardly anything was being sent my way. Jeremy paid only what the law required to avoid going to jail.

Jeremy's parents would later claim they had sent gifts and money. They would further claim that I sent them back. Imagine that.

It was a difficult balance, to weigh the tender heart of Ringer, who desired his father's love, against my anger at needing money from Jeremy to take care of him. Money would never feed the thirst in my son's heart and mind to know his father, so I decided to let him visit his father. I hoped that once they met in person, his father would soften and help us for his son's sake.

One day, my sister called out of the blue. She and her husband had hit the jackpot with a huge government contract. War and terrorism had been lucrative for people in their field. "How are you? I mean, how are you doing financially?" she asked. "I've been so busy and stressed that I haven't had time to talk to you." When I explained my situation, she graciously and generously offered to put up the money to help me get on my feet.

"Just go out and find yourself someplace to live and we'll help you with the money," she said. "You can start to pay us back a bit at a time in a few months, if you can."

She graciously promised she'd phone my landlord's office and settle my overdue account. Although I would still need to attend a scheduled court hearing, it seemed like a bullet had been dodged. Delusional hope that I would shortly acquire gainful employment filled the air between us, and I felt relieved. It seemed as if some of my fears and anxieties had been recognized. Help was on the way.

This same sister had helped me the previous Christmas by sending a surprise check for rent and presents. I was unspeakably grateful for the new offer of support. The burden of worry eats up most of one's energy when one is unemployed. Positive thinking is not enough to survive on.

My sister somehow understood my plight. She reached out to me. She brought hope to my weary, disillusioned spirit. I hung up the phone and told Ringer. We giggled with happiness. Somebody cared about us! Somebody knew we existed! The call had come in as we were curled up together in my bed reading and planning his trip to visit his father. It had been a hard road for the two of us up to then. But I began to feel safe from the threat of eviction and woven in a loving web of support. Desperation was transformed into confidence. The passion of confidence melted my heart into a puddle of utter humility. I was grateful I could care for and protect my precious son.

For the next several weeks, Ringer and I scouted places to live and finally found a cute, little apartment to rent. We were excited. Our hearts were lighter because our hopes were real.

Two days before my eviction court case was to occur, on Wednesday afternoon, I called my sister around three o'clock to tell her that I needed to give a deposit to the realtor. In one rushed moment, she simply and sharply stated, "I just spent $14,000 on black velvet curtains for the dining room and I want to get another set for the foyer."

Hot anxiety bubbled in my gut. Adrenaline hijacked me.

"We won't be helping you," she blurted out.

I never spoke. My throat was padlocked.

Annoyed, she heard my breathless silence. "I don't want to talk about it," she said and hung up.

Just like that. *Click.*

A lightning rod of silence cracked through my mind.

Then anxiety began to roar off in the distance, like a tidal wave on the move. My entire nervous system went into shock. I got numb. My mind filled with images of Ringer. I had no home for my son. Sensing impending disaster, I was engulfed by a helpless mindset as the roaring wave of reality grew louder. There was no escape. I was poor and swiftly slipping deeper under the waves of poverty. The drippy, clinging presence of misery flooded my mind.

Moments after hearing my sister's words, my legs collapsed. I found myself on the floor. I needed it to hold me so that I would not keep falling.

My arm reached for the phone and I called the apartment complex office. My mouth told them to go ahead and evict me. When they asked me why, in a flat voice I replied that my sister had backed out on her offer of support. She'd spoken with them weeks earlier and they were waiting for her check. They had planned to drop the judgment. Things had all been worked out.

There have been moments in my life when I wanted to die—not commit suicide, just die. There is a significant and subtle difference. There can come a point in life where one simply realizes that one's body is suffering immeasurably. When the nervous system is almost at a shutdown point, one can be convinced that dying is a good way to stop the suffering. That's how I felt as the pain of my situation rose up and consumed me. I longed to be nurtured in the warm, caring arms of love and compassion. Now a fantasy of death brought me powerful images of comfort.

Many people have judgments about dying by one's own hand. Our minds have been trained to believe, *Suicide is for the mentally unstable and for cowards.* The reality, however, is that many people think about death quite a bit—even sane and brave people. There can be dignity in wanting to stop our pain. There is honor in being honest about our feelings of wanting to end it. It is courageous to face the painful inner truth and keep going. We experience a moment of truth that reveals our strength when we can stand on the precipice of pain, allow the heart to experience it, and then choose to go on. That is real dignity—not the denial of reality.

Suffering will come to each of us. It is not usually the "will of God," as my mother might say, but the will of human beings. We love each other. We hurt each other. I was suffering from the decisions of people, including some of my own. I had about ten days before the sheriff would deliver a letter asking me to vacate the apartment. I felt there was no point trying to change that.

Lying there, on the floorboards of apathy, stillness simply blanketed me. Its weightlessness pinned me to the ground. My skeleton went rigid. My muscles collapsed. Living was automatic. My vital organs prepared for survival by succumbing to a minimalistic need base. Self-preservation simply occurred. Desire did not feed it. Delusional hope had made it worse.

Reality seemed to soothe it. I had failed. I'd failed to keep my business. I'd failed as a mother. I'd failed as a citizen. I'd failed as a sister. In the absence of money, I had failed. I believed I was not socially fit and felt like an enormous burden to society.

Doom politely took first chair in the symphony of my existence. There were no heroic tunes chiming in my ears. No. I barely had enough strength to breathe. A clock ticking close by me kept me grounded in the reality that my situation had not changed. I gave up.

Then, my ears heard someone pounding at the door. Movement was not an option. Even my breath understood that.

That someone kept knocking. "Amber! Amber! It's Shannon," I finally heard.

The mood within me startled me. Darkness whispered to me like an ancient, dear friend, "Let go. Let go. You can stop the pain."

The pounding continued.

Finally, I moved. I crawled across the floor, over to the door, and rose up. As I opened the door, my dignity slipped out through it. For there stood the building manager, Shannon, in tears, and her tears offered me my own release. Toxic tears gently began to roll down my face, easing the dammed-up ache in my shredded soul. Shannon reached out and I fell into her arms.

Shannon held me for a moment and then I let her guide me to the sofa. With a few muffled words, she handed me a check. "This is all I have. At least make a car payment and don't lose that. I will help you more. I just don't know how yet."

After Shannon left, thoughts of Ringer bubbled in my head. I knew he would be home soon from his friend's house. For him, I assembled my composure. For him, I knew I had to act.

The next morning I began by writing a letter to my sister, pleading for her to reconsider her decision to withdraw her support. Then in a move of stifling desperation, I began making calls and writing letters to county agencies, churches, and any other organizations I could think of that might offer assistance, advocating for myself as if it were not me for whom I sought help. From this burst of activity, I managed to raise several thousand dollars, which combined with Shannon's gift of money, was sufficient to pay some of the back rent I owed.

A few days later, one of the agencies I'd written a letter to asked me to come in for a visit. I met with a female minister, who said, "I am so moved by your story, Amber. We are going to help you." Of all the things the church decided to assist me with, can you believe, it was my car. Because I had borderline poor credit and no job they decided I needed to hold on to it in an effort to maintain my creditworthiness. I'd put in enough money for the car to be useful in this way.

Compassion. It hurts in a miserable, tender way.

Tears kept the floods rising even as charities poured out whatever they could spare in funds to me. My spirits lifted, but I was still jobless. I learned that my credit ranking and its reflection of my recent bankruptcy were part of what was hindering me from finding gainful employment.

For weeks, I walked through gate after gate of misery, deprivation, and intense sorrow. But for the sake of Ringer, who was too young to be informed about such things, I smiled, prepared meals, did the laundry, and made the bed. I only allowed myself to collapse when he was out.

Containment—not avoidance, but containment—was critical as I led both of us through this dark period. Support from a few loving, generous souls along the way aided my ability to lead.

After a few weeks and no word back from my sister, we were preparing for my son to meet his dad. Ringer had gone outside to find a friend, but came back suddenly. The car was missing! I had not parked it in the garage. I thought that since the charity had made two car payments on my behalf I would be safe for a while. Yes, the arrogant car dealership had greedily repossessed the car. No call. They took the money I'd paid them *and* the vehicle—and that was that. They had that right and I didn't have a dime for a lawyer, or the mind, to fight their decision.

My brain shut down in self-preservation. It knew. It understood.

Ringer's actions knocked me further into awareness of my poverty. He'd come directly to me one day, wearing his best clothes, looked me in the face, and plainly stated that he was going to go door to door to sell our computer, TV, and whatever he could sell. He was thirteen. My mind and heart snapped as I weathered another violent thrust of reality.

I conjured up an image of courage, knelt down before him, and smiled, saying, "That's okay, sweetheart. We won't need to sell anything." I hugged him, doing my best to express my mind's entire definition of confidence through the embrace.

The image held. It held until I put him on a plane to see his dad. I still harbored hope that his dad might help us when he got to know and came to love my beautiful Ringer.

I also had hopes that my sister would have a change of heart and come through. When someone is lost in a downpour of money, however, it can be very difficult to cast a glance towards the pain and needs of others. She'd had enough pain in her own miserable life, and money was providing a temporary salve for the wounds of her years of suffering. Even in my desperation I knew what was happening to her. Part of me was happy that she could go out into the world of material beauty and to use it to create a beautiful home, have nice things, and create some sense of safety for her wounded heart and mind. She deserved pleasure. Still I was sliced through to my core as I experienced her rejection of not just me, but more importantly, of her nephew, my innocent young Ringer. My empathy for her journey of immense pain conflicted with my deep, deep longing to provide safety for my son so he would not know the same suffering we had as children. This created a turmoil in me that ate at my emotional flesh. It felt like maggots were feasting on the deadness of my ability to move toward hatred. My love for her was infinite. I stood frozen in a web of compassion and intense love for the two most important people in my life, my sister and my son.

My sister did not understand that while the social and economic impact of 9/11 had brought her wealth, it had also brought total devastation to others—and I was one of them. People did not understand this. My own mother did not feel I deserved the support. Because she could see my talents, she did not understand why I could not find a job. Truly, I don't blame my mother or my sister for their attitudes. After all, my mother had taught my sister to share her belief that she was "not my keeper." My religious mother usually had some Bible verse she could whip out on any occasion to validate her point. Sadly, when an idea comes from the Bible, well, it seems there is no chance for someone like me.

My favorite copout from my mother was: "God never gives us more than we can handle."

God may not. But I've found that people often do.

The day after my car was repossessed I called a friend in the car business in a frazzled state of neurosis. It turned out that my credit was good enough to get a poor person's loan; meaning, I got to buy a used car on a payment plan with a steep 19 percent variable interest rate. Although people will provide all sorts of helpful solutions that cater to the economic cycle of survival of the wealthiest, the price tag for those of us who are less fortunate is usually much higher than for those who have greater means. Everyone knows this does not make sense in the grand scheme, yet it is the reality. Those are the "rules." Pay to play or drop out of the game. That's that.

I took the deal. I had a vehicle and never looked back. A genuine curve even graced my lips as I did. Hope confused me. It had nothing to do with the facts of my situation. It created delusional expectations for me that were not supported by events. People kept telling me, "It can't get worse than this. You will see. Have hope, Amber. Have hope." I wanted to believe. Ringer's confidence in me also increased when I came home with a car.

I ached quietly when he boarded the plane to visit his dad. By then I had begged Jeremy to help us. I innocently believed that when he met his amazing son, his heart would open and that he would understand why sending money was both needed and expected. The people in his life viewed me as a bad woman, as trash. His girlfriend had once called me a bitch and a cunt on the telephone. That's what we do, as a society, to the spouse who raises the children. The idea of giving money blinds us to the idea of a human life. I do not know what stories had been created to justify not taking responsibility for Ringer. The only threat Ringer and I posed to him was that of living up to his paternal obligations.

Wealth can be a social fortress that separates people from one another. It becomes a podium, a platform for platitudes. Fantastic stories are created that nurture the arteries of self-worth. Poverty is powerful enough to do the same. Wealth is an oxygenated idea of happiness and safety, while the toxicity of poverty is pumped from the social veins to be released, cleansed, and rid of as efficiently as possible. Both are viruses and neither holistically addresses the social needs of human beings.

Unconditional love and compassion, on the other hand, are powerful syringes that can be utilized to inject the highest vibrations of healing into tattering minds, hearts, and searching souls. We have *evidence* of such things. Yet, we are infants and toddlers still learning to believe we are worthy . . . still learning to understand that we are capable . . . still learning that we are connected to everyone and everything. Ringer profoundly needed his father's love. Jeremy's father, old and outdated in his attitudes, denied his grandson not only money but his grandfatherly love. He had never forgiven me and Jeremy for marrying against his wishes when we were young. He denied his own son love, support, and acceptance. Money was his fantasy. We were "trouble" and a threat to his fortress. In turn, he taught his son to be just like him: to run, to deny, and to do everything he could to maintain some dramatic sense of false nobility about being a man. Money often cloaks such cowardice. Money has a way of hiding unpleasant things about people who look collected and clean, drive nice cars, and seem socially responsive. Money turned Jeremy and his family away from the grace and gift of a human life, their bloodline: Ringer. How is it possible to deny a son, or even a grandson?

What cowards have we created in our irresponsible fathers? My own father was a coward, too. As an adult woman, I located him. As you'll recall, when I asked him why he had left my mother alone with seven children, he replied, "Because I did not have the money to support all of you." He ran instead of joining forces with my mother and experiencing the love of his children, which is a responsibility of adulthood. Society has allowed weak men to behave this way for a very long time. For years, we as a people have left burdens for mothers and their children to bear because there has been no accountability for men.

Ringer was scared, but nonetheless he really, really longed to meet his dad. I was stunned at the depth of pride I felt for him as I dropped him off at the airport. His bright, courageous face masked the depth of his boyish desire to get to know his dad. His heart was wide open.

As he waved goodbye to me, my son still had no idea that my sister had backed out on her offer to help us. He was counting on me to be there when he came home—and I wanted to be, but I had no idea myself of what was yet to come. My troubles were far from over.

My days swiftly passed in miserable angst as I continued to call local charities, begging for help. It later became clear to me that this arduous task of asking for help would powerfully engrain within me a deep sense of self-worth. Awareness would develop that I deserved help and support, and that I deserved to have my basic human needs met. The day came when Shannon told me that I could technically live in the apartment for only another 60 days before the sheriff would throw me on the street. The charities had only covered the back rent. I would owe any additional debt and my credit would be further ruined. She was doing everything she could to stall the process, but her hands were tied. I was going to crash. No matter what I did, my hope wasn't floating. We were drowning. I could not save my son's life without saving my own.

There were no shelters to live in. All of the extra hotel rooms in the entire northern Virginia region had been purchased by the government to house other homeless, jobless families. I am certain my sister was unaware. Most people were. Social services told me that if I could not provide a home for Ringer, they would take him from me. That was the only assurance they could provide. No place for both of us, but enough room to separate us. My nervous system continually crashed against wave after wave of reality.

To add to my crappy, entangled situation, endometriosis began to ravage my cervical, rectal, and pelvic regions, reminding me of my matriarchal failure. I was bleeding in massive clots. Stress fed the appetite of my condition as I fought viciously to keep my medical insurance for the surgery I needed. One kind woman at the health insurance company, who suffered herself from the same problem, made it possible for me to get surgery. Because I'd been a customer for nine years, she was able to pre-authorize the surgery, but nothing thereafter. That droplet of human kindness carried me from one moment to the next.

The fighting required for managing the stress in my life sucked out my vital energy. Madness seemed like a viable option. At night dreams of crying women would gush through my mind just like the blood pouring from me. I do not know how I made it through. It wasn't God. There were no angelic, winged beings hovering over me. There were bills, and bill collectors, debts and debt collectors, and they outweighed and outnumbered the few compassionate souls that extended themselves to me. Effort is noble, when one is so heavily taxed. And only effort, every ounce of it I made or received, can be attributed as being the source of my survival. Without the fractional doses of others' efforts on my behalf in addition to my own, I would have been consumed by my body's lack of ability to keep living. People and their concern for me mattered.

I surrendered to calling Ringer's father and asked him to take temporary custody of Ringer. His arrogance during that call threatened to provoke me into a murderous rage. I think he foolishly felt like a knight coming to the rescue when he shared his idealistically made plans of how he and his girlfriend had always wanted a child. They wanted to give Ringer khaki pants and polo shirts, and had football playing fantasies and images in mind of the thirteen-year old "young man" he needed to be. With mountainous restraint, I urged Jeremy to be tender, loving, and understanding with Ringer. I urged him to think of the psychological ramifications of trying to change him. He simply denied all "that emotional stuff."

To this day, my son has learned, as men before him, to do the same: deny what hurts. He anxiously modified his natural feelings and learned to be aloof instead, in order to survive. Plunged into the depths of his despair he would perish. People modify reality. Ringer learned to do the same.

"It's time Ringer learned how to be a man," Jeremy said, in his best manly voice.

Screams echoed in my head. I felt a sensation of claws cut through my fingers. The protective mother, the bitch energy, growled in madness. I violently forced myself to accept the volcanic vomit that bubbled and oozed out from my mouth as I signed over papers to Ringer's ignorant, insensitive father. I had no choice.

When Ringer found out that he would not be coming home as originally planned, my mental infrastructure finally collapsed. I broke. I died 1,000 times when he begged me to come home. I can neither bear to write, nor can I cleverly find the words to describe my emotional drowning when I heard his tears begging me, "Don't do this, Mommy." Hell is some other author's job to describe. I didn't have to fear going there anymore; we were already living in hell. I remember how his soft little pleas turned into a rage, a self-protective mechanism to help him manage the unbearable pain of separation and loss I'd created. It was my responsibility to accept his rage. He was a kid. I was his mother. I could not tell him that I'd lost everything, including our home. I did not need him worrying about me. *Instead, he thought that I did not want him.*

His father made things worse. He could not accept how hard this decision was for Ringer. Men did not cry in his family. They simply "strapped them on," drank alcohol, and spent money on pleasures to numb their pain.

At this point in my story, we've had a lot of sympathy for me. Here is where it has to slow down because we must move on to our sympathy for Ringer. As a society we try to create all sorts of clever crap to convince ourselves that kids are resilient. That makes us feel better, doesn't it? That makes "hope" a happy little thought. Well, I'm here to say that kids are not that resilient. They grow only because the violent, brisk rush of evolution forces all of us to do so. But kids do not create the pain adults put them through. Society puts our kids in pain by denying them basic needs. Human beings are vile creatures hell bent on destruction when it threatens our safely-created realities, our money, or our rights. And remember, all of us were kids once. Were we really so resilient?

As the days and nights blurred into one another, three things happened that steered my mental boat on a new course. First, I used to walk my faithful, loyal, loving dog, Neo, as often as my endometriosis would allow. We'd had him since he was a pup. One day while walking in the woods I met a female photographer. Hungry for some bite of an intelligent diversion from my mental torment, I expressed some enthusiasm for her trade. As a result of doing so, she offered me a part-time job paying $15 dollars an hour to help her organize and go on photo shoots. I graciously took her number. Once she and her dog left the woods, I dropped to the muddy, wet earth and smothered my tears in its fragrant nectar. I could smell fall in the soil. I did not want to get too happy or for that matter even to tell anyone. Too many losses had had their way with me.

Secondly, I finished writing Chapter 7 of this book. With the intelligent opportunity to make a dignified dollar, I had a little wind in my lungs. I knew I would not make enough from this job to pay for a place to live, but it was a start. I remember the weekend I forced myself to write about the rape. I barricaded my apartment, putting a chair in front of the door. I closed all the blinds to create as much darkness as I could. I needed it in order to find some source of light inside of me so I could find the courage to write. I took blankets and made a tent over my dining room table, and then Neo and I camped out on the floor below with my computer.

There were moments when I could not write more than one sentence at a time because I felt like I was re-traumatizing myself. Why did I press on? By the weekend's end I had finished my writing. I wrapped myself in my blankets late on that Sunday evening, sat with my dog on my porch, and cried in heaving spouts. Neo never left my side. I was very worried about where he would have to go when I had to move. I was not sure if I could bear another loss. Truly, I was not sure. I could barely afford to feed him.

One night, a few women friends actually forced me out of my apartment. I looked terrible. They took me to a local club where I drank alcohol compliments of them. I hated the noise, the smoke, the people, and the bitter taste of the alcohol. My wayward friends thought they needed to fix me up with some good-looking macho guy—as if that would solve anything. That's just what women think, isn't it, that a man will solve their money problems? They did not know the full extent of my pain. But that was how I met Odeh.

Odeh was a Palestinian and a Muslim. He was so darn sweet while he was drinking. Both of us were vulnerable. We hit it off that night. A few days later we went to my home, played drums, drank more wine, and talked. That was it. The next day when he left he promised he'd call, and he did. From that night forward he came to me in the night to love me. The touch of another human being was violently beautiful. He brought food for me at times and helped with a few car payments. But he was a loner. He'd call during the day to make sure I kept living. "Open the blinds. Let the sun in, Amber." He held me closely, but could not bear it if I cried.

Odeh had a good job and worked hard. He liked to drink beer. It aided him in handling his pain about missing his family back home and being a Muslim man in a world hostile towards him. He lived with a fear I had no awareness of, the fear of being taken away, accused of any sort of crime, or blamed for the actions of terrorists. We were both swirling in the aftermath of 9/11. But I was totally unaware or troubled at all by his background. I was entirely absorbed in his love and kindness toward me. Charities and strangers had become my family. They kept me connected to my own humanity.

Unfortunately, Odeh's kindness and gentleness were laced with rage for being blamed for things he could not control. His words could slice me to pieces. He'd been torn from his family at the age of fourteen. He woke up one morning in the home of his huge, loving family to find his bags packed. He was shipped to India to finish high school and get a college education. His parents had moved him for his own protection. Odeh had seen many horrible things in his young life and too many of the young men in his community ended up in prison. Occupied Palestine did not offer a stable environment for loving parents to raise a child. Never to return to his home, his bitterness at being alone in the world gnawed at him, despite his naturally loving nature.

Even with our cultural differences, I felt Odeh's plight and he felt mine. We were both miserable people. In the quiet of the night, safely loving each other, both of our youthful, innocent spirits would emerge, until the daylight would remind us of reality.

After meeting Odeh, my sister reconnected with me and spoke with me about the possibility of giving me job. Odeh and I went to her home for Thanksgiving. Once it was discovered that Odeh was not an American citizen yet, my sister's offer to hire me was recanted. Because of their pending "security clearance," it was decided that both Odeh and I might somehow be a threat to the future of their business dealings with the government. That's just how things were.

Thrust back into my plight, Odeh was the only person I knew who was willing to help me. Neither of us was thrilled about it, but he was all I had—and he cared for me deeply. He offered me shelter, food, and his love. His gesture of human decency reminded me that I was worthy. There were no other offers out there. I had to survive. Ringer was out there waiting for me.

With my eviction notice pending and my surgery scheduled, I then found out I also had appendicitis. Odeh asked his brother if I could move in with them as I had nowhere to go. I was exhausted, swimming in a lap pool of chronic pain. I would need at least six weeks to recover.

Then, I lost my job. The photographer could not afford me any longer.

I've got to pause here and add something else significant and strikingly powerful. I had received all sorts of job offers from men for "alternative" kinds of work, everything from posing for pornography to stripping and prostitution. I'd get excited about a call I'd get from my resume, only to feel very unsafe during an interview in the home of some home-based businessman needing "support." I had men offer me a place to live for free—in exchange for sexual favors. I had all sorts of offers that fed on the greedy appetites of perverts.

People do not *want to realize* the pressure poor women are under that makes us that much more vulnerable to predators. Women typically take responsibility for the children. What happens when the father abandons that responsibility? We judge the mother. We then make the single mother a hero. We empathize and vote down social programs that might help her. We keep her in that role, so that we elucidate her plight. It illuminates our own wealth. It makes it brighter and keeps us feeling safe in the fantasy that we are better off.

Even my own mother, who raised her seven children on welfare, judges other people who get assistance. Isn't that extraordinarily ironic?

Love is not a virtue in our culture, unless of course it is a commodity. On a global level, emotion has sociologically come to be viewed as a weakness or "feminine." Unless of course it becomes romantic, an illusion of the soul not connected to actual events.

So I ended up living with Odeh. He and his brother took me in. There was no one else.

Life was painful.

Some people have tried to rationalize the profound grief I feel with words like *karma*. There simply seemed to be no other way for them to understand the mudslide I was ensnared in. *Karma!* What a convenient path around the direct route to reality.

I closed my eyes against the stab of my mother's words when, in the depths of desperation, I called her one day and she candidly explained how she'd encouraged my sister to buy the black curtains and enjoy the fruits of her labors because I wasn't her responsibility. Truly, she had no idea of my struggles. Surely she would not have so ignorantly said those stinging, nasty words if she had known, right? I cried silently. It was healing. Both anger and compassion gnawed at this latest wound. My brain flew fast and hard from the reality of her ignorance. My heart understood it quite well. I had fallen and my family was not going to follow me there.

This is why a woman like me would chose to live with a man who would blame her for being raped. *Do you get that?* Let's call it tolerance in exchange for survival. Women are keenly skilled at this. They tolerate for their children. They tolerate so they do not have to sell themselves. Even still, some tolerate because they are afraid to make it on their own. History shows extraordinary strength and tolerance from women. Odeh was one of the only ones willing to show some measure of compassion. I had to provide my beautiful body shelter. I still loved it—even though it felt like I was almost dead. I needed a place to heal from surgery.

Before moving in with Odeh, I had to let go of my sweet Neo. A teenage boy and his mom adopted him. They had a nice home and adored him. I said goodbye to my best companion as I prepared myself for whatever storms were yet to arrive. The day I let him go, he knew I wasn't coming back. His brown eyes pleaded with me, echoing and torturing me with memories of Ringer's pleading tones. We'd had Neo since he was a fluffy, brown-eyed puppy. He belonged to Ringer. Neo had tugged and pulled me through every ounce of my pain as he pushed me each day to survive. He had forced me to laugh, which forced me to heal. He'd licked my tears and pulled the covers off of me, gently using his mouth to take hold of my hand, to get me out of bed. He was always at my side. He'd ferociously watched over Ringer. He was a part of Ringer's heart.

A few weeks after moving in with Odeh, I received a call from the woman who had adopted Neo. While her son was taking him for a walk, he broke leash and was hit by a car. He had died at the vet's office. I was devastated, flat-lined, and swallowed in a brutal spiral of grief.

Odeh forbid me to cry in his presence. He could not bear to see me suffer because he lacked the integrity of strength needed to allow me this loss. He could not protect me from the harsher realities of life. His powerlessness and fear were deeply shrouded in an edgy anger and dismissal of my grief. Men were supposed to be strong, he believed, and strength was fed by denying the reality of the experience of women.

The day Neo died I walked until I could walk no further and found my way to a tree. I wrapped myself around it and cried out my agony. Hours later, with the sun down, I made my way back and clung to the dark realm of sleep.

The day arrived for me to have surgery. My mother had contacted my sister and told her of my newest plight. Knowing I'd be alone most of the time while Odeh and his brother worked, my sister offered to pick me up after surgery. While staying at her beautiful home, she graciously doted over me, showing me genuine kindness and compassion. She then offered me a place to live and after a few weeks of recovery had me move my clothing and some small personal belongings into the wonderful private bedroom I'd been in.

One day after bringing clothing from the garage where my things were being stored and from Odeh's house—purses, shoes, toiletries, and other items—she politely, but matter-of-factly, asked me to remove all my belongings from the room she'd provided, telling me it was because her stepson and his girlfriend were coming for a visit.

There was not enough time for shock to formulate itself in my mind. "What's wrong? Where do you want me to put my things?" I asked in a plethora of acidic anxiety.

"On the floor in the other guest bedroom. Remove everything. They will be here for one night, but I want them to have the king-sized bed and private bathroom."

Poverty provoked my sister. Impressions from childhood days would attack her periodically and my weakened presence activated her senses to a point of great emotional discomfort. She was afraid for me.

I understood her. I knew her need to create what made her feel clean, safe, and sheltered. Money could do that at some level. Her guests needed the best. I was a sore spot so I needed to be hidden, cleaned up, put away. I understood. I truly did. A river of profound sadness engulfed me as I felt the soil of my shame in her eyes. Compassion's eye gently led me to the next moment of life.

My stunned expression and emotional momentum must have shown on my face. In a highly agitated state, she said, "If you don't like it, you can move out." Without another breath, she then added, "For that matter, I can't handle this. Just move out. I don't want to deal with any more of your shit."

People do things. There are explanations. It is up to me to choose anger or anguish.

Anguish provided me an understandable pain. Anger would have defeated me. Perspective gave me the opportunity to understand and to let it go. People harm each other. Some know what they are doing. My sister did not.

I know. I lived my childhood with her.

As I swayed in the emotions of my own misery, love kept its thread through it all. She was my favorite. She was a portrait of the unkindness that her life had been.

I wrote about my family history before I told this part of the story to illustrate the environmental imprint that embedded certain coping mechanisms into me and my siblings. The raw brutality of her childhood molded her, infected her, and dominated what remained. Each unconscious act against me was her own body's intelligence guiding her toward survival. My plight was a neurological threat to her environment. A potential threat to her attempts to maintain a home in which she could create her own happiness. Too much interpersonal connectivity was dangerous for her. Poverty hit a nerve. She logically wanted to clean me up and make things pretty again. I knew this all too well, for I had spent a lifetime doing the same.

At that time in my life I did not fully grasp this. Stress was toying with me and rational thought simply was not possible. Anger would not have served me then, and still does not serve to engender a productive outcome even when I now have the mental infrastructure to understand some parts of her mind and volatile heart. But I love her. I always felt for her in my heart, her preciousness poisoned and me unable to protect her. We all were.

After leaving her home, Odeh took me back although his disgust for my family and his frustration with my weakness was getting to him. He despised weakness and emotional fragility. People truly have very little capacity to feel deep emotions. He was the hero here, taking in a fragile woman. Typically males have such titles, and publically we don't often focus on the emotional impact of traumatic experiences. We summarize traumas—safely. We glamorize them—creatively. Or we deny them with fervor. To show too much compassion only meant he'd have to open his heart to what was buried deep in his cavity of memories, and that was truly more than he could bear. I don't blame him either. Society has taught our men, and now our women, to be strong and resilient. It is "heroic" to bravely move through things while shunning the emotionality of our experiences.

The radio in my head sang songs of panic, chaos, despair, and failure. The symphony in my soul cried out its love for Ringer. Everything outside of me reminded me of my social inadequacies and shameful existence. Compassion and surrender were the calling of the spirit. I hated this. I resented it and fell victim to my own resistance. Only weeks later, Odeh informed me that he and his brother would be traveling to Egypt for three weeks for a wedding and that I had to leave. I had a few weeks to get out. Still recovering from some setbacks from the surgery, unemployed, and penniless, I anxiously asked if I couldn't remain and housesit.

"Did you actually think you could just stay here while we traveled?" his brother responded.

Aware of his brother's distaste for my presence, I pleaded my case. I had to live. I had to survive for my son. I was soul bound to this mission. My heart's every beat was aligned with Ringer. My pleas fell on deaf ears. Odeh and his brother felt they had done enough. The compassion meter had run out. They would leave. The house would be empty, and I was not welcome any longer.

Odeh in his own strange way felt sorry for me and hated me at the same time. He had zero tolerance for my "weakness." He would often say to me, "This is life, Amber." I guess that he felt he needed to prepare me for the hell he believed life to be. Mercy is not always a value shared among survivors. It's rarely shared among men, especially when money is involved.

I held in my retort in the face of Odeh's brother's insensitivity. While living there, I cooked, cleaned, and did my best to be very pleasant when they were home. But these dutiful traits were expected of women in their culture and so had very little value. I went to bed that night and never said a word. Toxic anxiety ate at me. I felt it so deeply that the flesh of my ears burned.

The next morning I called my friend Andrea and asked her to help me. She said, "Absolutely, I'll be there in one hour." In that one redeeming moment, I began to pack. Both Odeh and his brother were at work. Every item I packed strengthened me. I felt bold. What fueled my resolve was his brother's final word on the matter, "Did you think you could just stay here while we traveled?" Yes, I did actually. But that power was not mine and he knew that.

The power to leave on my own was mine. His truth, his reality, had pushed me to make a move quickly. Dignity breezed back in as I opened the door to change. A healthy dose of anger pushed me to the edge of my nasty shame and light winds of inspiration caressed me. I was mindful not to overdo it.

I made another call to a woman with a soul, Shannon, the building manager at my old apartment complex. I told her I needed help. Without hesitation, she said, "Come on over and live in your storage garage. It's free. I'll help you when you get here, but stay out of sight of the upper management."

"You go, girl!" echoed in my head. I knew I would rather live in that garage than to be a burden to others. Yes, a burden. Most lack the courage when you simply do not get up and change things. People who "have things" lack the intellectual capacity to comprehend that it simply takes time for someone to recover. I did not drink. I did not use drugs to cope. I lived through it all, raw and festering with the darkest of human emotions a person can tolerate. It scares people. They need to hurry up and hide things, and then to act like "it" just did not happen. As a strong person, I understand that very few other people had the intestinal fortitude to witness my suffering. I am grateful for those who did.

I could feel the wheels unwinding in me as Andrea and I stuffed her SUV and my car with my things. I had no money, no job, and no home, yet I could feel the winds of freedom call me home to myself. Free! I could taste it—the freedom of being on my own—even if it was in a garage.

We arrived and unloaded my stuff. Andrea gave me $40 and said she'd be back the next day. And then it hit me, the rise and fall of grief, the ebb and flow of raging storms. I sat in the wreckage of my torment. Even though the winds of freedom had uplifted me, the darkness of the garage now collapsed upon me. Still, I was not strong enough to rise up and walk again.

I sat up my bed and surveyed my home. No bathroom, kitchen, or windows. It was a tomb. In its darkness I slept, and dreamed, and cried until my sorrow became beautiful, and I was achingly compelled to compose: to write. I slept and fantasized about death cleansing me of my sorrows, and holding me close to her bosom. By flashlight, I read books by Anne Rice about vampires and felt at home in my mental tomb. I felt I could go on for days in the dark, deathly home I lived in. No one would find me if my body stopped breathing.

I actually believe it would have been easier at that point for my family and most people if I had died because my death would have relieved them of knowing the reality of my situation. Mourning would have been much easier. Whispering tearful phrases, like "It's a shame," would have provided a convenient script for their behavior and a much easier way to face the mess.

Writing released the poison in my mind. I wasn't strong. People simply projected that fantasy on me. It seemed to ease the possibility that they might need to actually do something more. Writing and thinking about the truths of my past, brought crashing experiential moments of apathy. Sometimes, all I could write were a few words at a time before the well of grief erupted. I hated writing. A few times, here and there, the release of the stench of my words would soothe me. Writing was my friend and my fiercest enemy.

Leaving Odeh was the most empowering move I'd made that year. In doing so, I broke a dependency pattern and commanded some respect for myself. He and his brother were shocked that I had moved out so quickly. They had doubted my courage and my will. So had I. Their truth, their reality, forced me to see it.

I suffered while existing in that garage. I'd lost it all: a successful business and all the pretty things I'd used to run away from my core self, my core experiences. Yeah, I'd had it all. I had fit in with society quite nicely before my business crumbled. It was painful to face my-self living in that garage, pissing in a bucket, and continuing to look for value within myself.

Writing helped me to remember my youthful courage, strength, and impenetrable resolve. It was in there. Like many people do, I'd hidden it in the attic of my personality.

Days and nights passed, courage grew and then collapsed. More events were yet to occur that would remind me of the world's harshness. One day I excitedly answered my precious pre-paid cell phone. It was a call from California. I knew it was Ringer. A girlfriend had bought me the phone and the minutes so that I could talk to Ringer. Instead, on the other end of the line was the voice of a self-righteous and indignant public defender from the Juvenile De-tention Center in California. Ringer had run away from his father and the courts were trying to keep him in their care because of his "unfit parents." Ringer was not doing well. This overzealous court-appoint-ed attorney proceeded to verbally excoriate me with her version of me abandoning my son. He was clearly in his own hell. I felt it.

People who did not know my story often took the liberty of ver-bally sodomizing me concerning motherhood. That's how violent it felt. Many gave me verbal slam after slam about my inadequacies as a mother and my weakness, while others sang the hymns of my strength. Those two contradictions aided in the crippling of my men-tal status. All these people trying to make sense of Amber: blaming and claiming were much easier to do than actually getting involved.

I did not get the chance to tell this woman what had happened. Her judgment was swift and unyielding. She was going to take him from me. She had no idea I was standing in a garage. She was under the impression that I'd given him up for a "better lifestyle."

"You rich people are so selfish," she bitched, "shuffling your kids around like that." My minutes ended her harshness. The phone went dead. My choked up words remained in my throat and their threads to my story remained congested in my head. My son would remain in her care. I realized and powerfully understood that Ringer probably had to hate me in order to survive.

I closed the garage door and did not open it for three days, not until the smell of urine and the overgrowth of funk in my mouth forced me to go out and get air. The thought of losing Ringer pushed my hollow mind around the next bend of movement.

Unemployed and penniless, I continued to force myself to eat crackers, and I willingly slept in the tomb where I lived. I dreamed of Ringer. I dreamed of death. My will was tethered to deep emotional roots that shifted within the barren soil of my psyche. It was eroding. I could bear no more pain in this lifetime. Longing for death eased my suffering somewhat because I knew I could end it whenever I was ready. I could unharness my existence from the reality of my plight.

But my heart's deepest love called out for my son, Ringer. I loved him beyond my soul. I could not leave him no matter how much life hurt me. He fueled my strength. My brittle heart hunted like a scavenger for any remnants of love and will. Memories of Ringer were excruciatingly painful, but I knew I could not shut down my heart or I would bury my love for him. Love shoveled me through every aching moment of my days. I found myself challenging life like a foolish drunk. "Bring it on you bastard. Bring it on. You can't break me."

Love did that. Love for Ringer.

So, on I went. I continued to breathe and to delve deeper into the unknown within me. The darkness inside of me was almost soothing. The silence was healing. I now knew that God did not exist outside of human fantasies. I was both the light of my joy and the darkness of my sorrow. I kept searching for a glimmer of light within me. It had to be there. Where had it gone?

I vomited on words like "love" and "human kindness" when random strangers would show up with food and maybe a little cash. Yes, random people phased in and out of my nightmare. I had a pennies' worth of strength and would force out a pessimistic, "Thank you," even as each stranger offered no judgment. These wingless people extended to me from their own limited bounty. They brought with them love and compassion.

And then, my distrust would raise its hand and rebuke them. I did not trust their kindness. I told myself that they felt sorry for me or that they would win the "most kind" or "most generous person" award at some patriarchal church. I judged it was their religious "duty" to help me and not an authentic act of compassion.

And back into my nightmares I would spiral.

Friends occasionally found the courage to visit, although it truly was unbearable for them to witness me this shattered. Sometimes I slept for days. Living in a garage, very little light would get through. Death became the landscape of my dreams. It spoke to me. I welcomed sleep.

One day I took a walk. I'd longed for my Neo. As I walked, a man approached me. He asked if we could talk. Lifelessly, I replied, "What the hell." We made our way to a public gazebo. And then he spoke. "You know, I remember you from somewhere. I saw you walking down the street and I felt compelled to ask you to talk to me."

Sarcastically I wondered if he was going to hit on me. Finely laced in pessimisms, I wondered if he thought he might fuck me or have me blow him for some change. I remembered calling him a prick in my head. I waited.

He said, "I don't know what I'm doing or why, but I want to give you this and tell you that God loves you." And then he handed me $40 dollars as tears flooded his eyes.

My innocence—that part of me that still held my sweet spirit as high as a kite, the part that still loved dragonflies, fireflies, and snow-flakes—perked up. That's the gift he gave me: the rekindling of my innocence, the white light within me. That part of me that missed her daddy and mommy, deeply longed for clean sheets, a very big hug, Ringer, and Neo.

Quietly, I looked up at the man and into his eyes. I gave him a glimpse of my pain with gentle tears. I told him I loved him and he left. He'd witnessed his own compassion through me. I watched him struggle to compose himself as he reintegrated back into humanity. It was not God who handed me $40 dollars; it was he who had felt compelled to help me. He had known of my struggles for some time and had finally taken a moment to reach out. Maybe it was easier to say "God" did it. Maybe he felt shame for feeling so much.

I could not battle the warmth that flooded me and I did not know what to do with my money. So I walked to a local office sup-plies store and I bought a sketch pad and some colored pencils. I snagged some snacks, went home, left my garage door open, and began to write and draw.

Every time I prepared my battle gear to fight against all the people I hated, someone, one human being at a time, would appear and make some offer of human decency that would mend my warrior wounds and add to my cup of dignity.

My heart was slowly mending. The better days of my youthful spirit resurfaced and brought out giggles and grins as I prowled my way through the apartment complex at night, sneaking showers and taking a dignified crap in the community pool bathhouse.

In time, an employment opportunity came along through Shannon. After a nerve-racking interview and successfully overshadowing my desperation with social skill, I landed a job as the director of sales and marketing for an amusement park. No one had a clue that I lived in a garage because I was wearing an Armani suit.

There were moments when I was working in my new office that sadness would envelop me, the presence of humility was toxic. Just to eat food, good food seemed precious. I became excited about the theme park, the fun, sun, water, and joyous occasions.

I missed my son. Every time my spirit began to catch the wind, I thought of him. The weight of his absence and of my failure would press down on me until I desired to be buried in my garage as if I did not exist at all.

I had failed him. Could I rise up to meet this? Could I rise up to meet him?

In July 2004, I found a place to call home—for both of us. It was a basement rental without a kitchen and with only one bedroom. I took my first paycheck and moved in. I also applied for financial aid and registered for college classes. I wasn't mentally prepared yet for Ringer to come home, but I longed to see him smile and felt a suffocating guilt for what had happened.

Time passed. Shyly and fearful, I began to smile again. Outside of work and school I remained indoors, having no desire to connect with the world.

But I had a home.

I hated my book. I felt pregnant with it and it was getting bigger. At the same time, I was also maddeningly possessed to keep writing it, to keep nurturing it out of me. The words were alive. Even when I tried to run from them, they haunted me in my dreams. Having dreamed of infinite circles of women, each one telling me, ""You said you would," I sensed that I'd made some sort of promise to myself and women everywhere that I would rise up with the power of the written and spoken word and give voice to the shameful atrocities women and children have endured. Perhaps it was the genetic echo of the history of womanhood embedded in my ancestral cellular architecture, or perhaps it was my own internal subconscious map communicating with me—something was bringing images these atrocities to the surface for transcendence.

I don't entirely understand why, but I knew that I was meant to write this book. I had to give voice to my experiences in order to heal them. Being female hurt. Writing about it hurt worse because I had to slow down to relive and face the memories of what had stunted my happiness. While crying helped soothe my misery, writing helped me get rid of it. I had to use my voice to find freedom.

I hated my past. I wanted to forget it. Memories, quite frankly, would not have it that way. They just kept coming. Many, many labor-intensive hours of therapy was another process that helped me cope with my circumstances and heal the wounds of my painful past. My mind was very active at times and depressed at others—I was tormented by fragments of thoughts and images.

Shortly before getting the job, a social worker introduced me to the county social services department of mental health. Once again, I started getting therapy.

I fought quixotic diagnoses and against meds. Labeling and drugging me would not alleviate my pain and wipe out the truth of my past or of history. I remember one experience I had with a psychiatrist while living within my mind's mania. While in an intake interview, he said to me, "So I hear you have grandiose ideas about writing a book or something."

I actually chuckled, wondering if he was sex deprived. "Grandiose?" I inquired.

"Yes. Oftentimes when mentally ill people struggle, they get grand ideas about things they think they can do."

I took the challenge. I nestled a little more comfortably in my chair and boldly declared, "Yes, I am writing a book and I'd like to win the Pulitzer Prize in the category of redemption stories." My heart shuffled with electrical energy. I loved my boldness. I laced it with a dose of arrogance just to give him something to ponder.

"Well, what makes you think you can do that, Amber? You are living in a garage and very, very depressed."

It is so funny to me, how a "professional" thought he could ascertain my self-worth and potentiality within fifteen minutes or by reading a few notes taken by some person who had spoken to me on the phone in a moment of my deepest despair.

I told that guy, "So, if I were rich or came from a different family background, would you have the nerve to suggest that I cannot do something as bold as this? Do you actually think that just because my life has fallen apart, I cannot get up one day and do something as grand as writing an award-winning book? You have no right to suggest that I am not capable of doing anything I damned well please in my life."

He was an old guy. I projected that he admired my spunk and clarity of thought. I did not care, I'd already lost enough. I was not going to let him take the goal of writing my book away from me as well. Our session ended. After that session I was referred to a woman therapist who remained my counselor for eight years and engaged with me in a highly supportive manner.

I remained actively candid with my therapist. I remember once asking to speak frankly with her. I told her how much I wanted to die and how afraid I was to feel happy. She asked me, "Do you have a plan?"

"Yes," I replied.

She sat quietly.

Nervously, I asked her if she was going to do anything.

She replied, "No." After a pause, she continued, "Amber, death is your mind's way of telling itself that you can stop the pain. I've seen many things in my lifetime and I can't imagine your pain. But if you think about death and choose to live, then you know that you have chosen."

It was funny because in that moment I gained respect for myself. I had chosen to live. Constantly thinking about death was just my mind's way of coping with its suffering. I knew I could end the pain. But I was choosing to live with it and that empowered me.

Run from anybody who uses outdated clichés like, "Honey, you've got to put your past behind you" or "Never look back," or my personal favorite, "Get over it." Simply mark these people up as ignorant and move on. Respect for one's truth is earned. Survivors are not heroes. We are simply people who have lived through extraordinary experiences. We just need support from people around us to make sense of it all. We need this to live. We need this to forgive.

I've struggled with my feminine heart many times. Tears—even for women—seemed so cowardly. Why had I been taught not to cry? For whatever reason I learned to resist crying, it affected me worse because I was a woman and subject to monthly moods and thoughts that made me want to cry. My fight with my own femaleness violently jostled me, as I had always found safety in the masculine drive for competition, for possessions of things and people, and through the denouncement of human suffering. I hated both sides of the platform. Over time, I came to recognize that people can be both tough and vulnerable.

I've spent most of my life in judgment of my soft heart and I'm tired of it. I hurt. I cry. I am either a woman or I am not. Strong people cry because they have the courage to handle it. I am the essence of the feminine energy, the Gaia, the energy of the Earth. Because I am a woman, I possess the ability to birth children and to create as Gaia does. But the matriarch, the mother of the world, has been battered and shamed and cloaked in ignorance. She's been dominated and her image has been suppressed. Society asks women to love, then expects it, and then tells them it is a weakness. How clever. How brilliantly clever. We humiliate women by not paying them fairly and denying them title, respect, and power. When our women run for public office we actually talk about their clothing and hairdos instead of their minds, skills, and policies.

Humans have emotions. The electromagnetic pulse of the human heart is measurably 1,000 times stronger than the brain. The potential power of women, intensified by our maternal love, is exponential. No wonder I'd rejected patriarchal gods and gurus. Living in the garage, I found my feminine wings that could feel, expand, and rise up powerfully from tragedy. I learned that as a woman I have a social privilege denied to men, the privilege to feel, to hug, to be soft. In yoga, this is known as the yin energy, and it's the core strength of a warrior of honor, which is what I am.

Already suffering from post-traumatic stress disorder, the events 9/11 had bumped me off the edge. On a deeper level, I surrendered to the violence. I ferociously began to reject all things soft and lovely. All of it. Violent men had flown planes into buildings, physically killing people and smothering the survivors. History provides enough evidence to show that men will keep playing cowboy and Indian until they learn to feel, to love, and solve problems with yin attributes. I collapsed from accepting that I would not live long enough to see that change in human history. My own president had created a war based on "godly" male values about "good" and "evil."

When will women, when will we, put a stop to the violence? When will we become intolerant when we are not accepted for our feelings, opinions, and boundaries? When will we protect our sons from being raised on misguided and imbalanced values? When will we women teach our men to love and nurture our sons and daughters equally, with honor and dignity? I had hated the world of men for as long as I can remember. Nine-eleven gave me the final piece of evidence that I needed to collapse, to hide the feminine side of my nature, to ignore the gifts of love and compassion that were abundant within me. At times I hated women more for letting men be violent than I hated men. What happened to our voices? What happened to our will to say no? Why had it been shamed, beaten, or raped out of us and where were the stories of the women who had survived and stood up? *Had we sold out for comfort and safety instead?*

In December 2004, I received a phone call from my son desperately pleading to come home. By this time, he'd run away from his father again, found drugs and alcohol, and was living on the streets. He and his father did not see eye to eye. His father did not believe in psychological trauma. Instead, he contributed to Ringer's belief that alcohol was the solution to his problems, as his own father and mother had before him. Alcohol was a way of life.

Ringer's father had no compassion for his aching teenage son. The harsh words he had spoken to his son about me had only added to Ringer's intense suffering. The boy now hated and loved me. He had been botched up by an assortment of confusing feelings that most adults could not handle. When I heard his voice, I told him to get someplace safe and call me back. He did. I had just enough money to get him home on a plane from Las Vegas to Washington.

All my friends had advised me to hold off on bringing Ringer home. Like them, I knew that my mental state was fragile, but my thirteen-year old son's seemed far worse. How could I leave my kid stranded, living alone on the streets coping with the hell in his head? My mind, will, and heart were still shredded, but some of the parts had mended. I missed him terribly and prepared myself for the road ahead. We'd both descended so far down in life that the road to our restoration might ultimately take us to the very edge of total destruction. Could we survive our reunion?

I did not want to love anyone.

I did not want to face the pain of failure as a mother.

Love hurt badly.

Loving myself was awkward and difficult.. But love kept pulling me toward Ringer. The day after the phone call, I went to pick up the young man I'd dropped off one year before. Right away I saw he had changed. He was very thin, with hollowed skin and eyes, and he was very cool and distant when he hugged me. He did crack a small smile. Oh how I had missed that smile that had been with him since he was born! And then he backed off again.

There existed a push and pull of trust and distrust, anger and then love, then distance, then anger, then rage, then a flow of bottled-up tears that he'd been holding, and then we were back to love again. This was the emotional landscape that was to guide us home again to each other.

Minutes turned into hours and hours into days. With each passing day after Ringer moved home there were new challenges to overcome. His anger and teenage moodiness combined with my misery and tragic poverty had shaped his view of life. He was desperate for security. I was even more desperate to provide it. His high school teachers and principal did not understand. He didn't fit into their system of doing things. They were focused on test scores. Eventually, Ringer's troubled days at school led to his expulsion. Attempting to manage the situation led to me getting fired from my job. Stress consumed me as we survived cashless weeks, food pantry rations, a giftless holiday, job rejections, and, once again, no money for rent.

One day, in a confused and honest plea to receive strength from me, Ringer wisely yelled at me, "I'm going out. I'm going to do cocaine, alcohol, pot, whatever! Are you going to sit there crying, or are you going to get up and come after me?"

I was shell shocked and stunned. I did not move. He raged out the door.

He had struck a chord. He was asking for me to have enough strength for him. What a powerful, brilliant young man. I softly smiled, faced my fear of loving, and went after him.

Ringer fought me. But I caught a glimpse of that smile—for one second—a knowing smile, as I forced him to come back home. He had needed me to fight him and to love him enough to bring him home. What a champion!

Our children are our champions.

Ringer's challenging of me to do better did not stop there. He hated me because we did not have money, because I was too weak to handle things, because I would not take a job at McDonald's, because I was moody and cried, because of the basement we lived in, because his father did not love him, and because our dog had died. He'd lost so much more than me and I seemed a complete failure to him. At times his disgust for me turned violent.

He'd learned to bury his deepest sorrow, because "only women cry, Mom, don't you know that? Men are supposed to handle everything and be tough."

People have asked me how I became the woman that I am. I could not finish this book until I had the answer. It was something I'd lost my belief in until I understood the demands of the heart of my son. The answer is love.

Love.

There is no other possible answer.

My love bent like a tree being viciously blown by the violent storms of Ringer and life. My heart regrouped every single time.

Some of its branches were broken, but its trunk, the foundation of its strength, always stood rooted, ready to meet another day. I knew that life itself would one day reveal the truth of my love for Ringer, despite the tragedy of my life before he came along, and the fact that his presence in my life compelled me to grow.

That is the strength of a mother. That is the strength of this woman. That is also the strength of human beings. Our bodies are designed to survive, to protect us, to care for us—no matter what. Like the Earth, they will eventually fall, and it is up to community, to human beings with our magnificent capacity to love, to create and innovate in order to rebuild each other, rebuild the Earth.

That task requires the strength and vulnerability of love.

I have hated love since I was a child and have ruthlessly rejected concepts of love. People taught me to do this. And yet, this one young person, whom I am honored to call my son, won me over with his deep yearning to receive the strength and vulnerability of my love.

Love is the answer. Love saved my life. Love made the blood that moves through my heart richer and more vibrant, and radiantly allowed the flow of this life force to feed every cell of my body. My human heart was ready, waiting, and available to heal me. Loving my son taught me to love and respect myself more deeply. I had to learn this valuable truth in order to continue living as I do now.

Forgiveness provided another platform for growth. The hardest person to forgive was me. Blaming myself, this was the only logical explanation. Punishing myself was necessary for my transformation. But once I figured out that my innate nature held endless potential and accepted my life, my experiences, successes, hopes, failures, and mistakes—all of it—I let go of blame and punishment. Within the landscape of love and forgiveness, I changed.

Forgiveness is a journey. It does not happen through denial. The type of transcendence of pain I underwent does not happen overnight. One must walk in the reality of one's own life and actually experience it through the path of the human heart. That vibration took me to the edge of my existence only to be caught by the strength of the soul. It was waiting at the edge of my deepest fear. It delivered me to the mouth of compassion and set me free.

I have become an authentic human being. Me. I am lovable. I know this about myself. I have been a witness to my authentic capacity to love for my entire life. Tattered, shredded, battered, bruised, violated, and withered, I still love myself passionately. I love. It is still there.

Aren't those the sweetest words of this entire book?

The many years of vicious conflicts and challenging moments with Ringer have given me a framework to reflect upon and what I have to offer. I've grown to admire my strength, to dig deeper, and not to fear that which resides within me. I am imperfect. I still have challenging moments. I also know that I have grown against the enormous odds of doing so. I know that I am powerful beyond measure. I have witnessed my beautiful self as I lived through some very tragic moments. I have witnessed my life.

Not so long ago I made a list of the things I love. Ringer, tulips, dragonflies, kittens, horses, corn fields, lighthouses, raging storms, tidal waves, ball gowns, big band music, planets, the smell of soil after it rains, fishing, hot dogs, the ocean, dogs, and wild green onions.

I love. After all that life has been to me, I still love. Life doesn't make you stronger. Love does. Life just provided me the opportunity to figure this out.

These days I giggle. I meditate. I've chosen to believe in God on the seventh day of each week and to believe my horoscope on Tuesdays. I'm considering believing in karma on Thursdays since otherwise I simply cannot make sense of some human behavior and mental distortions. I practice yoga and teach at least twelve yoga classes per week, and I train teachers through my Yoga Alliance-registered school. I also have found my voice to talk about previously unspoken tragedies that occurred in my lifetime without shame or guilt.

The time has come for us women to lift up our voices, honor our wisdom, and be heard. The time has come to stop bad things from happening to our children, our sisters, our mothers, and our friends. We must stop making excuses for our loved ones when they go astray; we must say no to them and bear the burden of that choice. The time has come for us all to reclaim our essence, uplift our hearts, and redeem all that is beautiful about life within us—no matter what. We must love ferociously within boundaries that protect the very essence of love.

I have arrived at my authentic self. I am a champion warrior of the heart. Today, I am a writer, having fulfilled my dream from when I was twelve to write a story about my life for the whole world to read. I have reclaimed the voice of the confused and terrified young girl I once was. I have given her the freedom to express herself. I have given her a life that others threatened to take away. I have fought the warrior's battle and now, as a strong and powerful woman, rise up to meet all of reality that comes my way. I do this because love will always bring me home again to the deep, dark beauty of my soul.

EPILOGUE

I fell into the lap of death. It licked me clean and threw me back out there.

 I paused for a moment late one night, as I was headed from my car to my home. The spring air was crisp, remnants of winter still clinging to the change in season. The sky was crystal clear and scattered with the moon and stars. Aloud I affirmed that one day I would die and the ruling chaos of destruction would not matter in the moment of my death. I held the moment tenderly and consciously planted it in my cellular and neural memory.

As a lover of mathematics and science as a child, I knew about the abundant beauty on this planet and of the skies. I felt it. For years I had dreams of "knowing everything." I would wake up in the night and have exhilarating moments of knowingness. No matter the season, I would then run outside to ensure that I was awake and try to anchor the experience that all of life made sense. In the morning after the dream, I would only remember that I knew everything and I understood that what I would need in this lifetime would make itself known to me.

On occasion I would dream of flying and feel the presence of earthly things, items and people reaching up for me, trying to latch on to me during a flight to freedom. I had dreams of flying into the midst of human beings and showing them the light within me. In most, I hid my inner beauty, the same radiant light I now experience through meditation and yoga.

In one dream, I was walking in a playground amid a group of young women. I wore a cape from which light poured out like rays of the sun as I moved. Danger was close by. The women scattered to distract three men dressed as kings, in fancy clothing, who had come to see me. They'd heard about this female with radiant light and healing powers, and needed to see her to "make sense of it" and to squelch the musings of their townspeople. One of the women hurried me into a building where machinery—some sort of generator—was housed and I hid behind it.

Ultimately, the men found my hiding place. As they stood there, they authoritatively looked directly into my eyes. I knew fighting them would lead to captivity, so I decided to open my cloak just enough to allow a slither of the radiant light of my love to shine forth. I knew the full strength of my light would overwhelm them. One by one, the men's eyes softened, wisdom seeped into their consciousness, and then I glided past them.

Change is something we must do as individuals. I have learned to do this without bitterness and rage through practicing and teaching yoga. For me, yoga is not a mythical or magical experience, but a physical one, although it was originally created and utilized in India as a sacred way to train men to be warriors. That's why we have the postures known as Warrior 1, Warrior 2, and Warrior 3. Since then, it has spread worldwide, even being used to train athletes.

When I first studied hatha yoga sixteen years ago, I learned of its origins in India, a culture thousands of miles away. As my practice matured and I sought more information, I was shocked by how the poor and women were treated in India. I knew then that the yoga I would teach would embody principals that reflected the twenty-first century, where women are not held back.

For two years, I studied a style of Korean yoga in which health and wellness are cultivated not just through physical movement, but by working with the energy of the body and emotional transformation. From this I learned to maintain a deep sense of calm despite the chaos of life.

Next, I studied Kripalu Yoga in Stockbridge, Massachusetts. When I arrived to attend one of their thirty-day teacher training courses, I was a warrior, strong in vinyasa yoga and the harder poses. I was edgy, or what we in the yoga community refer to as *yang-like.* Here the brain is in a beta state, active, busy, productive, competitive, and "strong."

Two weeks into the program, I learned of love and compassion. I learned of acceptance, imperfection, the joy of not having superior balance, and the relief of letting go of self-imposed and socially imposed pressure to be the best. I learned to stumble and regroup. I learned to push further when I desired to collapse. Most importantly, I learned how to respect my body.

I came home to my community in Virginia with a deep yearning to move to Kripalu full time, but found myself flooded with job offers as a teacher. That was good news, except that I was afraid to show all the love in my heart when the students in the yoga communities I served wanted a yang-like workout. The manager of the gym where I began working then, an aggressive type-A personality who knew nothing about yoga, wanted to ensure that I was pushing my students hard enough. He said that the students only cared about fitness. Standing before me in each class in that facility, near Washington, D.C., were fifty or sixty people who knew little about yoga and lived in one of the most affluent and powerful suburbs on Earth.

Balancing soft-hearted yin energy with the yang energy of a strong mind and body is a transformational process. Coming home from

Kripalu, I was presented with the opportunity to take risks to teach in this manner—to risk rejection. Sometimes I wouldn't even attempt it. Yet, each time I taught an overly aggressive class, I felt depressed. I knew that my body was trying to tell me something. I suspected I might be projecting my fearful thoughts and feelings on my students. Perhaps they, too, would be open to experiencing a more compassionate yoga.

With all I had learned in my life from trauma and violence, it was my heart's yearning that beckoned me to take a chance and begin to weave softness into my classes. I began allowing longer periods for Savasana, the Corpse pose, which is the final resting position that completes every yoga practice. I began to tell stories and use softer music. My classes were packed. As I began to teach yin yoga, I used my creativity to incorporate aromatherapy, sounds, colors, and restorative poses to teach these good people how to relax, breathe, and soften their hearts. I told healing stories from my life. There were times when I actually felt ashamed to appear vulnerable in front of so many people, but then, one by one, my students shared their own stories of personal transformation with me. I was reminded over and over that all of my life's experiences thus far had been needed for me to truly understand and feel compassion for their suffering.

Teaching yoga and working with people one on one called me to smooth the gruffer, more defensive edges of my personality. Each class provided another wave of tension inviting me to transform my heart and soften the ebb and flow of my voice, my words, and my behavior. Negativity and aggression do not land well on others. They create barriers and anxiety. Power is not respected when it is delivered that way. The yang energy, the warrior energy, the one that meets the world and its challenges head on, can be powerful, however, it needs to be fed by the yin energy that heals wounds and rejuvenates the very cells of our bodies. The yin energy of love, which feeds our happiness, our beings, our joy, and our tenderness, brings others close to us. As it experientially embraces us, we are biologically impacted. Then the brain produces hormones that biochemically make us feel better. These softening and heart-warming neurochemicals are not mushy. It's the innate chemistry of being human.

Perhaps science serves us best through its ongoing discoveries about the mysteries of the human body, knowledge that makes it safer for people to open up. I am wise enough to know that as a species we are evolving, and although all the transformational processes that are now occurring will not be completed in my lifetime without a doubt people, one by one, can find more of the happiness they desire by moving through emotional healing processes, exercising their bodies, eating healthier foods, and surrounding themselves with very good people.

The first time I went to Kripalu, I was broke. A man who was building a health and wellness center in West Virginia granted me a scholarship to attend the course. Upon my return, I was supposed to lead his yoga program. While working together, he made several unprofessional gestures toward me, which I deflected. Two days before I was supposed to go, he withdrew both the job offer and his $1,000-dollar donation. I was enraged by this man's lack of integrity and for misplacing my trust in his word. But in my life, things can occur that turn out just right.

My sister, the one with the black velvet curtains, called out of the blue right in the midst of my sorrow. She asked about my trip, happy that I had an opportunity. I confessed and allowed my vulnerability to be present with no expectation in return. She simply asked, "How much do you need?" After telling her, she hung up the phone and paid the tuition. Two days later, I was on my way. My sister is single-handedly responsible for the gift of teaching yoga that I now experience in my life. Redemption is a very powerful transformative tool, and it is possible and available for all who have the hearts to feel, the minds to decipher, and the will, motivated by love, to hold the posture of life. Obstacles cannot stop its momentum. In accepting my sister's gift and going to study yoga I redeemed my life.

I found myself talking to my students one day about how after 9/11 I did not believe in peace, and that I had spent a good portion of my life mocking it. I then shared my new belief that if each student in that room, in that moment, opened their hearts to peace, joy, light, and love, it would be real in that moment. That truth became radiantly clear to me as I witnessed each of them resting and peaceful. I told them that no one could ever, not ever, take that inner experience away from us once we had gathered together as a community in peace. For those few shared moments we felt the breath and light of peace within us. Each similar experience of listening to my wisdom guide my students enabled me to teach the hungry student with myself.

Not long ago I finally felt ready to end my then thirteen years of arduous, intense psychotherapy. I knew it was time to go. A major milestone. Or a private victory, as Stephen R. Covey would say in *The Seven Habits of Highly Effective People.* I made this decision because I knew that I could meet the world as it was, face reality, and skillfully find my way home again to myself. Yoga and therapy, and much help along the way from others, have uplifted me when I did not have the strength to do it alone. This is the message of community. Love and support one another.

I believe in reality and have almost no attachment to hope. I know many believe that to be unhealthy; however, it is healthy for me. Reality is my best teacher. Things happen or they do not. I publish and I am successful or I am not. I open a yoga studio and I am successful or I am not. I do not hope for things now. Rather, I step up, speak out, and live my life according to my own value system and remain mindful not to impose on the values and beliefs of others.

The reality is that there will be moments when life challenges us. When governments challenge and mislead people, and abuse their power, it is an opportunity to rise up against the mounting unhappiness that we as human beings bear when groups of people are corrupt and greedy. We can come together and renew ourselves with dignity, mutual respect, and honor.

True social change will require a massive emotional overhaul of our mental infrastructure. We will be required to experience more of our vulnerability as human beings. That isn't a comfortable experience for most people, especially those with enough money to buy their way out of emotional reality. It's not just the rich who do this, of course, but the middle class in pursuit of as much material matter as they can possess. We all do this whether we spend our money at Wal-Mart or Bergdorf Goodman, or on the stock market or cock fighting. Any amount of money can provide us with a very sexy, distracting path to pleasure. Drugs, sex, alcohol, gadgets, clothing, cosmetics, boats, airplanes, and other luxuries can be effective emotional Band-Aids as we make our way through life. It's usually only a health-related or near-death experience that snaps our focus back on health and well-being of ourselves or others.

Change is always occurring. I believe this emphatically. I believe that change for the best is happening on our planet and inside human beings. Each of us must do our part. We already have poetry, songs, books, movies, role models like Mother Teresa, charities, and natural disasters to loudly illustrate the need for continual community action and intervention. I can only wonder if the genetic coding in our younger generations will overcome their ancestral heritage, the echo of historical injustices, the subtle undertones of the songs of futility, as they begin to grasp the truth about governments, organized religions, special interest groups, and wealthy campaign contributors who try to buy our leaders' influence in exchange for more social power.

People too often feel powerless. I have lived my entire life with this awareness. But even in the absence of much hope, I discovered that small, tangible possibilities can emerge and evolve if only through the shift that happens inside one human being at a time. I refuse to live my life anymore feeling as if I cannot contribute to the positive evolution of humanity through generous acts of human decency, thoughtful acts of intelligent participation, and honorable actions of compassion for others. I will not give up on that possibility ever. Decency, participation, and compassion have meant so much to me—both given and received.

Let me be clear. To this day I fall way short of the standards of perfection. I fall way short on the standards of the highest ideals. I fall short of being the best, the greatest, or the most at anything at all, and I do not desire to be these things. I live secure in the knowledge that despite my limitations I can step out of my comfort zone and inspire people to open their hearts and heal.

Genetically and environmentally I acquired the gift to question everything. I was never a follower, at least not for very long. I have paid the price for my individuality. But I have always been able to move about freely and to challenge what lay before me when I did not agree.

As individuals everyone has power. We have an internal freedom that cannot be abused by laws, judges, politicians, or those who would seek in any way to control our behavior. We can choose to be aware and to act differently toward one another day by day, minute by minute, breath by breath, one cell transforming at a time. You can do this, too. It is not magic.

Common sense tells me that if I run a traffic light I may harm someone. Speeding can be dangerous. Therefore, I gladly participate in following social laws that serve our mutual good. However, I am also keenly aware that three people can commit the exact same crime with three entirely different outcomes. I guarantee you that the person with money and connections will get off free; the person with money alone will get a slap on the hand; and the poorest person will be convicted, not only in the courts, but socially as well. Newspapers will print tales of their crime as tales of social justice and law in action. This sort of injustice angers me. It makes me want to collapse when I realize how very little I can do about it. We all know inequity is real and yet we continue to run, like mice, around and around the same wheel of social problems.

Let us not collapse, however. As individuals we have the choice to exert power over our personal behavior, make honorable choices, and use our hearts' compassion to serve and help someone. I feel myself inspired just knowing that we can do this much—even in the face of larger issues, like social and economic injustice. My own way to exert my personal power and serve is to write and to teach and take care of my body. I study the human body, follow as many of the advances in science and medicine as possible, and keep my mind open for more knowledge. My voice and the written word are my heart's salve for emotional and intellectual violence in the world. I am responsible for my environment and how I live in it. I choose to live well.

I have many judgments and biases. I've learned them along my path of evolution. Some I have consciously allowed to develop further, others I prefer to eliminate. I maintain a ruthlessly introspective inward gaze, aimed towards myself, and do my best to watch my responses to the social realities that surround me. Sometimes, I overload and react. It happens. Humility is the result of self-reflection about why I judge or discriminate. For example, I have judged the poor because I've not wanted to look at or deal with their problems. It's depressing. It reminds me of being poor myself. I've also judged black women because of television stereotypes that have infected my brain and yet I've admired the raw, edgy strength of black women I've met and felt sisterly compassion for them when I stopped judging them for our differences. Also I've judged white men for atrocities committed against women, Native Americans, African Americans, the Chinese, the Japanese, and others who were blatantly considered less than human in the history of our country. Some judgments are healthy for me, like judging corporations that feel justified to abuse their power to pollute the environment or exploit their workers.

When I sit still and stew, or when I suppress reality, I get tense and feel depressed. I once heard a psychiatrist say, "Depression is the silencing of the soul." Action, for me, relieves this internal tension. I purposefully choose to affect my own environmental DNA and then pass it on everywhere I go. As individuals we do not need platforms or wealth to be powerful, all we need is to express a voice guided by the heart even in the simplest of places, like a gas station.

Ignorance is a tool used by those in power to keep people looking the other way. Ignorance suppressed the voice of my mother as she submitted to the tyranny of the patriarch in my childhood home. Ignorance gave rights to the members of the religious group that judged and shamed me for being a cheerleader in high school. Ignorance cleverly woven into our sources of news and entertainment create and maintain barriers between ethnic groups that otherwise might be unified. Ignorance is more violent than nuclear weapons because it creates societies that are depressed, unhappy, and dependent on material niceties that cannot fill their souls.

After living in a garage in misery and being judged as a mother, abandoned by my family, and almost forgotten by my country, I've learned that peace is a feeling experienced after the padlock on the human voice has been unlocked. I have learned that peace is the aftermath of taking responsibility for reality, not singing songs and planting flowers while looking the other way. Peace can only be deeply experienced after the doors to the heart are opened and the voice heard. I teach yoga, write, and speak. I do not close the fifth chakra, the human voice; nor do I aggressively push my agenda out into the atmosphere. I breathe, I teach, I speak, and I write. That is my redemption. That is my life's small contribution. That is how I hold steady when tsunamis and earthquakes wage war with humans, and when wars among humans create massive disharmony and enormous grief. I teach, I write, and I speak. That is my task.

Our genes only determine part of who we are as human beings. The environments we live in and our ability to accept or deny them also become encoded in our cellular architecture. If you would like to leave your imprint on human history, contribute positively to the plight of another. Uplift and support other people, animals, or the Earth. Leave bad relationships. Let go of the attachment to money, the safety, the lie. Consider these acts your private victories, celebrated without need for kudos, awards, or compensation. Just experience and flood your cells with the sensations of compassion, love, and happiness. In this way, you can help change our path in history and pass on new environmental traits, like genetic code, to future generations.

Depression and boredom are clear messages from your body that you need to learn, grow, connect, and change. It is that simple! Once you get this, you have a choice to respond.

Anxiety is like sitting before a car wash of change, afraid of all the scrubbing, cleansing, and rinsing required to get through it.

You and I will not change the world. We will not. We can however, change ourselves. That really is the ultimate power of a human being. Because no matter who is running the show, we as individuals have the power to choose, to live an internal life of dignity, a valued life of honor, and a principled life of compassion with an unlimited supply of self-acceptance. Change begins when we can accept ourselves exactly as we are. That is a foundational principal for personal and interpersonal growth, one person's contribution toward evolutionary change that is now critical to our survival as a species coexisting with other species on a planet that serves as our home.

The formula for both survival and transformation is to never, ever give up. Random things happen in the presence of perseverance that are relevant and significant. I know this. I know this because I have lived it. I know just how badly it hurts sometimes to keep pressing on.

I get a vision in my head from time to time of a field of bright pink roses. Up close they look and smell beautiful so that I rush in to take in the scent. It is not until I am in the thick of these beautiful pleasures of nature that I realize they have prickly thorns. At that point, there is no turning back, or going left or right, because once I'm in the middle no matter which direction I move I will be cut and bled by the thorns of life. That's how I view life. There is no other way to fully experience the rose garden of living except to go straight through the middle of it. Take in all of its beauty and simply accept the thorns as part of the human passage.

By the way, you don't have to handle my pain. Let me set you free. Do not bend your heart for me. I have already done that. Others, however, are desperately waiting for you.

May your soul find comfort here.

ACKNOWLEDGMENTS

Thank you to all who have tolerated and loved me. Thank you to my sister, for her growth, her love, her truth, and her black velvet curtains. Thank you to my mother, for her growth and for respecting me more as I have taken my place in her presence. Thank you to the sister who knew all along and supported me. Thank you to my spiritual sister, who brought me the possibility of mystery and brought me closest of all to my spiritual, feminine nature.

Thank you to my dear friend, John; to lifelong friend and personal angel, Pierce; and to others who have stood by me all of these years: to Jila, who gave me shelter and sacrificed her own need for money for me and my son; to the Smith family; to Shannon; Samantha; to Odeh, who extended far from his comfort zone to care for me; to Gaines, whose belief in me is unwavering; to Maria, whose steadfast encouragement helped me see myself more clearly; to Lynne, Steve, Charlotte, and Maryam who had a direct impact on my ability to flourish in the yoga studio while writing; and to the many, many others whose kindness fed me, sheltered me, and gave me the strength to redeem the truest nature of my being, my authentic self, bright, brilliant, and beautiful.

Most of all, my deepest of thanks go out to my son, Ringer, whose courage far surpasses my own.

RESOURCES

Yoga with Amber, Roots Yoga Studio, LLC
Sterling, Virginia 20164
Telephone: (855) 550-4032
Website: www.loveyogawithamber.com

CONNECT WITH AMBER VIA THE SOCIAL NETWORKS
Join Amber's online community and receive updates about classes and events.
Facebook: www.facebook.com/Amber.Shakti
https://www.facebook.com/RootsYogaStudio
Voices of Women Group:
www.facebook.com/AmberBSkylar
LinkedIn: www.linkedin.com/pub/amber-shakti/57/807/55a
Twitter: https://twitter.com/AmberBSkylar

YOGA TEACHER TRAINING PROGRAMS
Yoga Teacher Education Training 200 Hour Program: A nine-month-long program that is an inquiry into self. Visit www.yogaalliance.org to read the course syllabus.

Yinoga™ Teacher Training, 100-hour Program: Intense training on the central nervous system, the eleven systems of the body, anatomy, the use of blocks and props, alignment, and working with special populations, as well as for stress and pain management. The coursework is inspired by Amber's own experiences of post-traumatic stress disorder, anxiety, and depression.
For more details on these programs, visit:
www.loveyogawithamber.com.

CORPORATE TRAINING PROGRAMS FOR HEALTH AND WELLNESS, AND YOGA FOR STRESS, BACK PAIN, AND NECK PAIN

For details visit: www.loveyogawithamber.com.

KEYNOTES AND SPEAKING ENGAGEMENTS

Amber B. Skylar is available to present lectures to women's organizations, political forums dealing with violence against women, and women's studies classes. Among other topics, her talks may include: Rape and Recovery, Homelessness and Recovery, Recovering from Domestic Violence, and Yoga for Women's Health.

For details, visit: www.rootspublication.com.

RECOMMENDED ORGANIZATIONS

Woman Within® International

www.womanwithin.org

From their website: Woman Within® International is a global not-for-profit organization that provides a sacred place for women to discover the power and beauty that reside within them. Our mission is simple: To empower women. Over 12,000 women have experienced our core program, the Woman Within® Training Weekend.

Kripalu Center for Yoga and Health (Stockbridge, Massachusetts)

www.kripalu.org

From their website: Kripalu is a 501(c)(3) nonprofit educational organization. Mission: To empower people and communities to realize their full potential through the transformative wisdom and practice of yoga.

ABOUT THE AUTHOR

Amber B. Skylar is a single mother, army veteran, yoga teacher, yoga studio owner, first-time author, and motivational speaker. She champions the human body's capacity for healthy adaptation and invites women to speak out and overcome societal limitations. Enduring poverty, emotional turbulence, and trauma in her youth, Amber grew painfully conscious of the significance and injustice of social stratification. Years later, dealing with the effects of anxiety, depression, homelessness, rape, and post-traumatic stress disorder, she undertook an intensive study of the human body—in particular the nervous system—as a means of survival.

Amber was raised in a family headed by a single mother in urban Ohio. Attempting to make sense of an austere, violent, and abusive childhood, one day she sat on a rooftop and promised herself that she would write a memoir of her life in order to speak on behalf of the silent. Just twelve, the promise reflected the purity of her heart and the nobility of her vision. Almost forty years later, the radiant and haunting memoir *Colors of Amber* powerfully realizes that promise. Smoldering for decades, Amber's voice burns incandescently.

Amber is the founder and master teacher of Roots Yoga Studio (Yoga with Amber) in Sterling, Virginia. As a Yoga Alliance registered school, Roots Yoga Studio provides yoga teacher training and leadership programs, workshops, and daily classes. Training and classes are designed for therapeutic benefit and emphasize navigation of pain and stress for productive daily living. She also presents to corporations and others organizations, and works with private clients.

Amber B. Skylar resides in Northern Virginia with her pet cat, Kikio.

Made in the USA
Middletown, DE
27 July 2020